SHIFTING SANDS

ALSO BY JUDITH SCHEELE

*The Scandal of Continuity in Middle East Anthropology:
Form, Duration, Difference* (as co-editor)

*The Value of Disorder: Autonomy, Prosperity, and
Plunder in the Chadian Sahara* (as coauthor)

Legalism: Rules and Categories (as co-editor)

Legalism: Community and Justice (as co-editor)

*Saharan Frontiers: Space and Mobility in
Northwest Africa* (as co-editor)

*Smugglers and Saints of the Sahara: Regional
Connectivity in the Twentieth Century*

*Village Matters: Knowledge, Politics and
Community in Kabylia, Algeria*

SHIFTING SANDS

A Human History of the Sahara

JUDITH SCHEELE

Profile Books

First published in Great Britain in 2025 by
Profile Books Ltd
29 Cloth Fair
London
ECIA 7JQ
www.profilebooks.co.uk

1 3 5 7 9 10 8 6 4 2

Typeset in Garamond by MacGuru Ltd
Printed and bound in Great Britain by
CPI Group (UK) Ltd, Croydon CR0 4YY

The moral right of the author has been asserted.

A CIP catalogue record for this book is available from the British Library.

ISBN 978 1 78816 645 4
eISBN 978 1 78283 763 3

dedication?

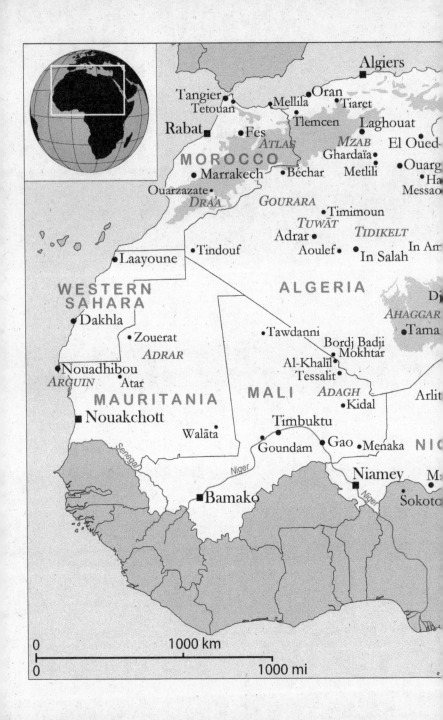

CONTENTS

INTRODUCTION

DESERT LORE

I love all waste
And solitary places; where we taste
The pleasure of believing what we see
Is boundless, as we wish our souls to be.
Percy Bysshe Shelley, *Julian and Maddalo: A Conversation*, 1818–19

If you want to travel overland from the Chadian capital, N'Djamena, to Faya, the main town of the northern Chadian Sahara, you will probably, after some searching, find yourself directed to the 'Parc Faya'. When you get there, you will discover an unmarked, mud-walled courtyard in a peripheral part of town. The only sign that this is a crucial transport hub for everyone desirous of traveling to the Chadian Sahara are a few dusty boxes of Libyan biscuits piled in a corner alongside two tired-looking four-by-fours, clearly not in a state to go anywhere anytime soon. Outside, the broad, unpaved streets are animated, with street sellers hawking fresh peanuts, cooked food and paper tissues, but here, everybody is more quietly occupied, waiting. Passengers shelter under the makeshift mud-brick awnings that line the edges of the courtyard; although the hot season has long passed, the heat is overwhelming, the air heavy with the smell of kerosene and gas. Lizards do their interminable push-ups on the

I

walls; flies settle on dusty bundles of luggage or inspect leftover food wrappers.

At night people find a quiet corner to roll out their mats, mumble a prayer and sleep lightly. Transport – in the shape of a battered four-by-four pickup truck or a desert-going freight truck – may show up at any time, perhaps in the very early hours of the morning, and only the first on board will be able to depart. Faya is a difficult place to reach – unless, that is, you have your own jeep and know the way through the dusty plain of the Bahr al-Ghazāl and the shifting sand-dunes of the Djourab that stretch for hundreds of kilometres between N'Djamena and Chad's extreme north or if you have privileged connections to the army and can hitch a lift. Otherwise, your only option is to wait. There are no regular services, but private drivers often stop by to take on some additional load or a few paying passengers. The thousand-kilometre journey, all but the first 80 of which is off-road, can take anything from forty-eight hours to six days, with hardly any settlements or provisions available on the way.

On my first trip, two Toyota pickups finally appeared on day three to take us at least as far as Moussoro, 300 kilometres north of N'Djamena, where the Sahelian drylands gradually turn into the Sahara proper. Their drivers assured us that it would be easy to find onward transport from there. And they were right: Moussoro had just been the scene of an important demobilisation campaign of the Chadian army and security forces, presided over by the late Chadian president Idriss Déby himself. As many Chadian soldiers are recruited in the north, demand for northbound travel was high. I found a spot on the back of a battered and unreliable-looking jeep with about twenty of them, returning after decades of service to a 'home' they barely knew. They were all past their prime and bore visible traces of former fighting: scarred faces, missing fingers, a limp. They all still wore the

khaki turban, sign of their military status, and most had not sur-
rendered their weapons. When the bumps on the road jolted us
together, I could feel shotguns hidden under boubous, revolver
butts in my back, in addition to the knives that are part of the
normal outfit in much of northern Chad.

The jeep quickly proved itself as unreliable as it looked. Day
after day, either stuck in the sand without any equipment to dig
us out or waiting for the engine to cool down, we grew hungry,
tired, irritable. The monotony of the landscape – first sand-
dunes, then the endless flat, dried mud of the Bodélé Depression,
dotted with an occasional tent made from woven mats as grey
as its surroundings – did little to alleviate the growing tension.
On day five, all twenty-odd of us finally abandoned the vehicle
and its driver 30 or 40 kilometres outside Faya and finished the
journey on the back of a freight truck. Two hours later, the town
came into view at the bottom of a vast sandy depression: greyish
bushy date palms as far as the eye could see, crumbling mud-
brick houses, rubbish heaps, an impromptu market, scavenging
goats, wrecks of Libyan tanks, all blurred by the dust. Men in
patchwork uniforms met the truck and its passengers, staring
at our passports upside down and barking out orders without
visible effect. My fellow travellers quietly disappeared. They
hardly stood out in a town that looked like a ruined garrison
anyway.

I was to stay in Faya for over a year in order to write a book
about the town's history and contemporary life. With time, the
oasis would gradually reveal its hidden beauty to me. I would
learn to ignore the presence of armed men everywhere, to take
them for granted – as everybody else seemed to do – and recognise them for who they were, regardless of their dilapidated
uniforms: brothers, cousins, uncles to my new female friends;
talented storytellers; passionate card players; loving parents.

Still, this first trip stayed engraved in my memory, if only for the striking contrast it presented with the Sahara of the popular imagination: the Sahara here was a flat, brown place with no elegant golden sand-dunes in view, criss-crossed by aging broken-down jeeps rather than camel caravans, inhabited by disgruntled soldiers rather than dignified veiled men behind their camels, and with no carefully tended slender palm trees swaying in the breeze. Yet it held much more truth, interest and depth than age-old external fantasies about the region.

Deserts are central to the Western imagination. Moses, Jesus and Muhammad all went to the desert in their search for truth. Countless American hippies in the 1960s and 1970s followed their lead. *Star Wars* battles were filmed in the Tunisian Sahara; blockbusters from *Lawrence of Arabia* to *Game of Thrones* were staged in the Moroccan south. Novelists from Gide to Bowles sent their protagonists to the desert to experience both boundless pleasure and unspeakable desolation. This is where Saint-Exupéry met the Little Prince and the English Patient came to grief; where, today, high-tech Euro-American imperialism falters in the face of the sheer determination of mysterious veiled men in plastic slippers. And of all the deserts in the world – from the Gobi to Arizona, Antarctica to Siberia – the Sahara, the world's largest hot desert, just an easy flight away from Europe, is the one that many people around the globe most readily think of: it is the Desert as such. Other deserts might approximate the Sahara – might be even hotter or more extreme – but they are never quite the real thing.

Easy as it may be to summon up ready-made images of the region, these fantasies make it difficult to discern the 'real' Sahara and the people who call it their home. 'Timbuktu' in English parlance stands for the end of the world, as does 'Tataouine' in French; their real existence may be doubted and in any case matters little. The Sahara 'guards its mystery', as tourist brochures readily assert, and this mystery participates in its appeal. But ignorance, like knowledge, is never just given but socially constructed. In European and arguably also in much Middle Eastern thought, the Sahara has long acted as the convenient antithesis of civilisation, as a canvas onto which to project fears and desires, without too much interruption by unruly fact.

The contemporary Sahara, meanwhile, is depicted mainly as a site of tragedy inhabited by nameless (and usually numberless) victims of humanitarian catastrophes or natural disasters. If the media carry any stories about the region, they are about civil war in Algeria and Libya; genocide and slavery in Sudan; military putsches in Burkina Faso, Chad and Mauritania; Islamist bombings in Morocco; refugees in Western Sahara; kidnappings and beheadings in Tunisia; revolution in Egypt; drought, famine and rebellion in Niger; or Islamist upheavals and foreign military intervention in Mali. Behind these barely sketched-out states and their intractable problems lurk more familiar 'global' threats: desertification, terrorism, 'waves' of clandestine trans-Saharan migrants and 'climate change refugees', all set against the unpleasant background of extreme poverty. The Sahara covers parts of eleven countries, four of which are counted among the poorest in the world, while at least six others make Western headlines mostly as theatres of endemic conflict and warfare.

The Sahara is thus a place not only of fascination with purity but also of obsession with danger, a place whose 'emptiness' is all too readily filled with the nightmares of contemporary imaginations. Of course, one cannot blame the media for favouring the spectacular – and many parts of the Sahara have indeed been shaken by a series of political, sociological and ecological crises. Yet clearly this is not all that can be said about the region, with its almost 8.3 million square kilometres (3.2 million square miles), almost one-third of the African continent), several million inhabitants, and a corresponding variety of languages, cultures, societies, livelihoods, settlement patterns, human ecologies, sophisticated agriculture, complex transport systems, and striking capacity to innovate. This book is about that other Sahara: not the 'wastes' of the romantic imagination nor the flattened terrors of news bulletins but the highly differentiated space in which Saharan peoples and, increasingly, incomers from other parts of Africa live, work and move.

Saharan Journeys

My own engagement with the region goes back for more than twenty years, first as a visitor, then as a trained social anthropologist, carrying out research with traders, migrants, pastoralists, and agriculturalists in southern Algeria, northern Mali, and northern Chad. Much like my first trip to Faya, these twenty years have been a gradual process of unlearning all the things I thought I knew, about the Sahara itself but also about the world beyond it. The Sahara itself, its people, its history, even its geography, is hidden behind a jungle of preconceptions that have developed over the last two millennia. These preconceptions have changed over time, leaving behind sedimented layers of unspoken assumptions. While this book is primarily concerned with the Sahara as seen from the inside out, we must begin this process of unlearning by shaking down our assumptions and holding them up to the light in order to be able to discard them where necessary.

Two closely related and mutually constitutive strands of thought guide these assumptions. On the one hand are perceptions of the geographical area that we call the Sahara, at the crossroads of the Mediterranean, the Middle East and sub-Saharan Africa. These perceptions continue to be informed by a particular form of orientalism, a strong imperial legacy, Europe's and the USA's conflictual and largely hostile relationship with Islam, state-centred constructions of mobility as a problem and racial assumptions about 'white' and 'Black' Africa, about who belongs where.

On the other is the notion of the desert itself, with its many near-synonyms, such as *wasteland*, *wilderness*, *badlands*; words that can be used for places that are highly exotic or else close to home and that have great metaphorical power. The great deserts of today – the Sahara, the Arabian deserts, the Kalahari, the Gobi – have all been pretty much in place for the last 65 million years, with periodic climatic variations. This means that the great literate traditions of the old world all developed in close proximity to deserts. Deserts play an important rhetorical part in these traditions as places of retreat and purity, of truth and the absence of worldly distraction, yet also as places of perdition, fear and temptation. Both the devil and God dwell in the desert, and, blinded by the desert's mirages, it is not always easy to figure out who is who.

Around 1375, Prince Joan of Aragon offered Charles VI of France a precious gift: six richly illuminated vellum leaves bearing a map of the known world, centred on Jerusalem, probably drawn by the Majorcan Jewish cartographer Abraham Cresques. This document, kept at the French National Library and known as the Catalan Atlas, not only is a masterpiece of medieval map-making but also contains what is probably the first visual depiction of the Sahara by a European author. Cresques' Sahara is a busy place, peopled by veiled men on camels, military tents, slave merchants and, most prominently, a seated Black man wearing a crown with a staff decorated with a fleur-de-lis, holding a golden nugget the size of an apple. The gilt of crown and orb still shimmers from the page 700 years later. This is Mansa Musa, the fourteenth-century king of the Mali empire, whom contemporary historians have dubbed the richest man in history.

Cresques' map was highly original. It drew on two cartographic traditions popular at that time: a mappa mundi, a depiction of the world as represented in scripture, and a portolan, a coastal guide for navigators based on their direct experience. The attempt to combine those two forms led Cresques to adopt a vertical aerial perspective, a perspective that, before the times of air travel or aerial photography (which was developed in the 1850s), was largely a feat of the imagination and advanced mathematics. One earlier map had adopted the same perspective and featured the Sahara: it appeared in the *Tabula Rogeriana*, an atlas commissioned by the Norman king Roger II of Sicily in 1138 and completed by the Moroccan-born and Andalusian-trained cartographer al-Idrīsī in 1154. In it, however, the Sahara beyond the Atlas Mountains hardly figured.

For the most part, neither Arab geographers nor Saharans themselves imagined the space they traversed or inhabited in this way. The earliest accounts of the Sahara are not abstract drawings but concrete narratives of travel, or itineraries. In the fifth century BCE, Herodotus famously described the Sahara along a straight line leading from the Nile to the Niger Bend, with 'peoples' spaced at a convenient distance of ten days' travel from one to the other. Arab travellers from Ibn Hawqal in the tenth century to Ibn Battūta in the fourteenth similarly described trade routes, with much practical attention to how to get from one place to another; they were almost exclusively interested in supply points and 'civilisation' on the road, not in the 'unheeded Berbers' whom they dimly perceived as living in the vast spaces beyond their own itineraries. Al-Idrīsī himself accompanied his maps with lengthy texts that adopted the classic format of Arab travelogues, enlivened with anecdotes gathered from Arab tradesmen whom he had met on the North African coast, showing that he considered an aerial perspective a poor substitute for travel narratives.

What, then, happened when Cresques and geographers after him adopted a different perspective? The most obvious result was that the Sahara started to look empty, as spaces that quite simply had not figured in itineraries – because the external travellers who wrote travelogs were discouraged from going there or because nobody wanted to go there anyway – suddenly had to appear on the map. Cresques' solution to this was simple: he filled all available gaps with large images illustrating principally European commercial interests, adding a few written anecdotes taken from Marco Polo's thirteenth-century *Book of the Marvels of the World*, and made them large enough to fill all the available space. This practice, however, quickly fell out of fashion, and by the nineteenth century, colonial maps of the Sahara mostly showed nothing at all apart from a scattering of mountains and largely imaginary lines along which, supposedly, travel was conducted. The idea of the Sahara as an essentially empty space had found its perfect visual expression.

While itineraries are uncompressible – each day of travel has to be accounted for – an aerial perspective permits manipulations of scale. Where the Sahara is concerned, this usually means zooming out. Enormous as the Sahara is, maps often reduce it to a smallish and rather uniform smudge, with most relevant physical features left out. (This is the equivalent of producing maps stretching from Galway to Novosibirsk, Portugal to Turkmenistan, or New York to San Francisco with no mention of, say, the Alps or the Rocky Mountains). On these maps, the Sahara usually appears in a unified shade of light brown, suggesting a region that is empty, barren, and everywhere the same. Oases rarely figure, and features that are crucial to local populations – salt mines, good pastures, perennial water sources – quite literally drop out of the picture. National borders are often left out or criss-crossed by many-coloured arrows pointing in all directions, suggesting porosity and frictionless connectivity over vast distances. This is not an image that can help us understand how people live in either the contemporary or the historical Sahara, nor how they understand their own position within it. Our first job, then, is to complicate this representation by adding nuance and heterogeneity.

Often, such general maps also convey a particular sense of time. Take, for instance, standard maps claiming to represent 'trans-Saharan trade' from, say, the seventh to the nineteenth century on a single map, with routes that seem to be fixed features of the landscape. Imagine just for a second anybody trying to do the same for even a small corner of Europe or North America on the basis, perhaps, of the continuity of Roman or colonial trade roads. This not only misrepresents actual movement on the ground – as we will see, the logistics of camel caravans and the vagaries of Saharan pasture make the very notion of a 'trans-Saharan route' an oxymoron – but also somehow implies that the Sahara is timeless, that nothing ever changes, and that both its environment and its people are situated beyond history (at least until the arrival of Europeans and their imperial armies in the nineteenth century).

A contemporary offshoot of this vision can be found in military and strategic maps, which also tend to adopt a vertical aerial perspective on a continental scale. In 2004, US Lieutenant General Wallace C. Gregson Jr described the Sahara – in a particularly badly chosen metaphor – as a 'swamp of terror', concluding with the ominous warning that 'trouble comes from ungoverned places'.[1] This was the beginning of what the anthropologist Jeremy Keenan has called the 'banana theory of terrorism'.[2] Take a moment to look at a world map: if you zoom out enough, it is easy to trace the banana-like arc of 'ungoverned places' stretching from Afghanistan via Syria, Iraq and Somalia across the Sahara to Mali and Mauritania. All places Western audiences have heard of, usually in conjunction with state failure, ongoing civil war, ominous terrorist threats, rampant poverty and destruction. Add a few arrows stretching from Afghanistan to Western Sahara, and the banana indeed begins to look threateningly large, spanning, as it does, half of the globe and bringing the 'terrorist hotbeds' of Central Asia into uncomfortable proximity with Euro-America. This is, of course, primarily an illusion of scale; if you zoom in, it quickly becomes apparent that the overland journey from Afghanistan to Mali is a long and arduous one, hardly suitable for jihadi (or any other kind of) mass terrorism. But these images are powerful political statements in their own right, creating fear and a perceived need for intervention.

The Sahara: Bridge, Barrier, or Laboratory of World History?

Beyond General Gregson's 'swamp of terror', the Sahara has long been spoken about through a series of metaphors specific to the region: as an inland sea, as a bridge, as a buffer zone, as a barrier that cuts the African continent in half. This language suggests an insurmountable civilisational frontier supposed to have cut off *sub-Saharan* Africa from the rest of the world for most of history. Contemporary borders, and the concentration of the region's major cities and densest populations to the north and the south of the desert, tend to support this view; even North Africans sometimes forget that they are as African as their sub-Saharan neighbours.

Although French colonial distinctions between 'white' and 'Black Africa' have fortunately been relegated to the rubbish bins of history (or have they?), their underlying (racial) assumptions often persist. In everyday perception, North Africa continues to be seen as an accidental appendage of the continent and its resident 'Arabs' as never quite African enough – although North Africans account for roughly 18 per cent of the overall population of the African continent and Arabic is spoken throughout much of Islamic Africa. This classification turns the sizeable Black population of North African countries (estimated to be 15 to 20 per cent of these countries' overall population) into strangers in their own lands and simply erases Black Saharans – arguably the majority of the overall Saharan population – from the picture, without even mentioning all those whose lives defy simplistic classification along these lines.

Another view, popular in global economic history, suggests that the Sahara has never constituted a serious obstacle to cross-regional interaction but rather has furthered it, that it has been less a barrier than a bridge in African history. This view is a clear improvement on the first, if only because it accounts for long-standing histories of commercial and religious exchange and works against all-too-well-entrenched colonial stereotypes of Africa as a continent outside history. Yet seeing the Sahara as a bridge assumes that its primary purpose is to be *crossed*; historical agency is attributed primarily to non-Saharan travellers brave enough to face desert hardship. This view is responsible for the all-too-familiar images of light-skinned North African traders leading camel caravans in a straight line across the otherwise empty space of the Sahara, facing incredible hardships caused by a hostile environment and uncouth desert raiders, about whom nothing more is said. It has also led to attempts to understand 'trans-Saharan trade' uniquely in terms of demand and supply on the Mediterranean coast, which carries into contemporary analyses of 'trans-Saharan smuggling' of guns, drugs or people. Beyond a few road cutters and raiders, Saharans rarely feature in these accounts.

This image of Saharan emptiness and passivity has deep roots in the historical record. Classical authors such as Herodotus and Pliny knew of the Sahara from distant hearsay only, whereas Arab travellers, versed in the same literary traditions, were able to add information gleaned from interviews with traders or even from their own personal experience. Although it is not always easy to parse fact from fiction, empirical information from literary convention in these accounts, it is clear that the Sahara was anything but empty when these writers began to describe the region from the tenth century onwards. Arab travellers were impressed – often grudgingly so – by the bustling cosmopolitan cities and high levels of Islamic scholarship they encountered on their journeys.

And yet, blinded by their own cultural and racial prejudice, they mostly attributed these qualities to the beneficial influence of fellow Middle Eastern and North African travellers and merchants, with whom they tended to lodge and interact. In the tenth century, the Arab traveller Ibn Hawqal described Saharan pastoralists as 'tribes of unheeded Berbers who are unacquainted with cereals and have never seen wheat or barley or any other kind of grain. They are for the most part in a state of wretchedness and their dress is a piece of cloth worn sashwise'. For his near contemporary al-Istakhrī, these people were quite simply 'isolated Berbers who have never seen a settlement and know nothing other than the remote desert'. Four centuries later, Ibn Battūta met them, too, as they held up his caravan, to his outrage, in the middle of the holy month of Ramadan.

For all those writers, the contrast with Arab trading towns couldn't have been greater. According to Ibn Hawqal, Sijilmāsa, in southern Morocco, was 'inhabited by people from 'Irāq, and merchants from Basra and Kūfa, and the men from Baghdād… . They, their children, and their trade flourish'. The impression he gives is one of a hardy Arab diaspora in an otherwise empty or savage land, reproducing itself independently and somewhat miraculously. He makes no mention of the many others involved in these Arabs' lives – the cooks; the servants; the guides; the providers of camels, food, transport, lodgings – or of the local wives who presumably made it possible for the 'Irāqī' merchants to have children in the first place. In the eleventh century, al-Bakrī similarly notes that 'most of the inhabitants of Awdaghust [in what is now Mauritania] are native of Ifrīqiya [present-day Tunisia]'. He, however, does mention local 'Black women', although hardly in flattering terms: 'Black women', he says, are excellent cooks, who are sold at 100 *mithqāl* per head alongside 'pretty slave girls with white complexions'.[3]

One of the first North African writers who broke with this tradition and attempted to understand the inhabitants of the Sahara on their own terms was Abraham Cresques' contemporary, the North African polymath Ibn Khaldūn. Abū Zayd 'Abd al-Rahman b. Muhammad b. Khaldūn was born in Tunis in 1332. A man of letters deeply involved in local politics, he spent his life moving between the capitals of the Maghreb, with occasional stints in prison, personally witnessing the fragility of all forms of political power and the rise and fall of kingdoms and princes (in which he often had a hand). Several times in his life, at moments of crisis, he sought refuge in the Sahara under the protection of Arabic-speaking nomadic tribes.

For Ibn Khaldūn, the history of the world was a cyclical confrontation between *badū* and urbanites. The Arabic word 'badū' has since given us the English 'Bedouin', but for Ibn Khaldūn, the term encompassed all inhabitants of the *bādiya*, or wilderness, whether they were nomadic, sedentary or somewhere in between and whether they spoke Arabic, Berber or any other Saharan language. According to Ibn Khaldūn, what made the badū different from city dwellers was not so much their lifestyle as the hardships of rural life, which were caused by the harshness of the environment and the absence of protection granted by a prince. This welded the badū together through strong ties of solidarity born from the need for mutual protection. States, meanwhile, purposefully encouraged meanness, strife and cowardice among their citizens, for how would the latter otherwise have consented to paying taxes?

The bādiya is thus close to the European idea of a fundamentally anarchic 'state of nature', with the difference that it was seen not as a state prior to policed society but as the latter's constant structural counterpart that kept kingdoms and empires on their toes. Additionally, the badū had none of the innocence that European philosophers such as Rousseau would later ascribe to the inhabitants of the state of nature; they were politically quite as sophisticated as city dwellers, just much tougher. This was why, Ibn Khaldūn wrote, the badū usually won their battles against city dwellers, taking over kingdoms and creating far-flung empires. Once victorious, however, they were then themselves corrupted by the luxuries of city life. They grew lax and weak, their quarrels petty, until, after a few generations, they were replaced by new groups of badū.[4]

During the period in which Ibn Khaldūn penned his universal theory of history, he had once more sought refuge in the bādiya himself, at the fortress of Beni Salama near Tiaret in contemporary Algeria. The fortress still stands, commanding stunning views over the pre-desert. From his window, Ibn Khaldūn could observe each summer the arrival of thousands of sheep, goats and camels, still covered in Saharan dust, flooding the plains in an unstoppable flow of moving bodies come to graze on the post-harvest stubble; it is clear from his autobiography that he spent many a pleasant moment in the shelter of their nomadic owners' tents.

Ibn Khaldūn's notion of life in the bādiya, then, was not purely theoretical; although he was a born-and-bred urbanite, he had felt, smelt and tasted the world beyond the cities, suffered from its hardships and perhaps experienced it as a form of liberation from the artificially restricted horizons of courtly life. Although historical reality in the Sahara was often more complicated than his theories allowed for (the badū did not always win, nor was the distinction between badū and city dweller always straightforward), to date he is the only thinker of some international renown to have developed a political theory rooted in Saharan history, attempting to account for it on its own terms.

Narratives of Desertification

For classical, medieval and early-modern writers, deserts were simply part of the world as God had made it. This attitude changed beginning in the late sixteenth century as Europeans set out to conquer the world and to absorb its natural bounty into capitalism, spreading natural disaster in their wake. In the seventeenth century, geographers and botanists observed the destruction of much of the native flora on tropical islands such as St Helena and Mauritius first hand. By the mid-eighteenth century, they had reached the conclusion that the global environment was responsive to human degradation and that destruction might be irreversible. This was a clear break with the past, when nature had been understood to be basically unchangeable and thus inexhaustible. 'Destruction' for many of the thinkers in this period was equivalent to deforestation, a process that many had witnessed first hand in the eighteenth century as native forests across the Americas were cut and burned down at an extraordinary scale, in fires that could last for weeks, leaving havoc in their wake. The aim was to sell timber and to clear the land for colonial agriculture, but the result was often nothing but a charred and ruined landscape prone to erosion.

If, eighteenth-century botanists mused, deforestation could cause land degradation on this scale, it stood to reason that deserts everywhere were not natural occurrences but the result of mismanagement. These colonial reflections were paralleled, in Europe itself, by the gradual enclosure of European 'wastelands'. Heaths, moors, forests, scrubs and downs, which had previously been held in common, were redefined as unproductive land, fenced in, and turned into private property, in the process unmooring a good share of the poor who had relied on them for daily survival. One of the justifications for enclosures was that open access to these wastes encouraged 'slothful and wandering habits' among the poor. The term 'wastelands' gradually accrued negative connotations, becoming 'land wasted' as well as 'land for the wasteful'. It's no coincidence that the word's Latin root *vastus*, unoccupied or uncultivated, has given us both 'vastness' and 'devastation'.

Imperial and domestic reflections went hand in hand. It was a short step from the assumption that deserts were the result of deforestation to the idea that, with careful management, they could be rendered fertile again. George-Louis Leclerc, Comte de Buffon, claimed in 1778 that 'a single forest' planted at the heart of the Arabian desert could attract enough rain to render the whole area fertile.[5] Thirty years later, the early socialist vision-ary Charles Fourier made similar observations about the Sahara itself.[6] From the eighteenth century onwards, in European litera-ture, deserts were no longer perceived as natural counterparts of civilisation, or its necessary cyclical corrective; rather, they were viewed as civilisation's failure. Similarly, the people who inhab-ited both deserts and other kinds of wastelands – whether they were Saharan mobile pastoralists or the 'roaming gypsies' of the English countryside – gradually came to be seen as harmful in their own ways, as obstacles to 'rational' economic development.

In 1830, twenty-two years after Charles Fourier wrote about the Sahara as a wasted opportunity, the French army conquered Algiers, finding ample space to test out the new theories of desiccation and environmental degradation. Apart from a few regions in the mountains and a relatively narrow strip along the coast, most of the land which was to become Algeria was made up of semi-arid or arid steppes, and a good proportion of Alge-rians were nomadic or semi-nomadic pastoralists. Forests played an important role in local prosperity as sources of fuel, fodder and food, and they were, just like pastures and in some cases also fields, owned collectively and managed through selective grazing and fires. Many of Algeria's most venerable cities, such as Tlemcen and Constantine, had long thrived through their intimate connections with such hinterlands.

Where local farmers and pastoralists could discern in the landscape a complex pattern of access rights and opportunities, the French colonial officers, looking for the green, undulating fields of the 'abundant granary of Rome' that their (mis)readings of the first-century Greek geographer Strabo had led them to expect, saw only desiccation, mismanagement and sloth. Rather than questioning their classical sources, they blamed this 'degradation' of the land on its current inhabitants. A standard reference work on Algerian pastoralism, published in 1906, sums up the general consensus: 'The Arabs have been fatal ... it is their sheep, their camels, their goats that have ruined North Africa'.[7] It was thus incumbent on the French colonial regime to 'pick up the work interrupted for 1,500 years', that is, since the Arab conquest of North Africa and the fall of the last Roman colonies in the region.

This was to be achieved through protection, prohibition, sedentarisation and agriculture. The French colonial regime set out to protect the 'remaining forests', which were duly expropriated and closed to all forms of local use (and in many cases granted as concessions to national or multi-national companies, to exploit for the production of cork, for instance). Next came the absolute prohibition of controlled fires and the exclusion of livestock from protected zones. Nomadic or semi-nomadic pastoralists were forced to become sedentary through the expropriation of collectively owned pastures and the privatisation of land. Finally, the immigration of (reluctant) French settlers introduced intensive agriculture, which was eventually handed off to large capitalist enterprises relying largely on Spanish seasonal workers.

Tiaret, where half a millennium earlier Ibn Khaldūn had penned his *Muqaddima*, was and had long been surrounded by fields of rain-fed cereals, but it was also situated at the extreme north of Saharan pastoral ranges. Saharan pastoralists used to arrive at harvest time with their herds of camels, goats and sheep. The poorer among them sought employment as seasonal harvesters;

the richer sold goods they had produced themselves or carried north from the Saharan oases: dates, cheese, leather, wool and livestock intended to be sold for meat as well as the handwoven carpets and blankets for which they were famous. They then let their herds graze on the stubble left by the harvest, fertilising the fields year after year. Each year, pastoral families tended to visit the same agricultural families, and these alliances, often strengthened through marriages and religious ties, could last over generations. They bound pastoralists and agriculturalists closely to each other, creating ties that could be drawn on in times of crisis – which, in the unstable climatic environment of the pre-Sahara, were always to be expected.

The French colonial government saw the region of Tiaret as prime agricultural lands from which pastoralists and their destructive animals had to be excluded at all costs. Their policies initially seemed to work, as the first two or three harvests on newly enclosed fields worked with the latest agricultural techniques to produce spectacular yields. A few years later, however, the soils, deprived of their yearly input of manure, were exhausted; settlers had moved on and fields lay fallow, while nomadic economies had been severely harmed without their northern outlet. Overall, experts now estimate that the Algerian environment, where the vegetation had been relatively stable over centuries, suffered severe degradation from the colonial insistence on intensive agriculture in regions that quite simply could not support it. Deprived of their traditional human care-takers, forests died: deforestation in Algeria had never been as high as it was from 1890 to 1940.[8]

Repeated failures, however, did little to change French attitudes towards agricultural models. Indeed, many of the unspoken assumptions of nineteenth-century environmental theory, in particular the need to 'reforest' the region and the hostile attitudes towards pastoralists, still persist and resurface in global anti-desertification campaigns today. The word 'desertification' itself, which started to be employed in the mid-nineteenth century and is still current in external accounts of the region – indeed, in January 2021, another 16 billion USD were earmarked for anti-desertification programmes by international funding bodies – is symptomatic. It implies that 'deserts' are primarily a problem rather than complex ecosystems in and of themselves; it forecloses even the possibility of asking questions about the complex interplay that might link deserts to other areas and about those who dwell there and derive their livelihoods from this particular environment.

Technical Utopias

Given the failure of colonial agricultural policy, from the conquest of Algiers in 1830 until the discovery of oil in the mid-1950s, the Sahara figured more as a status symbol than as a physical region of human habitation or even as an economic stake in the scramble for Africa – to the point where, rifling through the colonial archives, one is often left to wonder why anybody bothered conquering it in the first place. (Mostly, it seems, to stop other people from getting there first.) For the French army, the vast and open spaces of the Sahara, unified under military rule, were primarily a stage for the display of grandiose, transcontinental territorial power, gained and maintained by reckless courage and political skill in the face of the most unforgiving environment on earth. British statesmen, on the other hand, mocked the millions of acres of 'light soil' which overly romantic French gullibility had made into the unprofitable semblance of an empire.

Yet for many in the late nineteenth century, the Sahara's

apparent unprofitability was merely a matter of time and ingenuity. If the desert had been a moral provocation to classical
and mediaeval authors and an environmental failure to their
successors, it now appeared as a technical challenge or indeed
as an opportunity to push technical innovations to their limits
through the construction of large-scale infrastructure that
in more densely populated areas would have met with fierce
popular resistance. Propositions ranged from plans to flood the
Tunisian Sahara – much of which lies below sea level – in order
to create an 'interior sea', which French colonial engineers hoped
would automatically create a milder micro-climate, to the construction of a trans-Saharan railway linking the Mediterranean
to the Gulf of Guinea. If the Americans had done it in the West
and the Russians in Siberia, there seemed to be no reason why
the French should not have their very own transcontinental
railway to open up their very own agricultural frontier – in the
Sahara.

French engineers believed strongly in the universal value of
their undertaking. They also thought that the Tuareg, as 'light-
skinned and blue-eyed Berbers', were kindly disposed towards
French ideas of civilisation. They therefore decided to send the
first exploratory mission to trace the route of the railway-to-be
into the Sahara years before the French army had finished conquering the region – despite repeated warnings by Tuareg leaders
that they would not tolerate an armed expedition on their lands.
In 1881, all European members of this expedition, under the ill-
fated leadership of Colonel Paul Flatters, were duly killed near
Tamanrasset in what is now Algeria's southern tip; of the nine-
ty-three members of the expedition, only twenty made it back
to Ouargla. This caused outrage in France but for a while calmed
the ardours of the pro-trans-Saharan-railway camp.

In 1905, the French army, equipped with machine guns and

a solid spirit of revenge, wiped out most Tuareg resistance fighters in the battle of Tit near the site of the 'Flatters massacre'.
This brutally ended Tuareg sovereignty in the Central Sahara,
but the costs of constructing a trans-Saharan railway (estimated
at 600,000 francs per kilometre) remained forbidding. By 1949,
when the project was finally shelved, only 252 kilometres had
been finished, most of it relying on Vichy penal labour. Spanish
revolutionaries, prisoners of war, Jews and local communists
had toiled in grim and often deadly conditions similar to those
imposed by other fascist regimes of the period, but to little avail.

No trans-Saharan train ever left Oran's central station for Timbuktu. Similarly, the interior sea never existed except on paper.
But both visions lingered on in the popular imagination and in
books from trashy 1930s bestsellers to Jules Verne's 1905 post-
humous classic, *The Invasion of the Sea*. Similarly, the idea that
'the desert' could be 'subdued', or at least rendered productive
and profitable through technological intervention, has not gone
away. Plans for a trans-Saharan railway have been replaced by
those for a trans-Saharan highway, put forward by the African
Union since the 1960s and now nearing completion. Although
Tunisia still has no interior sea, Libya daily pumps thousands of
litres of clean water from the Sahara to the coast via its Great
Man-Made River. Oil prospection since the 1950s has revealed
large, sweet groundwater reserves under parts of the Sahara,
which has since fuelled agricultural development in Egypt,
Libya and Tunisia, particularly in the coastal regions, where
fresh-water is often scarce.

In 1970, the former Algerian president Houari Boumediène famously declared that 'where Algerians advance, the
desert recedes'. A year earlier, he had launched a massive 'Green
Dam Project', intended to 'stop the desert' by planting trees,

in conjunction with the Ministry of Defence. Twenty thousand soldiers, mostly conscripts, were mobilised. Boumediène's 'Green Dam' angered local pastoralists, who systematically uprooted his trees, seen as encroaching on their traditional pastures. However, it inspired the then president of Burkina Faso, Thomas Sankara, to launch a similar idea in his country; this project was later taken up by the instigators of the Sahel-wide Great Green Wall (GGW). Launched in 2005 by the African Union and funded by the World Bank from 2006 to 2020 to the tune of more than 5 billion USD, the GGW was initially conceived as 'an 8000 km-long line of trees and plants across the entire Sahel, from the Atlantic coast of Senegal to the east coast of Djibouti – halting desertification and creating a huge swathe of green across the African continent'. So far, very few of these trees have materialised, and those few that have are mostly planted outside the desert proper – in areas where people know, from centuries of experience, that they actually have a chance of survival. Elsewhere, local people do what they can to divert GGW funds into projects closer to their own hearts: the construction of schools and medical centres, for instance, or a viable road network.

European interest in large-scale Saharan technical utopias persists regardless. Witness, for instance, the 2009 Desertec Industrial Initiative, which proposed to solve Europe's energy crisis by constructing a network of solar power stations throughout the Sahara and the Middle East. Connected to the European grid, these would meet 15 to 17 per cent of European electricity demands and provide an equal quantity for domestic consumption in the producing countries. By 2014, one financial and many political crises later, Desertec was abandoned by its European sponsors, only to be picked up by the Moroccan king Mohammed VI, eager to greenwash the country's international reputation, which had somewhat suffered from revelations of political oppression and torture in the 1970s, 1980s and 1990s.

Since 2019, three concentrated solar power (CSP) plants have been functioning in Ouarzazate in the Moroccan Sahara, totalling 2 million mirrors covering 30 square kilometres of land and producing 6 per cent of Morocco's electricity consumption. By 2030, the king announced, another two sites would be added, one in the disputed territory of Western Sahara, which has been under Moroccan military occupation since 1975. In both cases, vast stretches of local pastures have been redefined, in language oddly reminiscent of the nineteenth century, as 'unproductive wastelands', that is, as empty and so far unproductive space from which no dissenting voices will be heard.

From the Inside Out

So much, then, for the models and metaphors that have been used to make sense of the Sahara, from bird's-eye-view maps via models of bridges and barriers, wastelands and environmental degradation to imperial agricultural fantasies and technical utopias. With the benefit of hindsight, it is easy to see that they erred by responding to crucial preoccupations of their times rather than to the realities of the desert itself. Yet these models throw long shadows over our current understanding of the region and have crystallised into ideas that are often taken for granted – the 'free' and 'ungoverned' nature of nomads, for instance, or the necessary decline of mobile pastoralism, the 'unproductive' and somehow 'futile' nature of deserts or the bundle of values and preconceptions contained in the deceptively straightforward term 'desertification'.

Any approach to the Sahara has to take these ideas into account and pick them apart very carefully. But that is just the beginning. The real challenge is to find new ways of thinking about the Sahara by taking our cue from Saharans themselves.

September 2009, somewhere near the long border between Algeria and Mali. Ghali's truck moved at a snail's pace. I had been granted a comfortable spot in the cabin next to the oldest of the three apprentices; the other two young men were now perched on the back of the load, holding on tightly as the heavy truck bumped over rocks and jolted in and out of old tire tracks, baked solid in the unforgiving heat. There were other passengers on board, but they, too, had to sit out back – I was privileged, not so much as a foreigner, but as the only woman in the company. Moreover, I had been introduced to Ghali by his boss, an Algerian trader from central Algeria: 'Treat her', he had said, 'as you would a girl from the Tantawi family'. The Tantawi were one of the most influential religious families in the Algerian Sahara and beyond; they had hosted me so far during my stay in the Algerian south. And so Ghali and the others treated me accordingly: it took two days before anybody talked to me at all beyond a few respectful greetings. This was somewhat at odds with my aim of carrying out research with contemporary trans-Saharan traders, but it taught me an important lesson right from the start: the Sahara might look big on a map, but it is socially dense; wherever you go, people will already have situated you within their social worlds depending on who introduced you to the area.

Ghali was born and grew up in Tamanrasset in southern Algeria, but his family were originally from northern Mali. His parents were among the many pastoralists who lost most of their herds in the droughts of the 1970s and 1980s and migrated north. Since then, many of his family had drifted back south to the 'sweeter' lands of northern Mali; Ghali's job as a truck driver not only promised him a regular income but also meant that he could visit them on a regular basis, providing them with staples bought at a lower price in Algeria. Ghali's own experience of a pastoral existence was thus at one remove, but this didn't prevent him from identifying with it: '*Nahnu al-ruhhūl, we* are the nomads', he told me, grinning, including in a sweeping gesture his three apprentices, his Arabic-speaking truck-driving colleague, the few paying passengers, and, perhaps most importantly, the truck itself.

And he was right: it was very clearly his mobility that gave him access to the Algerian funds that in turn made the life of the rest of the family, in the bādiya, a possibility. Although herds have been reconstituted since the droughts, few herders can live off them alone, and all therefore need to have a son, brother, cousin or brother-in-law like Ghali. Although the situation was clearly exacerbated by the current economic, political and environmental context, this interdependence of different forms of life and sources of income has always been true to some extent. Hence my second lesson: to endure over time, everything in the Sahara has to be connected to something else. Facile categorical distinctions – between nomads and sedentary populations, pastoralists and agriculturalists, traders and peasants, white and Black – simply do not hold.

Like many other contemporary Saharans, Ghali's family was spread out over hundreds of kilometres, and he moved easily between different worlds, from the urban amenities of southern Algerian cities to the beauties of Malian pastures. Lesson number three: family matters, and this in turn means that women are crucial, as it is women who throughout the region are pivotal in the arrangement and maintenance of marriages and in charge of most of the everyday work of preserving emotional and affective bonds between people who might live thousands of kilometres apart. Yet if close connections are cultivated and strengthened through marriage, it is also through marriage that families become large, diverse, far-flung and complicated: intermarriages between different linguistic, occupational, geographical and status groups have always been common throughout the Sahara and indeed fundamental for the working of Saharan societies and economies – but this does not mean that they have ever been easy.

Family is not all: Ghali's connections clearly spread much further. He worked as a driver for a well-known Algerian businessman, which meant that he could cross the Algerian border both ways without any difficulties. He stopped at every Islamic shrine on the way, asking for spiritual protection on his journey but also invoking the very real protection of the saints' contemporary descendants. He knew where to drop off portions of the Algerian petrol that filled the truck's double tanks to curry favour with Malian officials, how to talk to Algerian customs officials, which of his many passports to show at the border, when to be humble, when to be loud, where to give gifts, where to pass unnoticed. Lessons number four: never rely on just one type of connection, and five: connectedness does not imply equality.

Ghali clearly loved the open air of the bādiya and, to the consternation of some of his passengers, spent the first day of our journey staying put in his favourite spot just outside Tamanrasset. He knew how to live in the desert and how to turn Algerian subsidised staples into delectable desert food; most importantly, he knew how to look after his truck and took pride in its strength and beauty. Yet he also knew that truck driving was backbreakingly hard work that would eventually exhaust his youth and that most of the considerable profits made by his work were reaped by others. He also knew that it was dangerous: during one of our trips, we were stopped by armed men looking for money. They let us go when they saw that there was a woman on the truck – that Ghali was, as he said, using the polite formula, 'travelling with family'.

This was in 2009. Northern Mali has since descended into armed conflict and war, the border with Algeria has been officially closed and Ghali has had to renegotiate his mobility with the new strongmen in the area. Yet whatever happens, there will always be a need for people like him – people who can connect places across national borders, supply them with necessary goods and maintain crucial ties at relatively little cost. Here, then, is the summary of his five lessons: connectivity is, and always has been, hard work, but it is essential to life in the region.

Ghali's five lessons inform the exploration of Saharan life in this book. It is divided into three parts – resources, movement and politics – of three chapters each. It follows a rough timeline, starting with prehistory and ending in the 2020s. However, the chapters are primarily thematic, and contemporary developments connected to particular issues (such as radical Islam or contemporary mining) are dealt with in the relevant thematic chapter. The reason is that this book is not a straightforward history but an invitation to think, together, through certain questions, to suggest different perspectives on current problems and to show the relevance of past events to contemporary concerns. Given the vast temporal and spatial distances covered in this book, these connections might otherwise pass unnoticed and more fundamental conceptual conclusions be swamped in seemingly straightforward facts. This also means that not all of the Sahara is represented in equal measure in all chapters, nor is this book exhaustive, as indeed it could not be, given the scale of the region and the depth of time treated here. In some places and on some topics, it is mostly an invitation to look for more.

Although this book has a strong historical and geographical focus, it is written by an anthropologist and remains indebted to anthropology in many ways. Much of it is based on fieldwork, that is, on direct experience of life in different parts of the Sahara and shared with different people, usually for periods lasting more than a year, in southern Algeria and northern Mali (2006–2009) and northern Chad (2011–12). None of the experiences recounted here, and none of the people described or cited, can stand in for the Sahara as a whole. I have attempted to represent their points of view and their internal diversity as faithfully as possible, but there are of course many others who, by the nature of things, I had no chance to meet or had to leave out – and there are probably as many things that I quite simply did not see or misunderstood. Anthropological fieldwork cannot be very directive, as people talk only if they feel like it and usually do so on topics that interest them. Nor do they necessarily agree with each other.

Most of the ideas, experiences and viewpoints presented in this book thus emerged from long conversations with Saharans themselves, who provided not just the 'raw material' of the book but also its frames of analysis. The purpose of this book is to escape long-standing external perceptions of the Sahara – and of other 'wastelands' like it – as timeless, unchanging, empty and passive. In order to do so, we must challenge many of our underlying assumptions about desert life, and perhaps about life as such. Saharans, historical and contemporary, have much to say on these topics; let us follow some of them through the chapters of this book.

PART ONE

WHAT MAKES A DESERT?

1

SAND, ROCKS AND YELLOWCAKE

Here is no water but only rock
Rock and no water and the sandy road
The road winding above among the mountains
Which are mountains of rock without water

T. S. Eliot, *The Waste Land*, 1922

When we think of the Sahara, we think of sand: large dunes, as far as the eye can see, blown into majestic shapes by incessant winds and only rarely disturbed by passing caravans. And indeed, sand is a challenge and a lasting memory for everybody familiar with the region. It gets into the eyes, the mouth, the food, the water; between one's teeth; up one's nose; into one's ears. Many Saharan settlements are periodically obliterated by wandering sand-dunes that force farmers to stand by helplessly as their lands, houses, irrigation systems and palm trees are suffocated by sand. There is absolutely nothing anybody, whether a local farmer or an international development expert, can do to stop a wandering dune – planting them with grass or shrubs might slow them down for a while, but the wind blows on regardless. Grain by grain, the shifting sand will cover everything in its path.

The effects of such dunes are devastating: deprived of air,

palm trees will die, gardens that had been carefully tended over generations will disappear, and houses will be rendered uninhabitable. Saharan horticulturalists therefore spend much of their time and energy protecting their gardens against sand by building walls and digging out trees: near Ouargla in southeastern Algeria, individual palm trees seem to be growing in deep pits, only their top leaves visible from afar, as generations of horticulturalists have had to dig down to be able to reach them, giving the whole area the appearance of a gigantic Swiss cheese spiked with heads of celery. In the palm grove of Faya in northern Chad, people have simply resigned themselves to rebuilding their lives from scratch every time the large sanddune that travels through the oasis every generation or so has passed through. The outskirts of settlements are studded with these dunes, with the very tops of palm trees still sticking out, visited at irregular intervals by their owners, who are helpless to prevent their slow suffocation.

Beyond the narrow confines of oasis gardens, it is not the sand in dunes but in the air that is most problematic. Sandstorms are always a possibility, and there are certain months of the year – in autumn and spring, in particular – when travel regularly grinds to a halt in the face of passing sandstorms. Drivers turn off their cars to protect their motors. Visibility is reduced to nearly nil, and taking a plane is out of the question. Not even a camel will budge, and only a madman would venture out into the storm. The only option is to wait, huddled for shelter behind the grounded car or resting camel, keeping one's eyes shut and one's face covered with a veil, drinking water protected from sand as best as possible, eating food made crunchy with unwanted mineral additions. Some of these storms can go on for days, imposing their own rhythm even on travellers who thought they were pressed for time.

In the Sahara, you simply cannot afford to ignore the environment. It is, quite literally, in your face, influencing every move you make, every decision you take, your daily rhythm, the way you sleep, what you can eat; clogging your eyes; parching your throat. Even within the solid concrete houses of air-conditioned northern Saharan cities, any of the frequent power cuts will immediately remind you of where you are, as will drives across vast open stretches of not very much at all, straight road pointing into an unfathomable distance, tarmac blistering in the heat of the day and sighing as it contracts in the freezing cold of the night – a place where you should never, *ever* forget your spare tire.

This book must start, therefore, with the sheer physicality of the Sahara, with the sand, rocks, salt-pans, mountains and dust where people must make a living, and have done so for millennia, but also with the natural wealth hidden within them, for those who know how to make use of it, which has made the region a focus of external desire and intervention for as long as records go back.

Dust and Deep History

Despite the overwhelming presence of sand in some places, glib descriptions of the Sahara as 'a large sandbox' or 'the largest beach in the world' are highly inaccurate. Sand-dunes (*ergs*) cover only about 15 per cent of the Sahara's surface, in the few 'great ergs' that are as beloved by tourists as they are difficult to cross for humans, beasts and jeeps. The rest is mostly rocky hard surface, or 'desert pavement', called, after the Arabic term, *hamada*, alongside major and minor mountain ranges, boulders, salt flats (*shatt*), gravel plains (*reg*), seasonal riverbeds (*wadis*) and large stretches of caked and dried mud, mostly in former lakes and riverbeds. Areas that were covered by lakes or wetlands millions of years ago are still recognisable in today's Sahara by their fine dusty covering and their absolute flatness and monotony.

Take, for instance, the Bodélé Depression in the Djourab in north-western Chad. Stretching over 150,000 square kilometres, it is absolutely, totally and unbearably flat, its soft, light brown soil covered in a grey crust that breaks easily when you step on it. This is, according to the prestigious science journal *Nature*, the 'dustiest place on earth'.[1] There is nothing here – no road, no settlement, no camps – save one or two stunted trees, their survival miraculous, and a few gutted tanks left over from the Chadian civil war forty years ago, ground down by the incessant dust storms that act like sandpaper on their chassis. Storms with winds that can reach up to 47 kilometres per hour rage for 100 days per year on average, funnelled by the Tibesti and Ennedi mountain ranges to the north. At 35 kilometres per hour, they start picking up dust. So much so, in fact, that scientists now think that the Bodélé Depression alone accounts for 20 per cent of the dust that can be found in the earth's atmosphere.

This rather unprepossessing place is where, in 2001, a Chado-French archaeological team found the flattened and fossilised skull of what many now think is the oldest hominid ever discovered. Called Toumai, or 'hope of life' in Dazagada (a variant of Tubu), he or she lived about 7 million years ago, roughly at the time when, according to evolutionary biology, humans and their nearest cousins, the chimpanzees, diverged. Toumai's discovery kicked up a lot of dust indeed: he or she lived almost 4 million years before Lucy and 1 million years earlier than the 'Millennium Ancestor' discovered just a year earlier, in 2000 in northern Kenya. For years to follow, archaeologists argued endlessly over his or her 'true identity': was Toumai a strikingly human-looking ten-year-old female palaeo-gorilla or a strikingly gorilla-like adult male early hominid? (It appears that differences between the two are slight, as 'human' and 'female' features on early hominids tend to converge.) Paired with the 1995 discovery, also in Chad, of the 3.6-million-year-old Abel, these are indications that the region that is now the Sahara was probably quite as central to the story of human evolution and migration as the Great Rift Valley.

The Sahara looked very different then, of course. Toumai lived at the edge of Mega Lake Chad, a permanent body of water covering 350,000 square kilometres, like the Caspian Sea today, which has since receded to 5 per cent of its former size. Nearby fossils of forty-five different species of animals, including twenty-five kinds of mammals, suggest a landscape that hosted cows, or rather their prehistoric equivalent, palaeo-giraffes, monkeys, some kind of big cat, elephants, rodents, horses and hippopotami. The presence of fish, sea turtles, sea snails, crocodiles and a large number of amphibious animals suggests a landscape of rivers and wetlands bordered by open savannah, which in turn was bordered by desert. As long as early-hominid finds had been concentrated in East Africa, archaeologists had speculated that there was a close link between human evolution and the desiccation that is observable in East Africa during that period. The idea was that our ancestors had to adapt to increasingly open savannahs and hence started walking and hunting in groups. Toumai radically changed this story, as he or she seems to have thrived on variety, abundance and choice and on the ability to range over a mosaic of strikingly different ecological zones rather than just responding to environmental pressures.

The maritime abundance of Toumai's world also explains the crucial role that the Bodélé Depression now plays in world climate. Its fine, soft soil is composed of silt from the bottom of Mega Lake Chad, which dried up about 6,000 years ago – a mere blip in world history, especially when compared to Toumai's venerable age of 7 million. During the winter months, constant storms turn this soil into dust and blow it west across the African continent. Much of it falls into the Atlantic Ocean, replenishing sea life with vital nutrients. The rest makes it across to the Amazon basin, where it provides half of the nutrients the Amazonian rainforest receives each year. The Amazon's own soil is notoriously sparse and nutrient-poor, and without this vital addition, it would probably turn into a 'wet desert'; therefore, the world's richest, most diverse and wettest ecosystem depends directly on its most arid.

The reason why the Bodélé dust is so rich in nutrients is that much of it consists of organic material produced by the lake – in fishbones rich, among other things, in phosphates. Hitching a lift with the dust are various micro-organisms, living bacteria, algae and fungi, leading to at times surprising faunal and floral parallels between those two areas and in stopping posts on the way – in the Cape Verde archipelago, for instance, where researchers now think that all endemic plants and animals have their origins in the Sahara.

The influence of this dust is as profound as it is voluminous. According to recent estimates, during the dry season, the Bodélé Depression releases 700,000 tonnes of dust *each day*. If we look at the Sahara as a whole, this figure rises to 1.7 billion tonnes of dust per year. This dust might be bothersome, obscuring the sun at times. It might be surreal, falling on the faraway streets of London, lingering for days in the cracks of pavements and on dustbin lids. It might be picturesque, as when red dust suddenly covers the snow-capped Atlas Mountains on the North African coast, tripping up disgruntled skiers. Or it might cause alarm, as when analyses revealed that the Saharan dust that regularly settles on cars parked on the street in Brittany is actually radioactive – courtesy of nuclear tests carried out by France in the Algerian Sahara in the 1960s. But it is a crucial part of the global ecosystem. As annoying as it might be, the world could not function the way it does now without Saharan dust.

As appealing as images of Toumai-like creatures, male and female, frolicking in abundant wetlands may be, the climatic history of the Sahara is not simply a straightforward progression from wet to dry. Instead, the region has long been subject to severe climatic variations, oscillating between periods of extreme aridity, when much of West Africa was desert, and 'wet' periods, when much (but by no means all) of the contemporary Sahara was covered in plants and dotted with permanent lakes, seasonal rivers and extensive wetlands. This was probably due to small variations in the earth's axis which led to shifts in the West African monsoon and hence to more or less rainfall, combined with periods of extreme cold ('ice ages') that immobilised water as ice and hence increased worldwide aridity.

Then, as now, changes in Saharan climate had an impact worldwide: wetter episodes allowed species to cross the area that is now the Sahara, while arid and hyper-arid episodes created barriers that led to increased speciation (the independent development of different varieties and species) on either side of the desert. This is called the 'pump theory', and it is a crucial part of evolution, including our own. To put it simply, during the wet Sahara, animals, people and plants moved into the Sahara, at times crossing it. As the Sahara dried out, they moved towards its edges, some north, some south, some east, and were, for a while, cut off from each other, developing their own cultural and, over time, biological adaptations. As the Sahara greened again, they returned, were brought into contact, learned from each other, mingled, migrated, moved around and interbred.

With new climatic changes, the whole process started over again.

Catastrophic as those shifts may have been for the individuals who lived through them, from the point of view of biodiversity and the ecosystem as a whole, the migration and diversity they encouraged contributed to the health of the larger ecosystem. The environmental history of the Sahara potentially provides ample grounds for the study of radical climate change and adaptation, but only if we let go of the simple narrative of a unidirectional change from green ('good') to brown ('bad') and pay more attention to concrete cases and specific regional adaptations over time. While the current, human-induced climate change is definitely *not* conducive to diversity, the Sahara's example demands that we reckon with complex regional ecosystems from the bottom up before pronouncing judgement on a seemingly harsh and protean landscape.

The latest of the Sahara's wet periods peaked around 10,000 years ago. By then, we start to have evidence of relatively widespread human occupation of different parts of the Sahara, most notably in what is now southern Morocco, in the Aïr Mountains in what is today northern Niger, in southern Libya and in the eastern Sahara near the Nile. (As we have seen with Toumaï and Abel, there had been much earlier occupations, but these people had all but vanished in the extremely hostile period which peaked 26,500 years ago.) It seems that, drawn by an intricate mosaic of wetlands, seasonal rivers, small lakes, and open savannah, as well as the abundant fauna that lived there, people slowly drifted into the Sahara from its southern, northern and eastern edges.

We should image them as hunter-gatherers, living near lakes and rivers, mostly sedentary. They made and exchanged elaborately decorated pottery, among the first to appear on the African continent. They corralled wild sheep, decorated Central Saharan rock faces with paintings and engravings of elegant round-headed people, built windbreaks and stone huts and processed plant food to cater for their tastes, but they had no interest in agriculture. There was no need indeed for the back-breaking labour that agriculture usually implies, as they could rely on the abundance of maritime foodstuffs that wetlands usually produce as well as trapping rodents and hunting cattle and sheep. Although this last wet period in the Sahara clearly saw important migration and networks of exchange, they were not necessarily the result of hardship but rather perhaps of curiosity.

Cows, Pharaohs and Irrigation

Six thousand years ago, the Sahara gradually started to dry up again until it reached, about 3,000 years later, its current condition, forcing all living creatures either to return south or head north or to adapt to an increasingly arid environment. The best-known of these adaptations featured in the rise of the early Egyptian kingdoms in the Nile valley, which emerged about 5,000 years ago. Their story has long been told as a historical oddity, or rather as a link in a social evolutionary chain that connects the earliest cities in Mesopotamia – incidentally, a landscape that was probably quite similar to the 'wet' Sahara – via Egypt to Greece and Rome and finally to Western Europe, leaping great chunks of time but especially making short shrift of geography. Egypt is, after all and first and foremost, in Africa, and although the Nile valley had long been connected to the Levant, the earliest archaeological finds both in Egypt and in Sudan show just how closely tied the Egyptian polity was and always remained to its Saharan surroundings. Pharaonic Egypt did not rise out of nothing, like a universal idea suddenly made flesh in a propitious environment.

For most of human history, the Nile valley had not even been seen as propitious: the earliest evidence of life in the area suggests mobile cattle camps at a good distance from the river rather than in the valley itself. There are also traces of elaborate cattle burials, some of them showing signs of early attempts at mummification (yes, they made cow mummies before they made human ones). This changed as rain grew scarce, and archaeologists now believe that the profound cultural and conceptual transformations that eventually brought about Pharaonic Egypt were probably sparked by Saharan pastoralists – then at the forefront of technological and social innovation – moving into the Nile valley, where they met hunter-gatherers who had just started experimenting with crops, although it was not until the fourth millennium BCE that anybody became truly sedentary. If this was the case, these pastoralists never abandoned their infatuation with cows. From their earliest depictions, Egyptian kings were shown as conquering bulls, surrounded by people with horns or bovine heads. Through subsequent millennia, many of the elements that were central to the mobile cattle pastoralism remained at the core of Egyptian culture, from an intense interest in animals via cattle cults to elaborate animal burials.

Other Saharans, pushed by the same factors as the soon-to-be Egyptians, probably headed south to what is now northern Sudan, where they founded the kingdom of Kush about 4,500 years ago. Kushites loved cattle. They buried cattle rather than humans and kept them even as ecological conditions further deteriorated, making cattle raising economically unprofitable. As in Egypt, well-irrigated agriculture here might have developed first to produce grain to feed cattle as pasture became scarce but people did not want to part with their beloved animals. In such a context, agriculture was probably not seen as 'progress' from mobile animal husbandry but rather as a way of saving it in difficult circumstances, perhaps in the hope that the climate would eventually improve so that people could become fully nomadic once more.

Fast forward 4,000 years, and Egypt and especially Sudan have become mere outliers, peripheral in a Mediterranean world now dominated by a recent upstart: the Roman empire. The Romans had rather clear notions about the inhabitants of the Sahara. These notions derived largely, like many Roman prejudices, from Greek sources, in particular Herodotus. Saharans to them were uncouth and dangerous raiders, barely civilised, and smelled of dung; they were ungovernable barbarians, living for the most part in tents or scattered villages of huts. For Tacitus, they were brigands, receivers of stolen goods, perhaps useful when employed as partners in raids but otherwise mere cowards and slavers. This poor opinion had long shaped images of the Garamantes, a Saharan people who lived in Fazzān in what is now southern Libya and who maintained close albeit not always friendly relations with Rome, until the Romans finally sent two military expeditions to Fazzān, leading to a Roman triumph in 19 BCE.

Although the first excavations in Fazzān, conducted by an Italian team, took place in the 1960s, European archaeologists and historians had long adopted Roman imperial prejudice wholesale. It therefore came as a bit of a surprise when, in the 2000s, a series of excavations undertaken by a British team from the University of Leicester uncovered the remains of a vast and complex urban civilisation, complete with city defences, elaborate burial sites, irrigated agriculture, evidence of far-reaching trade networks, and the remains of a public Roman-style bath-house. The Garamantes, it turned out, were not quite 'nomadic barbarians' after all but a society where people lived in large and well-built cities. They routinely imported large quantities of Roman staples, such as wine, olive oil and fish sauce; Roman luxuries, such as Roman glass and fine ware; and exotic trade currencies, such as Indian glass beads and cowrie shells from the Red Sea. They had some use for writing. They also grew, in the middle of the Sahara, water-guzzling cotton, presumably for their own local textile industry, of which much of the product was probably destined for export, and produced their own glass beads and pottery, probably also for trading purposes. They had very clearly turned Fazzān into a far-reaching regional trading hub, with a sedentary population estimated at up to 100,000 people – a population figure that in Fazzān has only been reached (and exceeded) recently after a slump that lasted for two millennia.

The ruins of this civilisation were there all along. The rather belated 'discovery' of the Garamantes tells us just how much external images of the Sahara have blinded us to empirical realities and of just how different world history looks when viewed from the south. The Garamantes also provide a key example of a socio-cultural adaptation to extreme climate change, which in turn transformed Saharan landscapes. Clearly, what had happened in Fazzān was comparable to what had happened in the Nile valley as formerly semi-mobile Saharan people, hunter-gatherers who kept some livestock or pastoralists who did some hunting and gathering, were forced by drying conditions to specialise. Some released their cattle, concentrating on goat- and sheep-herding and becoming increasingly mobile. Others settled in Fazzān near a gradually disappearing lake. As food became scarce, they started planting crops imported mostly from the East: grapes, dates, barley and wheat, to which they later added millet and sorghum from the south. The permanent lake turned into seasonal wetlands, then dried up completely. Local residents, now sedentary, had no other option than to dig wells, first shallow, then deep, and then to extend them, drawing on Eastern expertise, into the complex underground irrigation canals (*foggaras*) for which they are still famous.

These newly settled populations could survive and expand because they maintained close ties with their pastoralist neighbours but also because of their investment in trade, acting as a commercial hub between the Mediterranean world and the region that, at that very moment, was gradually turning into *sub-Saharan* Africa. It is clearly this trade rather than the Garamantes' local agricultural production that allowed them to survive and expand, to become wealthy and powerful. Most of the estimated 77,000 years of human labour needed to dig and maintain the foggaras was probably provided by slaves, acquired from further south in exchange for trade goods either produced locally or imported from the Mediterranean coast. Although we now call them by the convenient shorthand 'Garamantes', following Roman usage, the inhabitants of Fazzān at that time were clearly a motley and cosmopolitan bunch linguistically, culturally and ethnically, with quite as many (or more) southern as northern additions. No wonder, then, that Roman descriptions were so confused.

Landscapes of the Contemporary Sahara

Imagine a dusty plain studded with vertical rocks of bizarre shapes, forming a labyrinth of narrow and winding corridors. In the rocks' crags nestle small, spiky plants, greyish green from the dust. In a few shady corners, small permanent sources of water are indicated by dūm palm trees and shrubs that grow there spontaneously, innumerable birds cackling in their branches. Suddenly, before you turn a corner, a strong ammoniac smell. A large body of apparently stagnant water comes into view, black and reeking, with camel and other dung floating on its frothy surface, encased by the high, rocky cliffs reflected in the stagnant water. This is the Archëi *guelta* (permanent pool) in Ennedi in northern Chad. Far above, the sun beats down from a merciless sky. In the water, a herd of camels, bleating and urinating with joy (hence the smell) – they probably haven't seen any water for days, if not weeks. Their shepherds relax under an acacia tree in the corner; nearby rock art speaks of millennia of human passage and occupation. On quieter days, people say, you can spot dwarf crocodiles in the water, endemic survivors of a much earlier age. Today, however, the guelta resounds with the calls of happy beasts, reverberating from the steep rocky walls. It is difficult to imagine silence in such a place, full, as it is, of life.

Situated at an altitude of almost 3,000 metres (10,000 feet) above sea level, the Assekrem Plateau, 80 kilometres north of the city of Tamanrasset in southern Algeria, provides a view over range after range of chiselled rock formations in all possible shades of ochre. These are relatively young mountains, former volcanoes, but heavily eroded by desert winds into fantastic gothic shapes, reaching upwards as if to touch the sky. At night, temperatures can descend below freezing point; they are rarely above 6°C even on a warm night. In good years, after the autumn rains, the rocky mountain slopes suddenly and spectacularly turn pink, covered in wild sorrel as far as the eye can see. Two days later, all trace of this sudden abundance will be gone. Yet as all local goatherds know well, some moisture will remain trapped in rocky fissures and crags, collecting in small but precious pools. At the bottom of the valleys grow wild olive trees, lavender, palm trees, tamarisk, and various kinds of artemisia and acacias, providing firewood and toothpicks; on the plains between and beyond the mountains grow tough tufts of desert grass called *drinn*, which camels love and the seeds of which people harvest at times of famine. With patience, you might spot desert foxes, gazelles, mouflons, and many bird species, including eagles, ducks and two types of stork, all attracted to the permanent water sources and shelter offered by the mountains.

With floral and faunal wealth thanks to the mountains' capacity to attract rain and to store water, the Ahaggar Mountains have been central to regional livelihoods for as long as we can tell, to the point that one of the main Tuareg federations in the Sahara, the Ahaggar, is named after them – or is it the mountains that are named after the people? This is where the famous tomb of Tin Hinan, dating from the fourth century and containing, among other things, Roman coins featuring the emperor Constantine, is situated. According to Ahaggar legend, Tin Hinan was a Berber queen, as beautiful as she was commanding, who arrived in the region from the oasis region of Tafilalt in southern Morocco. She is considered the ancestor of the Kel Ahaggar, yet it is clear, if only from rock art dating back to the Holocene, that at the time of her arrival, people were already flourishing in the area. Because of the ecological importance of mountains, their biodiversity and the shelter they offer from extreme climate and marauding invaders, most major pastoralist groups in the Sahara are attached to and often also named after a particular mountain range, from the Mauritanian and northern Malian Adrar via the Ahaggar and the Tassili in southern Algeria and the Aïr Mountains in northern Niger to the Tibesti in northern Chad, alleged place of origin of the Tubu, or 'people of the mountains'. One look at the slopes of the Ahaggar, after the rains have fallen, can tell us why.

Arguin, on the Mauritanian Atlantic Coast and, like the

Ahaggar Mountains, now a national park, is on UNESCO's World Heritage list. No mountains here, but sand-dunes as far as the eye can reach – which isn't very far. With the intense moisture coming off the Atlantic Ocean and evaporating in the desert sun, this coastal strip is, more often than not, covered in a dense fog which provides moisture in an area where it rains even less than elsewhere in the Sahara. The relative humidity in the air routinely reaches 60 per cent, and the constant haze lowers temperatures – maximums are around a mere 27°C – and protects against the merciless blaze of the sun.

This is the one part of the Sahara with relatively diverse, drought-resistant endemic scrub forests covered with lichen and interspersed with succulents, sheltering hyenas and honey badgers. It is also where, out in the ocean, the last colonies of Mediterranean monk seals live, mate and hunt, their loud barks occasionally echoing through the fog. Up to 2,4 metres long, they are the largest still surviving seal species and among the rarest aquatic carnivores in the world (there are about 700 individuals left). Monk seals are old creatures, and they have probably been at Arguin since prehistoric times, when they elected residence here because it is the place where three major sea currents (the Canary Current, the North Equatorial Current, and the Guinea Current) meet, providing seasonally a phenomenal abundance of fish. Thousands of migratory birds from northern Europe join them in winter on the Banc d'Arguin, a group of sandbanks just off the Mauritanian Coast where, in 1816, the French frigate *Méduse* – of Théodore Géricault's *Raft of the Medusa* – came to a tragic end.

This abundance of fish has also given rise to a very particular form of human ecology. In the constant vapour of the shore live the Arabic-speaking Imraguen, who have long derived their livelihood from seasonal fishing, especially of the flathead grey mullet, trading fresh, dried and salted fish with camel pastoralists further inland. They used to practice a unique form of nomadism, following the schools of mullet as they migrated along the coast. Today, they live in villages on the coast near the national park, but they continue to host pastoralist families from the inland or wealthy citizens from the Mauritanian capital, Nouakchott. These visitors desire to improve their health through a seasonal fish cure, especially as many of the wealthy Nouakchott elite now suffer from the ailments of a modern industrial diet: diabetes and obesity. Most Saharan pastoralist nomads, whether they are Arabic-, Tuareg- or Tubu-speaking, disdain fish, considering it improper for their consumption, but some make an exception for the grey mullet. As they say, it has been killed and bled in an Islamic fashion, in a way mastered only by the Imraguen – who drive the fish into shallow nets, some say with the help of dolphins, and then wade into the water to kill and bleed them by hand.

These landscapes of abundance are a far cry from the Bodélé Depression or even from the images of sand-dunes and sterile greyish-brown salt flats that we associate more commonly with the Sahara. What we need to retain from them is the notion of diversity that persists in marginal and fragile ecologies – a diversity that can be destroyed by even small changes or careless use. It is this diversity and the ability to derive and combine elements of different ecological niches, regions and zones that have made human life in the desert possible. This diversity, however, tends to be hidden from external descriptions and imaginations.

Take, for instance, the word 'Sahara' itself. It is derived from the Arabic term *ashar*, meaning a yellowish and reddish brown; although it is now used widely throughout the region, it has no historical equivalent in other local languages, whose speakers quite simply never conceived of the whole Sahara as one place. Different local-language communities had different names for the different deserts that they saw around them, much as in antiquity, when the Mediterranean was thought of as a succession of different 'seas' rather than as a coherent whole. The latter perception indeed requires the kind of aerial perspective that has now, as outlined in the introduction, become commonplace but that until the use of aeroplanes (and, today, satellite imagery) remained not a visual reality but a laborious construction, even for European explorers.

For people who had to make a living in the Sahara, such a perspective was of limited use. They tended and still tend to think and talk about space from the user's point of view. In spring 2012, as I was travelling with one of the first groups of tourists to visit the Ennedi in northern Chad, these different perspectives became blatantly obvious. As the tour guide (trained in the capital) was asking a local pastoralist to point us to a striking rock formation that he knew his European clients would appreciate, they instead described the way to the nearest permanent water source. For them, unused to European tastes, this was a much more likely place of attraction, beauty and joy than an oddly shaped rock.

Despite this diversity, we can nonetheless point to a few consistent principles. One of the main distinctions that informs internal perceptions of the Sahara is between areas where (human) life can be sustained and those where it cannot. The latter are designated differently, according to the language used, as *serir*, *tanzerouft*, *ténéré*, *awi*. Each carries much the same moral burden of desolation as the English 'desert' – spaces devoid of human life, empty of flourishing. Some of these words have been turned into place names by Western geographers, such as the

'Ténéré', a vast, sandy and mostly unoccupied plain stretching over 400,000 square kilometres in northern Niger. The Ténéré is a place where you can relish the sight of elegant untouched sand-dunes, stretching in all directions and turning both motorised and animal transport into an unmitigated chore, but it is not a place where any Saharan in their right mind would want to spend more time than absolutely necessary.

In the 1980s, the German anthropologist Georg Spittler noted that when you tell local Tuareg that Europeans tend to think of them as the 'sons of the desert', they laugh; they might be, at a stretch, the sons (and daughters) of a particular mountain range, or a valley known for its good pasture, but certainly not of the sandy and hyper-arid Ténéré.[2] This is not because they do not know how to go there or indeed travel through it; indeed some of the most important trade routes, such as the one linking the Aïr to salt mines in Kawar, cross the Ténéré outright. What they do not like about the Ténéré is therefore not the sand, or the hardship to be expected there, but its loneliness. They know that humans, to remain human, need company; this is what makes *akal*, the camp, different from *asuf*, the place of loneliness. Asuf is the abode of the Kel Asuf, *jinns* or malevolent spirits, and it is best to avoid them wherever possible. If they get hold of you, they will make you sick, or just sad with impossible longing. This is why, on the caravans across the Ténéré, even usually taciturn camel drivers talk incessantly, as conversation is the essence of sociability, which in turn keeps the Kel Asuf at bay.

People who spend too much time away from others might become 'like animals' and forget even the most rudimentary forms of human sharing and interaction. Local people place no value on being 'close to nature' in this sense, as in the European romantic tradition, and to 'get lost in the desert' is not a matter of spatial or even spiritual but rather of social confusion. At the same time, the growth to adulthood is expressed in a person's increasing ability to confront the outside world, to travel in ever wider circles, *without* getting lost or losing oneself; indeed gender distinctions hinge very much on the different forms of mobility open to men and women, respectively. Women are also seen, throughout the Sahara, as more vulnerable to jinns than men, especially when they are pregnant or have just given birth. Whereas in Europe, people tend to oppose nature to culture, the artificial to the biologically given, here, where anything human-made is a reassuring sight, nature and culture are one and the same. They are, together, opposed to 'loneliness': the absence of even the possibility of sociability and therefore of life.

Salt: The Essence of Being

These varied Saharan landscapes have given rise to an array of ecological adaptations by man and beast, but they also hide, to different degrees, mineral resources. Some of these, such as salt, have been exploited for centuries. This has durably structured Saharan space, creating trade routes marked by wells, markets and permanent settlements of miners in otherwise out-of-the-way places. Others, such as oil, gas and uranium, have acquired market value only more recently. As early as the late tenth century, the Arab geographer Ibn Hawqal noted that the king of Ghana (probably in what is now Mali), who was 'the wealthiest king on the face of the earth because of his treasures and stocks of gold ... stands in pressing need of the goodwill of the kings of Awdaghust [now in Mauritania] because of the salt which comes to them from the lands of Islam. They cannot do without this salt'.[3] A century later, al-Bakrī claimed that in the neighbouring kingdom of Gao, now also in northern Mali, people traded with salt, 'which is like money among them' and which replaced gold and silver as a currency.[4]

On reflection, it is easy to understand why salt might act as money: it keeps well, is easy to transport over long distances and can be subdivided into relatively standard quantities. And, in opposition to gold, it actually has inherent value: people (and most kinds of livestock) cannot live without salt, although they can well live without gold. 'It would appear strange', wrote the Scottish explorer Mungo Park of what is now central Mali in the late eighteenth century, 'to a European to see a child suck a piece of rock salt as if it were sugar. This, however, I have frequently seen; although in the inland parts the poorer classes of inhabitants are so very rarely indulged with this precious article, that to say "a man eats salt with his victuals" is the same as saying "he is a rich man".'[5] Saharans who lived near salt deposits were effectively sitting on piles of money.

Like the Saharan landscape that contains it, Saharan salt is highly varied from one region to the next, both in its chemical composition and in the form in which it occurs. The most common of these are *sebkhas*: low-lying, monotonous depressions, sometimes with seasonal or past lakes, that are covered in a crust of reddish-white salt, called earth salt, or *amersal*, that breaks when you step on it. This is not the kind of salt that can be turned into money, as it is crumbly, mixed with earth and difficult to transport; it is used for human consumption only if absolutely necessary. Yet pastoralists often travel hundreds of kilometres with their animals to earth-salt deposits that they particularly esteem to let their animals feed on the salt directly, and there was (and still is) some trade in earth salt stuffed in bags. Pastoralists usually choose the kind of salt they give to their animals wisely, mixing different kinds, each according to their own recipe and experience, but they all agree that without these 'salt cures', camels especially would die of constipation.

Rock salt, or salt that can be turned into money, occurs much more rarely, and there are a few known deposits and mines that have shaped Saharan history over time, from Awlīl, mentioned by Ibn Hawqal in the tenth century, via Kawār in northern Niger to Tawdanni, whence Timbuktu derived its dominant position in commerce from the fourteenth century onwards. Although Timbuktu is famous in European lore as a city of gold, it is in fact situated far from the West African gold fields, over which the city had no political control whatsoever – legend even has it that Timbuktu merchants had no idea where the gold actually came from. What the city did have, however, or could procure from its northern desert, was rock salt, which in turn could be exchanged for gold in the savannah and forests further south, some say at a rate of one to one. Salt slabs from the Tawdanni mines 655 kilometres north of the city, still hold pride of place in the Timbuktu market today.

In the eleventh century, al-Bakrī said that in the salt mines of 'Taghara' (which might be Tegaza, which is close to Tawdanni), 'the ramparts of the city were made of salt as also its walls, pillars and roof. The doors, too, were made of slabs of salt covered with leather'. This image of a place or city built from salt alone goes back to Herodotus. Whether or not it is true, given the barren environments of many of these salt mines, the use of second-rate salt slabs as building material might not be far-fetched. 'Tawdenni', as the French colonial administrator Paul Marty wrote in the early twentieth century, 'is situated in one of the most appallingly desolate areas in the world. There is not one bit of vegetation, nor any wood within a radius of 150 kilometres'[6]; contemporary miners in any case live at times in shelters made out of salt slabs, with roofs made out of tarpaulin.

As magical as a castle of salt might sound – shining white and glittering in the sun as if built of diamonds – it is excruciating to live, breathe, sleep and work in salt, drink salty water and eat salty food, all in a landscape both too flat and far too bright for human eyes. All food has to be imported, by the same traders who buy the salt and usually on credit, at vastly inflated prices. In permanent contact with salt, miners' hands and feet erupt in painful cracks and sores, and their bowels permanently cramp due to the bad water, which fills the whole area with its nauseating stench. Marty said of conditions in the early twentieth century, 'The inhabitants of Tawdenni are always at the brink of starvation, and food at the market is unaffordable. Every year, several people die of hunger or physical misery'. Conditions have not changed much since Marty wrote these words. Rock salt occurs in layers roughly 1 metre under the ground. It is mined with the same hand tools and equipment that were used when Marty wrote, as the low cost of labour does not warrant any investment in more sophisticated tools. The topsoil has to be removed, and slabs have to be cut and levered out whole in order to retain their commercial value. They are cut into rectangular shapes and stacked until merchants take them away. There is no shade.

It is not surprising, then, that miners were historically drawn from among the underprivileged, from those whose choices were limited: slaves, debtors, freed slaves and the poor but also occasionally young men who needed a lump sum of money fast, to get married or to start in business. From 1969 onwards, miners also included political prisoners, as the Malian dictator Moussa Traoré set up a penal labour camp in Tawdanni to which he sent those of his enemies he feared most. Hardly anybody came back alive, and the very name of Tawdanni still invokes terror throughout the country. The camp was closed, under international pressure, in 1988. Moussa Traoré was toppled in a coup in 1991. The salt mine, however, remains. Today, about 100 miners work there permanently. They are now recruited mostly from the north of the country, with the addition of a few sub-Saharan migrants on their way north who need to earn money so that they can travel on. Most of the salt is exported by trucks, but the occasional camel caravan can be seen during the cold season, slowly making its way south to Timbuktu, giving a (false) impression of permanence in a rapidly changing socio-economic and political landscape.

Sitting on money, then, does not necessarily make your life easy. Let us turn from the desolation of Tawdanni to the much lusher landscapes of Borkou in northern Chad, where run-off from the neighbouring Tibesti Mountains replenishes abundant shallow underground water tables, leading to some natural vegetation and an abundance of natural springs. Some of these feed a self-refurbishing natron mine on the outskirts of the town of Faya. To call this a 'mine' is something of an exaggeration: rather, picture a shallow natural open-air pit several kilometres across just beyond the dusty palm grove, surrounded by springs, its bottom criss-crossed by rather haphazard trenches that, once emptied, are left to crumble in the sun. Natron is a naturally occurring compound of sodium carbonate and sodium bicarbonate which has long been crucial to Mediterranean economies and industries. Roman and Greek glass-making, medicine, food, and the production of pigments, incense and glaze all relied on natron as a key ingredient. The ancient Egyptians in particular were avid consumers, as they used it to soak up the fat in bodies to preserve them for mummification. It took, according to modern estimations, about 400 kilogrammes of natron to mummify an adult fat-tailed sheep and perhaps half as much for an average-size human.

Although natron has been traded throughout the Mediterranean for as long as the historical record goes back, this was not the case in the Sahara proper. Although natron looks very much like ordinary salt with a slightly soapy texture, it spoils easily and has to be fresh, making it a poor substitute for money. In Faya in the late nineteenth and twentieth centuries, natron was therefore a sought-after resource but not a commodity. Pastoralists from further south and east would drive up their herds for annual salt cures, selling some cereals on the way and collecting a few bagfuls of salt lumps to take back with them, and that was it. Until, that is, truck transport became available and the markets of the Sudan – where natron is used in the cloth-dying industry and has a range of medicinal purposes – were suddenly within Faya's commercial range. Since the 1980s, a lively trade in natron has developed between Darfur and Faya, relying almost entirely on truck transport.

Natron mining is hard work. Blocks of earth weighing up to 50 kilogrammes each have to be levered out with crowbars, sledgehammers or axletrees and then lifted by hand onto dump trucks which can each carry between 25 and 35 tonnes. Today, you can earn on average 5,000 F CFA (8 USD) per day mining natron; this is a decent daily wage for manual labour in Faya, where jobs are few and far between. A truck-load costs the driver about 700,000 F CFA in labour and taxes; he will be able to sell that load for 2 million F CFA in Abéché in eastern Chad and for up to 5 million (8,400 USD) in Sudan. During the height of the cold season, up to six trucks loaded with natron leave per day for other parts of the country and abroad. The revenue generated locally by the mine thus amounts to between 40 and 100 million F CFA (67,000 to 170,000 USD) per month, of which more than half is syphoned off by local strongmen and government officials. From a free-for-all natural bounty, natron has thus become a highly priced international commodity.

Black Gold: Bounty or Curse?

Elderly people in northern Chad today still remember stories of their southern Libyan neighbours' extreme poverty before the discovery of oil in 1956. People in southern Libya were so hungry, they say, that when you gave them a piece of meat, they would chew it for a while, then put it in their pocket to chew again later. They would come to northern Chad, begging for old bones and animal skins, which they could sell back home to make soup, while people in the (then) much wealthier northern part of Chad would just throw these items away without a second thought. These stories are comments on the vagaries of history, often recounted to relativise what is seen as contemporary Libyan arrogance. But they are also historical reminders of a possible future: everybody knows that if both Libya and Algeria continue to exploit their oil and gas resources at the current rate, they will run out within a generation or two.

Large deposits of oil and natural gas were found in Algeria and Libya in 1956 and 1959, respectively. Algeria was at that time in the midst of its war of independence, the longest and bloodiest ever fought on the African continent. The great wave of repression dubbed 'the Battle of Algiers' (and immortalised in the 1966 eponymous film) took place barely four months after oil was struck at the caravan well of Hassi Messaoud, touching, by sheer luck, what remains even today the country's most productive oil field. In January 1958, the first consignment of Algerian oil arrived at the port of Bone (then Philippeville) under military escort, ushering in, it was said, a new period of 'European' energy self-sufficiency. By then, it was clear that the future of industrialised and industrialising nations would be oil; outside Algeria, the French government was painfully aware that there were hardly any known oil or gas deposits on its territory, which might explain at least some of its ruthless determination to keep Algeria French. Both the Algerian National Liberation Front (FLN) and the French government used Saharan oil as a bargaining chip, promising concessions to large international oil companies in exchange for political support (such was the world then, and such is it still today); nobody ever thought to ask the Saharan peoples' opinion about the rapid restructuring of the place they called home.

As a result of the subsequent oil boom, while southern Saharan countries such as Niger and Chad regularly vie for bottom place in the UN Human Development Index, both Algeria and Libya are rich countries. Libya's GDP per person from 1964 to 1986 was on a par with that of the US and above the European average. Despite years of civil war since 2011, it still stands among the highest on the African continent, just after that of the Seychelles and before that of Mauritius. Algeria is in the top ten, before Tunisia and Egypt. Both Algeria and Libya are rentier states, relying for most of their income on external trade; hence their governments are hardly accountable to their own populations – until they rebel with more or less success, as the Libyans did in 2011 and the Algerians, once again, in 2019.

Both governments have invested heavily in infrastructure in the south, where almost all of their hydrocarbon wealth is located, building schools and hospitals, roads, military garrisons and administrative centres and thereby irreversibly changing Saharan landscapes, societies and economies. Hassi Messaoud, the caravan well where the first discoveries of oil were made in

1956, has by now become a city of over 50,000 officially registered inhabitants and probably many more, as oil wealth attracts migrants from north and south alike. Roughly two-thirds of these residents derive their income directly or indirectly from oil.

The oil and gas deposits in the Sahara developed 400 to 300 million years ago, when the current Sahara was situated somewhere near Antarctica as part of the supercontinent Gondwana. Just a few decades have passed since the 1950s, yet the socio-economic changes of this short period have been profound, as the hazards of geology and of colonial border-drawing have led to lasting inequalities that, arguably more than any other factor, continue to structure contemporary Saharan landscapes – and relations between the northern and the southern Sahara.

In 2002, Niger suddenly made headlines when its president was accused of providing Saddam Hussein, then president of Iraq, with yellowcake (a type of uranium concentrate powder) for Iraq's (alleged) programme to develop nuclear weapons. Although clearly an absurd fabrication, this accusation drew international attention (once people had located Niger on a map) to yet another aspect of the Sahara's strategic importance.

Like oil in Algeria, uranium had been discovered in Niger's extreme north in 1957, at the very end of the colonial period. The first uranium mine in northern Niger, near Arlit, was opened in 1970 by the French state-owned company Cogema. By the 1980s, it was the source of 40 per cent of all uranium produced worldwide. Despite falling uranium prices, Niger remains the fifth-largest producer of uranium even today, with uranium ore accounting for 60 per cent of the country's exports. France alone needs between 8,000 and 9,000 tonnes of uranium each year to feed the nuclear reactors that produce – remember, no oil or gas – 72 per cent of its electricity, and although Niger today provides only a fraction of French uranium consumption and has since opened its territory to other (notably Chinese) prospectors, French state involvement in Nigerien uranium mining has been constant.

According to many Nigeriens, this involvement has been more than purely technical and economic; as many note wistfully, military coups always seem to happen when negotiations about uranium prices take a bad turn (from the French point of view). The resulting political instability is compounded by the great volatility of uranium prices on the world market. Activists claim that the impact on local health is considerable, reflected, for instance, in exceptionally high rates of cancer, but since Orano, the French state-owned company that owns the largest share of mines in the area, is the only provider of decent health care locally, no independent data is available to confirm or refute this idea. When, in 2010, seven foreign Areva (as Orano was then called) employees were taken hostage by armed groups and were redeemed against a ransom of €20 million, some locally might have seen the ransom as a form of compensation, a way of laying hands on the money that Areva is known to make on the backs of people's lives, livelihoods and futures but that it is otherwise very unwilling to part with.

The town of Arlit, where the main mines are situated, with its almost 150,000 inhabitants, stands out in a landscape where most human settlement consists only of a few tents or small oasis settlements. Until the 1960s, this was a particularly desolate patch of desert, flat, rocky and dry; between 1977 and 2011, the town's population grew fifteen-fold to reach today's (by Saharan standards) enormous proportions. The town itself is a mirror image of global hierarchies. Around a European compound, consisting of villas, schools, shopping centres, even a racetrack and of course a swimming pool, there are small villas for higher-ranking national employees of the mine, most of whom are recruited in the south of the country. Then dormitories for contractual staff. Then, as far as the eye can see, stretch the slums, inhabited by migrants from the south of the country and locals hoping to obtain at least a tiny fraction of the wealth produced here.

Houses in the slums are built from what people can find locally, often radioactive material taken from in or around the mines. Water is contaminated, and the constant wind carries radioactive particles through the town, its suburbs and nearby pastures. More recently, following international reports, the management of the mines has decided to destroy all contaminated equipment that locals might otherwise recycle by pouring chemicals on them that render them unusable by even the most determined. Locals marvel at this final act of what they consider wanton destructiveness. They know that they are permanently exposed to radiation anyway.

Not all mining, however, involves international companies and high-level diplomacy. In 2013, just after I had returned from northern Chad to the UK, I received an unexpected call from my friend Herdei, who lives in the northern Chadian town of Faya. She sounded very excited: 'People are finding gold everywhere. You must come at once, and bring a metal detector. Buy it before you get here because here, they have become very expensive'. Starting with Sudan in 2010, northern Chad in 2013, northern Niger in 2014 and Mauritania in 2016, a gold rush was sweeping the southern Sahara.

Local legend has it that the first gold deposit in northeastern Niger was found by two brothers, Teda pastoralists, in 2014 as they were herding their camels near the Chadian border. They kept quiet about their find, just going up there now and then to discreetly fill their pockets with gold. As time went by, people noticed. Family members had to be let in on the secret. Finally, they all decided to have a big party to celebrate their luck. This party attracted the attention of the army, and then all hell broke loose: everybody in the area, from Niger via Chad to Sudan, scrambled up there to pick up their share of easy wealth. Four years later, formerly remote pastures had been transformed into a 'landscape reminiscent of Mad Max', according to the *Wall Street Journal*.[7] In Tchibarakaten, for instance, miners descend into a hand-dug trench up to 350 feet deep with only a rope, a helmet and a prayer for security. They live in makeshift tents and shelters right next to their stake in the trench. By 2018, the Organisation for Economic Co-operation and Development (OECD) esti-mated that 10 per cent of the population of Niger, and similar percentages in Mali and Burkina Faso, lived in one way or another off the profits generated through artisanal gold mining.

Throughout the Sahara, conflicts soon broke out over who was permitted to work and, more importantly, tax the gold mines that were now springing up in northern Niger, Chad, Sudan, Mali and even southern Algeria and Mauritania. In the Tibesti Mountains in northern Chad, local self-defence com-mittees had formed almost immediately after the discovery of gold in 2013 to control gold extraction and especially to keep the greedier elements of the Chadian national army – those who were not themselves from the region – at bay. By 2018, this led to a full-blown military stand-off from which the coun-try's reputedly unbeatable elite corps had to retreat, to the late president Idriss Déby's great embarrassment. He clearly never forgave this, and until Déby's violent death in 2021 at the hand of a Libya-based rebel group, his army attacked the mine fields continuously under the pretext that he was worried that reve-nues from gold would feed armed rebellion.

In most places, the gold rush died down almost as quickly as it had begun, leaving its usual quotient of environmental destruction, of the wounded, dead and disappointed, coupled with the occasional story of glory and success. The various armies have gone home, as have the Sudanese miners. North-eastern Niger and northern Chad have returned to their normal state of wakeful sleepiness. Very few people have become rich, as even my friend Herdei had to admit. She herself never got her metal detector, and in any case, women largely stayed away from the troubled mining zones. As in earlier scrambles for the Sahara's many mineral resources, including salt and natron, gold might have been there for the taking, but wealth was reserved for those who had the means to make use of it, protect it and to transport it and who knew how to sell it. And as attractive as the Sahara's mineral resources have always been to locals and outsiders, Herdei knew as well as anybody else that in the long run, true wealth in the Sahara depends on other factors: most importantly, reliable access to sweet, pure, clean water.

2

LIKE THE DESERTS MISS THE RAIN

Aman iman (Water is life).
Tuareg proverb

Imagine, in the middle of the Sahara, a series of permanent lakes shimmering in the sunlight, some blue, some green, some reddish, all colours of incredible depth and beauty. They are surrounded by a dense belt of reeds, gently rustling in the wind, that protect them against excessive evaporation and where frogs croak as the sun sets at night. A mild breeze fans out the leaves of the nearby palm groves. Birds nesting in the reeds raise a deafening chatter as the evening falls. Any careless movement will release hundreds of them into the sky. Fish flicker away as you wade into the lake, tickling your calves as they pass. This is the romantic image of an oasis, a natural haven of life in an otherwise inhospitable environment. It is an image that is largely incorrect – oases only very rarely contain surface water and even less often occur naturally. Here, however, in Ounianga in northeastern Chad, it is real.

Declared a UNESCO World Heritage site in 2012, this landscape consists of eighteen lakes, some salty, some hyper-salty, some fresh, covering a surface of 20 square kilometres. They are constantly replenished from underground fresh-water sources and are surrounded by fresh-water springs that water the local extensive palm grove and irrigated gardens alongside shallow wells. Water is so abundant here, and so close to the surface, that palm trees do not need to be irrigated; they can plunge their roots directly into the shallow water table. People plant them near the lakes and then go off into the surrounding desert to pasture their camels, returning perhaps to pollinate them in the spring and most certainly in summer for the harvest. In such a setting, boundaries between a nomadic and a sedentary way of life simply make no sense.

Now imagine a landscape whose uniform flatness and brown hue would be oppressive were they not broken up by dense patches of palm trees with a few mud-brick houses sheltering in their shade. Here, there is no naturally occurring surface water. Little bumps of dust tipped with white indicate that this is a sabkha, or salty plain, produced through evaporation, a sure indication that we are at the bottom of a valley and that there must be some water nearby. In the distance are a few low and unspectacular hills, their brown a slightly darker shade. From each clump of trees, a neat row of simple shafts indicates open mud-brick wells, hundreds of them dug at equal distances, gently curving towards the hills, dividing the empty space between them. They are of exactly the same colour as the landscape, and although they look fragile – they are made of mud, which in hyper-arid conditions is never far from dust, and the wind worries them endlessly – they seem to have been there for as long as anybody can remember. This is the Tuwāt, a large and relatively densely settled oasis belt in the Algerian south, home to the foggara, one of the most sophisticated traditional irrigation systems in the world.

Or imagine yourself on a plane flying over the Libyan south, which again is mostly light brown, with a few darker shades indicating mountains. The heat is oppressive, even at high altitude.

Suddenly, large dark-green circles appear on the horizon out of nothing. These circles are scattered over the landscape in a seemingly random fashion, huge and absolutely regular, as if a giant had been let loose with a compass. Enormous irrigation machines, looking like giant cranes turning on a central pivot, spray water pumped from hundreds of metres below the ground over the crops, which grow dark against the light-brown soil in perfect circles; some are fodder to raise livestock, others cereals to feed the nation. This is the Kufra project, the late Colonel Qadhafi's pet agricultural development scheme; it is the only thing in Libya that can be seen from space. Although, sixty years after it was first built, the Kufra irrigation machinery has itself become an antique, those neat circles of vegetation seem the exact opposite of the randomly huddled, discrete mud-coloured wells of the Tuwātī settlement: the former drawn first on paper in an office somewhere, the other the result of centuries-old bottom-up investment and negotiation with the harsh realities of the sabkha, but also among the people themselves.

These are all landscapes made by water, but in very different ways. The naturally occurring Ounianga oasis relies uniquely on shallow phreatic tables and endemic reeds to protect against evaporation, with people's needs an afterthought. The Tuwātī landscape bears witness to humans' centuries-old engagement with a landscape that otherwise would be uninhabitable. The huge circles in Libya indicate how Saharan landscapes can be transformed radically and from the top down through the use of fossil resources – water as well as the oil used to pump the water to the surface – and technical ingenuity. Between them, they sketch out the history of water use in the Sahara.

The most common perception of the Sahara, and deserts more generally, is that they are places bereft of water. In fact, the problem with water in the Sahara is not necessarily its lack but rather its erratic distribution and inaccessibility: water in the wrong place at the wrong time. It regularly rains in some parts of the Sahara, especially on its fringes and in the mountains. In 2008, the inhabitants of the south-western Algerian town of Béchar watched, first with joy, then with terror, as in two days, 90 millimetres of rain – the average *annual* rainfall in the region – fell on their town, washing away the historic town centre and leaving many homeless. In 2016, floods devastated much of Moroccan-occupied Western Sahara. In January 2021, photographs went viral of snowfall in the Algerian Sahara. Scattered through the Sahara are seasonal rivers that run only a few days each year but in which a person can drown on a stormy day. Most importantly, the Sahara contains some of the largest reserves of sweet water in the world. These, however, are deep underground, and for most of human history, they have quite simply been inaccessible or accessible only through much human ingenuity and labour.

Over the centuries, sedentary farmers have developed many ways of gaining access to and stabilising capricious water sources, thereby bringing about that ancient miracle of making the desert bloom. This often came at a great cost to them of labour, time, capital and freedom. Indeed, historically, the majority of sedentary farmers probably did not so much choose this way of life as they were forced to adopt it by others more powerful than they. In such a context, irrigation and water distribution do not stand for but *are* society and politics. Following water's flows – or stoppages, wastages, shortages – provides a privileged entry into Saharan human ecologies, involving historical continuities as well as profound change.

Lakes of Sweet Water Locked in the Ground

We can think of the Sahara as a layer cake containing in some areas several overlapping underground water tables at different levels and in others none. Historically, the most important of these water tables was the one closest to the surface, the phreatic, or uncontained, water table – uncontained because it communicates with the surface and recharges directly through rain and drainage. This also makes it particularly vulnerable to pollution, as any oasis dweller trying to survive on shallow well water – with its vast array of nasty bacteria – can attest. Further underground, at depths between 200 and 2,500 metres, are profound fossil (i.e., non-renewable) water reserves that were formed several thousand or even millions of years ago. They usually contain very high-quality sweet water of the kind that, given water shortages everywhere, is increasingly becoming a global asset.

Like oil and gas resources, these water tables are distributed unevenly throughout the Sahara. Shallow phreatic water tables tend to be situated at the bottom of valleys, with springs and lakes forming at the base of hills. Imagine, for a moment, a cross-section of the layer cake. After a thin layer of icing, representing the soil, add a layer of water. Then imagine pushing up bits of the cake from below, creating hills and mountain ranges: as the top layer now slopes down, the water just beneath it flows down to the bottom of the hills if there is room and creates pressure if there isn't. Sometimes, if the top layer is weak or porous, this pressure is sufficient for the water to erupt as springs or spring-fed lakes. This is what produces Ounianga. Sometimes this pressure means that if you pierce the top layer at the right spot, water will spurt out of its own accord, creating a natural fountain as long as the pressure remains high enough – in other words, as long as enough water remains in the water table. This is called an artesian well. Before deep-well boring, the hollows, depressions and lowest points of mountain ranges were the places where water was most easily accessible, and these are therefore the places where people first settled.

The story is different for the deep fossil aquifers, the underground sweet-water reserves situated too low in the layer cake to ever reach the surface on their own. They are accessible only through deep-well boring and (usually) constant pumping. Their inaccessibility meant that they remained largely undisturbed until recently. The largest of these underground reserves, which feeds the large-scale industrial irrigation projects of southern Libya, is the Nubian Sandstone Aquifer System (NSAS), situated under northern Chad, northern Sudan, south-eastern Libya and Egypt. It stretches over 2 million square kilometres: the equivalent of two-thirds of the surface area of the Mediterranean or ten times that of the Great Lakes. It holds an estimated 150,000 cubic kilometres (150,000 billion litres) of fresh-water, which makes it the largest known fossil aquifer system in the world to date. The Northwestern Sahara Aquifer System (NWSAS), situated under Algeria, Tunisia and Libya, is only about half the size of the NSAS and contains one-third the amount of water. Yet it was the first to be exploited for agriculture though deep wells and has been supplying some of the more densely populated parts of the Sahara – Tunisia, eastern Algeria and western Libya – for more than a century. This is why it has been much more depleted than the NSAS, and its use is hotly contested.

Together, the NWSAS and the NSAS hold about 5 per cent of the world's fresh groundwater, which in turn accounts for 30 per cent of the world's fresh-water reserves. Smaller water tables are situated in northern Mali and Mauritania (the Tawdanni basin, named after the infamous salt mine) and in Niger, but they are difficult to access and have not yet been exploited much so far. After all, it takes more than just thirst to exploit underground water: money, for one. Also the political will and power to invest in heavy equipment, and of course fuel, to work the water pumps, which guzzle petrol at a prodigious rate. For now, North African countries have much more of all three than their Sahelian neighbours, and the 'free' water that fuels contemporary agricultural development in Libya, Tunisia, Algeria and Egypt is heavily dependent on regional petropolitics.

Like all geological layers, underground water tables are never quite flat but follow the relief of the soil. In the Sahara, they generally slope downwards from the south to the north. This means that regions where surface water – mostly rain – filters into underground water tables are rarely situated in the same countries as areas of intensive use. Above-average rainfall in the Tibesti Mountains in northern Chad, for instance, might result in an almost immediate rise in groundwater levels in the Dakhla oases in the Egyptian desert, 1,327 kilometres to the north. But it also means that if you pump water in one spot, effects will be noticed everywhere. The more Saharan water tables are depleted in the north, the less hope there is that that they might one day fuel prosperity in the south.

Add to this the fact that all of the large water tables in the Sahara cross national boundaries, and you can imagine the complexities of international water management in the Sahara and the temptation for strong northern states to control the water supplies at their source. Or rather, you can imagine how complex such management would be if it existed. For now, however, and despite the existence of a few international bodies, the rules are simple: take what you can for as long as you can. Age-old irrigation systems, like the one described in Tuwāt, and naturally occurring oases, such as Ounianga, are the first to suffer from this approach, as even a slight lowering of underground water tables endangers their survival.

Oases Are No Paradise

There is a long-standing association in Mediterranean and Middle Eastern literary traditions between oases and the idea of paradise. The English word 'paradise' derives from old Persian *pairi-daêzā*, literally a walled garden. In Arabic, the connection is even closer: *jinna* (paradise) and *jinan* (garden) are derived from the same root. And parallels are more than just linguistic: countless are the descriptions of the 'garden of Eden' as a neat horticultural enterprise with layers of fruit trees, pleasantly running water, abundance of all kinds and plenty of shade. 'Paradise', according to the Quran (which contains 166 references to gardens and a mere fifteen to camels), 'is the most prosperous place', while the Song of Solomon describes 'a large and beautiful *paradeisos*, possessing all things that grow in the various seasons', a garden 'planted by God's right hand'.

This long entanglement between oasis gardens and paradise has rubbed off on images not only of paradise but also of oases. Most people rarely stop to think about all the labour that makes them what they are – surely there are no gardeners in paradise – and they tend to be seen as entirely natural occurrences, a manifestation of divine (or earthly, according to taste) bounty. In fact, date palms cannot reproduce on their own but need to be planted, fertilised and in most cases irrigated throughout the year. Most other plants cultivated in their shade need constant care; therefore, there is no such thing as a 'natural' oasis – with the rare exception of places such as Ounianga. Nonetheless, the standard image of an oasis, found on screensavers and soda bottles, is of lush palm trees, their slender silhouettes reflected in an open lake with abundant vegetation all around, perhaps a few birds frolicking in the sand – and no humans in sight.

Some of this fantasy was translated into textbook images of oasis agriculture of the kind developed by and for early-twentieth-century colonial agronomists; these books describe it as a highly intensive and literally fruitful affair. Date-palms, introduced into the Sahara from the Mediterranean some 2,800 years ago, give shade and maintain the soil. Smaller fruit trees thrive in this shade, creating an artificial Mediterranean climate. On the ground, vegetables, cereals and fodder are grown in the double shade of palm and fruit trees. These crops are irrigated daily, and any excess water is sucked up by the fruit trees that shelter them. In this way, Saharan oases are highly efficient, produce everything anyone might ever need, seemingly without effort, and give a yield per square metre vastly superior to that of any other form of agriculture in what is essentially a Mediterranean garden transplanted into a hostile environment.

In practice, however, things have often been less pleasant. In the fourteenth century, Ibn Battūta described the (notoriously prosperous) southern Algerian Tuwāt as producing 'many dates which are not good... . There is no cultivation there nor butter nor oil... . The food of its people is dates and locusts. These are abundant with them; they store them as dates are stored and use them for food'.[1] Any other food, he wrote, including oil and cereals, had to be imported from the north, which meant that dates were grown primarily for the market rather than for local consumption and made the oases inherently dependent on visits from traders and pastoralists. More recent descriptions of oasis horticulture concur with this rather bleak assessment. In 1909, a few years after the French colonial conquest, the French colonial administrator of the Tuwāt described the 'material situation of the indigenous population' as 'none too rosy': most people lived on 'one single meal a day' consisting of 'a few dates'.[2] 'Stout people', as the colonial officer Martin concluded, 'are a real exception'.[3]

A thought experiment might tell us why. Imagine you want to set up an oasis. Well versed in Saharan hydrology, you have identified a promising depression situated near hills where water pressure in the phreatic tables might be strong enough to create an artesian well, or, with a bit of luck, you might find a spring. That failing, you know that you will find water relatively quickly by digging down. As in many Saharan depressions bearing traces of former watercourses or shallow lakes, the soil looks fine and seems suitably rich in nutrients. First, you need to plan and build a functioning irrigation and drainage system to carry the water to your crops and away again. If there are no springs, you also need to find ways of hauling water to the surface.

Before the arrival of motor pumps, Saharan populations developed many solutions to this problem, taking into account the minute details of the local landscape and geological features. All of them required a lot of manpower and usually also some degree of communal organisation. Take, for instance, the simplest and probably most widespread type of well in the Sahara: the *shadūf*, or counterpoise lift. It consists of a simple pivot, built right next to the well and roughly at adult human height, on which rests a lever. On one side of this lever is fixed a weight, perhaps a large stone. On the other a bucket, which today is usually made of plastic but would have been made of wood or leather in earlier times.

A shadūf can be worked by one person alone, standing on a board posed over the well directly opposite the bucket side of the lever. He or she pulls down the lever until the bucket hits water; they then let go, and the weight automatically pulls the bucket back up, now full. Once the bucket comes up, the person who sent it down empties it either into a basin or into a wooden shaft leading directly into the garden's irrigation canals. This shaft and the canals have been carefully set up and are regularly cleaned so that water will flow through them by gravity alone. Another person, perhaps a child, is placed somewhere in the garden to open and close irrigation canals as necessary to direct water to where it is most needed. The garden is subdivided into small patches surrounded by earthen ditches. Each patch is inundated in turn. Although working a shadūf is simple, imagine doing it all day every day, with your back bent, your hands rubbed bloody by the wet cord and your clothes drenched, whether with your own sweat or spillover water, it is difficult to know. You might last a day, but you certainly wouldn't want to start again the next. Unless you really have no choice.

Hence, in order to get at the water, you need more people, ideally people who have little say about their working conditions. It should therefore come as no surprise that historically, irrigation in Saharan oases was performed largely by enslaved people or landless freedmen (*harātīn*) who usually had few options other than to continue serving their former masters. To get your hands on enslaved labourers, you first need access to some form of exchangeable wealth and transport or to the means of violence necessary to raid faraway populations on your own account. Once the enslaved are settled in your oasis, you also need to be able to feed and clothe them, initially with little help from your own agricultural produce. Palm trees, needed to shade all the other crops, take decades to grow, mature and bear fruit.

Nobody can live on dates alone, and most dates were therefore grown not for local consumption but for commerce. This means that you also need to gain access to regional and trans-regional trade networks to exchange your dates for other types of food: cereals, meat and oil and butter, all the while weathering the periodic disasters that might strike, such as raids, plant and human diseases, water sources drying up or an unaccountable interruption of trade routes. The historical record of the Sahara is indeed quite as full of abandoned oases – where 'other than a sterile remnant of palm-groves, only decaying ruins and blurred traces remain', according to one example given by the Moroccan geographer al-Idrīsī in the twelfth century – as of flourishing ones.[4]

Irrigation canals, palm trees and, to a lesser degree, a dependent labouring population constitute immovable wealth – they cannot simply be carried away at short notice if threatened, as livestock might be. You therefore also need to strike some deal with neighbouring, more mobile populations, if only so that they do not come too often to help themselves to what you now consider to be yours or encourage your workers to desert. You should probably also invest in some kind of fortification to discourage excessive greed. Ironically, perhaps, this returns us to the idea of pairi-daêzā, a walled garden, with the emphasis this time placed on the wall rather than the crops. Throughout the northern Sahara, oases in fact tend to be referred to as '*qsūr*' (singular *qsar*) or fortresses rather than by the classical Arabic term '*wāha*', oasis. You might be familiar with the qsar of Medenine in southern Tunisia, whose curved roofs and superposed grain stores were used as the setting for Luke Skywalker's home planet of 'Tatooine' (named after nearby Tataouine) in the *Star Wars* films; historically, its high walls were meant to keep out not interplanetary armies but marauding nomads.

Lastly, and perhaps most importantly, you need a good reason to go through all this trouble. As the Moroccan geographer Paul Pascon concluded after a painstaking study of the local account books of the oasis of Ighil in southern Morocco, 'The considerable investments that are necessary to start the irrigation of the smallest plot of land, the cost of the development and the maintenance of intensive arboriculture in an extremely dry environment cannot be justified solely by their financial return nor even by general economy', as oases usually 'decline long before they have finished paying back the initial capital outlay'. Does this mean that the founders of oases were either overly optimistic or quite simply naive? No, he says, it shows only that they had some motivation other than economic gain.[5]

You might be in search of political glory or in dire need of putting some distance between yourself and a rival; you might be part of a persecuted religious minority hoping to build a stronghold far from the centres of power. You might be a minor saint, hoping for wider recognition by means of the age-old miracle of making the desert bloom; a pastoralist, wanting a safe space for storage and some agricultural produce to supplement your pastoral diet; or a hard-headed trader in need of a relay post on your trans-Saharan journeys. Most likely, you are motivated by a combination of all of these factors plus a spirit of adventure. We can therefore think of Saharan oases as an internal frontier attracting both the ambitious and the desperate from more populated regions to the north and south.

Not everyone wanted to fight this battle. Indeed, it seems to have been fought mostly by those who really had no other choice, that is, those who lived in or were settled in areas where access to water was difficult and required initial investment and ongoing collaboration. Conversely, where access to water was relatively easy, people seemed to prefer a more varied, more mobile and probably more autonomous life to the drudgeries of intensive oasis agriculture. An example of one such landscape, where water was relatively easily accessible, can be found just southwest of the Ounianga lakes in the northern Chadian Borkou.

The Borkou is a low and relatively flat area wedged between the dunes of the Djourab (Toumai's erstwhile home) and the Tibesti mountain range. Its capital is Faya, the difficult approach to which I described at the opening of this book. Around the town, endless rubbish dumps bear witness to the proximity of the former consumer paradise of southern Libya; small camel caravans cautiously pick their way through discarded aluminium cans, rotting carcasses and plastic bags. Beyond the town stretches its palm grove, around 5 kilometres wide and 70 long and still growing. Lush as it is, Faya's palm grove bears no resemblance whatsoever to picture postcards: no slender trunks surmounted by crowns of leaves, swaying elegantly in the breeze and sheltering carefully tended vegetable patches below, but rather prickly and stubby greyish bushes growing in all directions as far as the eye can see, planted directly in the sand and rock. Date-palms grow trunks only if they are regularly pruned, and here, clearly, nobody thought it worth the effort.

The phreatic water table in Borkou is accessible 2 to 3 metres below ground. There are many springs and permanent pools, although none quite as spectacular as those at Ounianga. 'If you want water', people say proudly, 'all you have to do is dig a small hole and wait until it fills up' – hence (almost) everybody can have their own well and operate it independently and undisturbed. This also means that palm trees, once they have reached a certain age, plunge their roots directly into the water table and do not need to be irrigated. Non-irrigated palm trees of this kind get less water and hence produce many fewer dates than irrigated ones, sometimes only one-tenth as many, and the dates that they do produce are small, wrinkled and dry. This leaves locals with two options: either irrigate trees year-round or plant ten times more trees and chew your dates hard. Most opt for the second solution, as it frees up their time for pastoral and other kinds of mobility for most of the year without having to give up on their share of dates, which continue to be an essential addition to daily meals and an important item of exchange with cereal producers who live in the rain-fed agricultural belt further south.

From a local point of view, in a context where true wealth is associated with livestock rather than agriculture and status and happiness with pastoral mobility rather than agricultural labour, this clearly makes sense. Permanent irrigation is the antithesis of pastoral mobility and moreover is recognised as a form of labour that might be necessary at times but is best avoided if at all possible. Each summer during the date harvest, the population of the sleepy Borkou palm grove therefore triples or quadruples, literally overnight, as pastoralists from throughout northern Chad arrive for the date harvest. They come with their animals, on foot, on the backs of trucks, many of them women, and set up their makeshift camps on the dunes near the town. All night, small transistor radios or mobile phones blare out the most recent Sudanese hits. Young people dance on the dunes, flirt outrageously, play cards and chat endlessly.

There is some debate at each harvest among the few sedentists who live in the palm grove year-round about who these people really are. Close relatives for some among them, owners of palm groves for others, nomads who have long held sovereign rights in the palm grove, semi-nomads who divide their time between a sedentary and a nomadic existence, allies of sedentists who share the harvest equally between them and in exchange look after the sedentists' livestock. Long-lost cousins or aunties, people who come to help with the date harvest and get their share in return or simply passing strangers who try to take advantage of the situation. What is certain, however, is that the harvest comes each year with its set of conflicts – sometimes fought out violently, sometimes settled amicably or with a game of cards – but also that nobody will go hungry in the end. Strange as it may sound, the Borkou, despite its unprepossessing appearance, is much closer to a place of shared abundance than the picture-postcard image of oases as a paradise of intensely irrigated walled gardens.

No Country for Individualists

The Nefzāwa is situated in southern Tunisia at the country's 'gate of the desert', just beyond the boundaries of rain-fed agriculture, and cut off from the rest of the country by a salt depression (*chott*) and a belt of sand-dunes. In Saharan terms, the region is relatively well watered and still counted more than 200 naturally occurring springs in the 1970s, when its complex irrigation system was described by the French anthropologist Geneviève Bédoucha.[6] Some of these springs were abundant enough to be shared among several villages, as was the case with al-Ghrīg, whose use for irrigation dates back to Roman times. Water flowed from the spring into a shared basin, whence it was divided into three main irrigation canals, each leading to a village. Water in each village was then distributed by 'turns'. This meant that every garden received all the village water for a short span of time until it was diverted to the next garden and so on until, after twelve days, the water returned to the initial garden.

These turns were measured by a village functionary called a *goddās*. As water flowed continuously, each irrigation system needed two goddās: one to work during the day and one to work during the night. Surprisingly, perhaps, given the absolute centrality of the goddās to village life, they were usually from low-status families, often of slave descent and more often than not locally categorised as Black. Turns were measured in units called *gadūs* that each lasted exactly 3 minutes and 20 seconds. They were measured with a water clock: a small cup with a hole at the bottom suspended over a basin of water. At the beginning of each turn, the goddās filled the cup with water; when it was empty, he knew that the gadūs was up. Once all the *gwādis* owned by an individual gardener were used up, the goddās blew a horn, and the gardeners – who usually knew roughly when it would be their turn – adjusted the irrigation canals accordingly. At every change, the goddās calculated the time that it would take for the water to reach the new garden and added it to the time allocated.

The goddās hence needed to have a precise map of the village in his head and to constantly pay attention to the tiny water clock. This, however, was not all. Consider that water rights were attached not to particular gardens but to their owners; that both gardens and water shares could be freely sold, lent, leased, hired, inherited, borrowed and shared so that water rarely simply passed from one garden to the next and the quantity of gwādis each individual was to receive changed all the time; that people often owned more than one garden, perhaps in different parts of the palm grove, and divided their water between them differently according to the season and the crops planted, and we can then just about glimpse the mind-boggling intellectual task that was the goddās'. In addition to a spatial map of the village, the gardens and their crops, he needed a full-fledged social map in his head too: who had just got married to whom and brought some water with him or her; who had just died, leaving his or her water to be divided among their heirs; who had just got into terrible debt and had to hand over some of their water to make up for it; who had generously gifted parts of their water to a poorer relative; who had just mortgaged their garden; and so on. Perhaps this is why the goddās had to come from a low-status family; otherwise, this detailed knowledge would quite simply have made him too powerful.

The connection between irrigation and community life goes even deeper in the Tuwāt, 1,000 kilometres south-west of the Nefzāwa. Here, in the expanse of grey flatness, there are no naturally occurring springs, and local communities were in charge not only of dividing water but also of producing it in the first place. All irrigation relied on hand-dug underground filtration galleries, or foggaras, that brought water from nearby hills to lower-lying oases through the force of gravity. Think back to the image of the layer cake with bumps: foggaras plug into deep underground water tables (in this case the NWSAS) at a point where they are above the level of the surface further down, that is, in the hills, and then bring the water to the oases, emerging where the angle is just right for them to come to the surface. This is where the oasis will be built. The underground canals are marked on the surface by wells dug at regular intervals. These wells provided access to the underground canals so that they could be cleaned, cured and repaired. In the 1950s, in the region of Adrar alone, there were more than 2,000 kilometres of foggaras – ten times the distance of the Paris Métro at that time – providing drinking water and irrigation to barely 40,000 people.

We can be fairly sure that these underground tunnels were modelled on Persian *qanāt*, the oldest of which date back 3,000 years. Thanks to recent archaeological finds, we can track their likely progression from Iran in the first century BCE via Syria, Egypt and southern Libya in Roman times. The Garamantes, whose Roman-era urban civilisation was described earlier, relied entirely on foggara irrigation. Foggaras were described in what is now southern Algeria in the eleventh century, although they might have existed there much earlier. From there, they continued their journey west and north to Morocco and southern Spain and later, with Spanish settlers, to the Canary Islands and South America. Foggaras are thus in themselves a proof of the far-reaching connections that linked out-of-the-way Saharan places such as the Libyan Fazzān and the Algerian Tuwāt to the heartlands of Middle Eastern civilisation.

Once foggaras have brought water to the oasis, it still needs to be divided. In the Tuwāt, people have opted for a division not by time, as in the Tunisian Nefzāwa, but by proportional volume. The water from the foggara flows into a basin and from there into one or two main irrigation canals; these branch out into subsidiary canals until they reach individual gardens. Every time a canal divides, water is split exactly through a *kesriya*, or a dividing comb, a triangular slope where small channels made of mouldable clay determine just how much water can flow into each smaller canal. Each change in water ownership is reflected in changes made to the kesriya and hence inscribed on the irrigation system itself. Whereas in the Nefzāwa, the goddās had a spatial and social map of the village in his head, here, the social relations within the village community are literally embedded in the always-shifting 'water metres' of irrigation canals.

Foggaras were traditionally built and subsequently managed by local assemblies, which we should imagine as a meeting of all property-holding heads of families in an oasis. These assemblies convened regularly and decided on everything that was of common concern: when the foggara needed to be overhauled, for instance, or prolonged, as sometimes happened when water tables ran low. Whether this could be done entirely with local labour and know-how or whether external help had to be called, requiring payment, and how to raise the money. Whose turn it was to feed the next group of visitors or to guard the walls that often surrounded such settlements. Who was right and who was wrong in the latest dispute over land or water. When the harvesting season should start. Who should be in charge of collecting rubbish in the streets. What should be done about so-and-so's widow, left penniless. How to react to threats made by a neighbouring strongman or indeed the sultan's tax man and how to rapidly collect the funds necessary to appease them. Who was entitled to sell, lease, rent or mortgage water to whom. In a setting where everybody's survival was bound up with that of their neighbours, we can understand why all of these questions were within the assembly's remit, as prolonged conflict and strife potentially spelled the end of irrigation – and hence of oasis life – for all.

We know this because many of these assemblies continue to function today but also because the Tuwāt was a highly literate society, and many assemblies kept registers when paper was available to do so. Membership in these assemblies depended on water ownership, which in turn was (at least notionally) proportional to the investment made when the foggara was first dug. It was then passed down the generations but could also be sold on or mortgaged, making ownership and membership rights quite as complex here as in the Nefzāwa. Maintenance work on the foggaras was paid for collectively. Most of the actual labour of maintaining foggaras (and the gardens they irrigated), however, was carried out not by the members of the assembly but historically by enslaved workers and freedmen who, deprived of ownership of water (even more than of land), remained economically dependent on their former masters. This made Tuwātī society appealingly self-governing and unappealingly hierarchical all at once.

*

From the 1950s onwards, deep-well boring gradually caused local water tables to fall. By 2016, more than half of the 2,000 foggaras in the Tuwāt had dried up, while water production in the others had been reduced by half. As soon as their foggaras dried up, members of irrigation assemblies were put to a choice to either abandon their gardens, to relocate to the new industrially irrigated perimeter or to attempt to 'repair' their traditional irrigation system using new technology.

The inhabitants of the qsar of Lahmeur opted for the latter. In 1989, their foggara had failed after the government had drilled a deep well just above it. Deprived of their own supply, the Lahmeur assembly decided to physically occupy the government borehole and divert its water to their own irrigation system, thereby depriving the whole region of drinking water. They also took advantage of a nearby government visit to block the road and kindly 'invite' the minister to look into their problems. This proactive approach to water management promptly bore fruit, and the Lahmeur foggara now functions again, 'strengthened' by a 150-metre-deep borehole whence water is continuously pumped into the foggara. The cost of this – which at that time was considerable – was and still is covered by the local agricultural department. In exchange, the Lahmeur assembly agreed to supply drinking water from 'their' borehole to the region as a whole.

The Lahmeur assembly clearly knew how to work local politics in Algeria. Most importantly, however, they succeeded in drawing on the support of everybody in the oasis, including low-status families of reputedly servile descent who until then had been excluded from water and landownership and hence from membership in the assembly. Their support came at a price: instead of reproducing the former, unequal pattern of distribution, the water from the newly 'strengthened' foggara was shared out equally among everybody who had participated in 'taking hostage' the government borehole. As traditional as the Lahmeur irrigation system might thus look, it has been profoundly renewed from the inside out to start again on a more egalitarian basis. Oasis gardens in Lahmeur are flourishing today, in striking contrast with neighbouring oases where no such consensus was achieved, mostly because former elite families were loath to relinquish their privileges. As a result, their gardens have dried up.

Making the Desert Bloom: Large-Scale Irrigation Projects

In Tunisia and across the border in southeastern Algeria, deep-well boreholing for industrial agriculture started in colonial times. Following its success, traditional oasis gardens were gradually replaced by plantations of deglet nour dates – literally 'fingers of light', transparent when held up to the light. They are the kind of soft, honey-coloured, melt-in-the mouth dates that you can buy in supermarkets throughout the world. They have to be eaten fresh or kept refrigerated, require large quantities of water and constant irrigation, and, until the late nineteenth century, were cultivated only in small quantities, as delicacies, while most of the crop was given over to much hardier dry varieties that can be stored for months and easily carried on camelback. You might have seen pictures of these deglet nour plantations taken from the air, with square dark-green gardens cut into the surrounding dunes, resulting in a striking contrast of shapes and colours. Two colours, that is: one shade of green, since this is a monoculture, and one of light brown, the uniformly sterile sand-dunes.

Despite Tunisia's relatively small size, it is today the world's leading exporter of dates, thanks partly to the head start it got in colonial times. This success has come at a price. Take, for instance, Oued Righ, just across the border at the heart of Algeria's deglet nour production zone. As you approach the town, you first notice the smell: damp, putrid, salty. Then you come upon large puddles of swampy excess water, the result of industrial plantations uphill whose fields drain into what used to be oasis gardens but have now turned into a reeking salt marsh that nobody should get too close to. If you touch the stagnant water or even just the slimy mud, all local children are taught from babyhood, your skin will burn, your tongue swell and your eyes water; if you drink it, your resultant diarrhoea might be lethal. While all traditional irrigation systems in the Sahara include provisions for drainage, this is commonly overlooked in large-scale industrial enterprises, as the former inhabitants of the oasis gardens of Oued Righ have learned at great cost. Fossil water, mined deep underground, is now freely released into the surface water table, creating swamps and salty crusts on formerly fertile soil and cracking it like seawater drying on skin.

The use of deep-bore drilling has moreover noticeably lowered water tables. By the late 1970s at the very latest, throughout the deglet nour–growing regions of southern Tunisia and southeastern Algeria, there was no more need for the complex social and technical arrangements that underpinned the laborious efforts of the goddās, described earlier. All surface springs had run dry. Instead, gardeners obtained water from government-run pumping stations. From the point of view of villagers, this meant that they now had to pay for a resource that they had long considered to be their own. Yet it also meant that community control over water was eroded, making it possible for all those who had long been excluded – the formerly enslaved, landless labourers, former nomads, younger brothers and sons, outsiders – to obtain their share of water on an equal footing. After all, they were all Tunisian or Algerian citizens now. Although water rates were kept artificially low through state subsidies, this also meant that gardeners had to give over at least some of their land to deglet nour plantations in order to ensure a steady income in cash to pay for water.

From the 1980s onwards, the state monopoly over water was gradually eroded, and private entrepreneurs started to acquire motor pumps to set up their own drilling sites. With the influx of cheap Chinese motor pumps, this has now become the most common way of irrigating gardens. On the Algerian side of the border, few farmers ever ask for permits to drill for water (although these are officially required), and government officials usually do not complain about private wells. Water access used to be more strictly regulated in Tunisia, but this changed with the 2011 revolution. One of the most immediate effects of the revolution in the Tunisian south has been the exponential growth of palm groves, as everybody could now buy a pump and settle down wherever they pleased, to the point that deglet nour cuttings, many stolen in Algeria, became a precious commodity on the cross-border black market. It is easy to call the resulting plantations anarchic and to point to the devastating effect that they will have on regional water management. But for many local farmers, especially of the younger generation, and those from families who had long been deprived of access to water and land, they quite simply spell liberation from centuries of exploitation.

Profound as deep well drilling's transformations of local landscapes, ecologies and societies have been in Tunisia and Algeria, changes were even more spectacular in neighbouring Libya, where sudden and extraordinary oil wealth meant that Colonel Qadhafi could splash out freely on the most extravagant irrigation projects. Ninety per cent of Libya is desert. Historically, agriculture was practicable only in a narrow strip near the coast and a few oases in the south. With the discovery of vast underground reserves of sweet water, this suddenly changed. Drill enough deep wells and the Sahara could, or so the Libyan government thought at the time, play the same role as the American Midwest had played in US history. Certainly, water pumping requires oil, but there seemed to be plenty of that too. If this sounds short-sighted, it was part of a global trend: today, 40 per cent of all agriculture globally, and one-third in OECD countries, relies on groundwater for irrigation. The problems that excessive groundwater use necessarily entails thus concern everyone.

The Kufra project, the first large-scale industrial agricultural project in Libya, was launched in the late 1960s, first by an American oil company as a favour-currying gift to the then Libyan king Idris I and then, from 1969 onwards, by Mu'ammar Qadhafi himself. Kufra was chosen because of its symbolic potential – this was where the Sanūsiyya Sufi order which had brought King Idris to power had long held its headquarters – but also because population density was so low there that little opposition was to be expected. The aim was to make Libya independent of food imports, which in the 1970s accounted for 80 per cent of the food consumed in the country. Giant sprinklers were attached to 500-metre-deep wells, irrigating perfect circles with a radius of 560 metres, covering 100 hectares each, in a region where up to then traditional oasis gardens had been measured in square metres. By 1975, 15,000 hectares of brown had been turned green.

The abundance of water did nothing, however, to solve the

other great problem of desert agriculture: transport. Building materials and labour needed to be ferried to the Sahara, while agricultural produce needed to be brought to the coastal belt, where 85 per cent of the Libyan population reside. Qadhafi eventually decided to change course and, instead of taking agriculture to water, take water to the coast. In 1983, he announced the creation of the Great Man-Made River. This 'river' was in fact two underground pipelines large enough to accommodate an underground train, one from Kufra to Benghazi and the other from Fazzān to Tripoli. Together, they stretch over almost 3,000 kilometres and constitute, according to Colonel Qadhafi himself, not only the world's largest underground water network but also the Eighth Wonder of the World.

Today, the Great Man-Made River pumps, each day and notwithstanding civil war, rebellion and the current political chaos in Libya, half a million litres of fresh-water from the heart of the Sahara to the shores of the Mediterranean, providing water for agriculture and for the rapidly growing cities on the coast. Many of the large coastal farms are leased to foreign companies (Egyptian and Tunisian but also European and US owned), and they employ – or used to employ – a largely immigrant labour force, with Egyptian managers overseeing Sudanese or Sahelian workers. They are as far removed from traditional oasis gardens as one can imagine: no three-level mixed horticulture here, no goddās ringing the horn to redirect the water at regular intervals. No community assemblies to manage harvest times, maintenance and repairs, and other communal affairs. No slaves. Instead, underpaid and precarious sub-Saharan workers, monoculture and especially the possibility (for the owners of farms or the capitalists who back them) to move out once the soil is exhausted or the water runs out. Which might be sooner than expected.

Saharan deep-well drilling draws on water deposits that formed, in some cases, many million years ago. There can be no doubt that overuse will eventually deplete them. The jury, however, is still out on what exactly constitutes 'over-use'. On the surface, it seems simple: if you take out more than goes in, this is unsustainable in the long run. But this apparent simplicity hides more complex questions about collective priorities and the kinds of temporal and geographical frames that ought to matter. Experts still squabble over whether, at the current rate of use, depletion is a matter of hundreds or thousands of years – which incidentally indicates both just how politically charged these questions are and how little we really know of the deep geology of the Sahara. If it really were a matter of thousands of years, would that make it all right? On the other hand, any amount of use of a fossil resource – whether water, metals, coal, oil or gas – is theoretically unsustainable. The question then is not so much whether 'water mining' is acceptable but *how much* of it is acceptable, by whom and for what purpose – and who should be able to decide.

Recent research indicates that Saharan underground water tables are not fully fossil, that is, that they do recharge, albeit at a very slow and as yet badly understood rate. Figures vary widely from one water table to another. Current use of the NWSAS, the water table that feeds most agricultural development in Tunisia and Algeria, would have to be reduced by 90 per cent to be sustainable; if not, water will run out in 150 years. The NSAS, on the other hand, seems able to replenish if current rates of use are maintained, despite Qadhafi's Great Man-Made River. But given the global rush towards agricultural land and clean water and demographic growth in Egypt, it is highly unlikely that current rates of use will in fact be maintained. And once Sahelian countries decide to start using their underground water resources more fully, things will look dire further north.

In 2015, in the southern Algerian town of In Salah, hundreds assembled in the streets, holding placards and shouting slogans about an issue that for once seemed to have brought together old and young, secular and religious, publicly committed and apolitical, men and women. The government had just announced that it would start shale gas fracking in the region. Algeria claims to have the largest accessible reserves of shale gas in the world, containing three and a half times as much gas as its conventional reserves; international figures place it third in global rankings, before the USA. The protest concentrated not so much on the irreversible environmental damage that fracking would cause (although this clearly mattered) as on the extraordinary amounts of water it would require: 10 *million* litres per well, of which a minimum of ten were needed per site.

No worries, claimed the government, since the NWSAS, on which irrigation in In Salah depends, contains an estimated 50,000 *trillion* litres. This would easily provide all that was needed, they said, with more to spare. Yet although In Salah, thanks to its distance from the coast, has so far been preserved from deglet nour–type monoculture, people know very well how these underground water tables work: once you pump on one end, water goes down everywhere, spelling the end of traditional irrigation systems in the whole region. In fact, geologists worry that fracking in the area would quite simply destroy the NWSAS altogether, thereby putting an immediate end to agriculture not just around In Salah but also throughout the Algerian southeast, the Tunisian south and much of western Libya. Although the Algerian government shelved its plans for fracking in In Salah in 2015, two years later, it signed its first contract with Total for shale gas fracking in neighbouring Timimoun. Access to sweet water in the Sahara has always been a hotly contested political issue, and this clearly will not change in the years and decades to come.

Sedentists in the Sahara have for millennia found an astonishing range of solutions to their water problem by coaxing water with great technical ingenuity towards their gardens. Other Saharans have opted for a different solution: not to bring the water to them but to go where and when it naturally occurs. In close symbiosis with other non-human animals, this has over time led to the development of many different forms of pastoral nomadism, to which we shall now turn.

3

CHERCHEZ LE DROMADAIRE

Milk your camels
their milk is worth more than crushed millet.
Al-Qasum ag Himi.[1]

In November 1975, the Moroccan army, accompanied by 350,000 Moroccan civilians brandishing the Quran, crossed the border into the Spanish colony of Western Sahara to claim it is as part of their own in what came to be known as the 'Green March'. On the other side of the border, they found a country that was predominantly pasture: at least half of the population of Spanish Western Sahara at that time were mobile herders looking after more than 50,000 camels (and perhaps the same number of sheep and goats) among them and constituting a population of about 70,000. By the time most of them had settled in refugee camps near Tindouf in Algerian territory a few months later, they had lost, sold or abandoned almost all of their livestock. Many animals died in the war, when wells were poisoned and pastures rendered unsafe. Others were taken across the border into Morocco, and yet more were abandoned by their owners to fend for themselves in a context of generalised drought. The few refugees who managed to bring their beasts to the camps were forced to slaughter them on site or to sell them to Algerian pastoralists at low prices.

The few camels that survived were appropriated by the Western Saharan government-in-exile. It would have been impossible anyway for their owners to keep them in the overcrowded army camps that were to be their new homes – impossible for them but also (which they couldn't have foreseen) for their children and grandchildren. The days when they were woken by camels early in the morning and went to sleep only after their beasts had settled for the night; when they slept in tents and on blankets woven from camel hair, drank camel milk and on special occasions ate camel meat; when large celebrations brought large numbers of camels together and conflict was managed through transfers in livestock; when camel ownership determined daily work and seasonal movement as well as social positions and marital alliances – those days were over.

Or were they? In contemporary Western Saharan camps, tents have by now been replaced by mud-brick or even concrete houses. Hospitals, schools and mosques show that people are here to stay. Mobility for young residents is about education, trade and international scholarships rather than the search for good pasture. Life depends on the continuous support of the United Nations and various NGOs, not on seasonal rainfall and one's ability to predict the herd's every want and need. Yet for the last decade or so, the grunting of camels can once more be heard echoing through the camps and the stench of camel urine pervades many a peaceful alleyway. The government-owned herd is grazing far away on the few pastures still left in the rump territory of Western Sahara, herded by salaried Malian shepherds (as most Sahrawis have grown up in camps and hence lack the necessary pastoral skill to do this themselves). The grunts are those of newly bought, privately owned camels kept in pens inside the camps themselves and fed, at great cost, with Algerian-produced industrial fodder. If, in the past, owning camels made you rich, you now have to be rich to own camels.

The camels' ostensible purpose is to provide milk, especially to the camps' elderly residents. Camel milk, seasonally abundant and difficult to store, used to be given away for free; today, it is sold in milk bars throughout the camps. Elderly women in the camps will quickly explain to curious visitors that there is, in fact, a disease called *eghindi* which attacks only true Sahrawis – a term which originally just means 'Saharans' but has come to designate the citizens of the disputed Western Saharan territories. Eghindi is caused by pollution and the consumption of brackish water and processed, overly salty food – the kind of food, in fact, handed out in aid packages throughout the world, and the Tindouf camps are no exception. Eghindi causes swelling of the neck, a burning feeling in the throat and stomach, and skin rashes and itching. It can be cured only by drinking fresh camel milk. Even in the unpromising circumstances of a refugee camp, camel husbandry is therefore no luxury but a vital necessity, essential for the survival of Sahrawis *as Sahrawis* – much as the Western Sahara government-in-exile-held herd out on the pastures indicates that Sahrawis have at least some control over some parts of the territory they claim as their own.

Camels have shaped the Sahara as we know it. They have made life in the desert possible: as providers of transport, food, water, salt and the raw materials for clothes and tents and as crucial instruments of war and political rule, they have been at the heart of most economic and political systems in the Sahara, whether nomadic or sedentary. Their value has never just been economic; they have been bound up so deeply with many a Saharan's self-perception that even today, they are understood by many to be intrinsic to their very existence. When Mu'ammar

Qadhafi, the late ruler of Libya, invited Western dignitaries to sit cross-legged under a tent and partake of a repast of fresh camel milk and stewed camel hump; when he offered gifts of live camels to various African rulers from the Gambia to Madagascar; when he insisted on his trip to Paris in 2007 that a Bedouin tent be put up in the garden of his prestigious Parisian hotel, and camel milk and meat provided on a daily basis so that he could properly receive his visitors, he was therefore not just following a personal whim but pushing one of the most consensual and prestigious markers of desert life onto the international stage.

Although the importance of camels in the Sahara can never be reduced just to their economic value, this is also not merely a matter of 'tradition'. Nomadic pastoralism makes rational use of lands marginal to agriculture, drawing on specialised skills that are fine-tuned to a difficult environment and inherently flexible. It produces a form of wealth – livestock – that is mobile and partible and thus adaptable to all kinds of economic and commercial systems. Livestock is, in fact, the only kind of capital (note, in English, the word's close etymological link to 'cattle') that *really* increases naturally, however much economists would like us to believe that money is able to do the same. Despite the oft-touted notion of pastoral nomadism as at best an anachronistic survival, it therefore remains an important part of local livelihoods today and will continue to do so in the future. The British anthropologist E. E. Evans-Pritchard, studying, in the first decades of the twentieth century, the cattle-raising Nuer of southern Sudan, famously quipped that there was but one way to understand Nuer political and social life: *cherchez la vache*. Following his suggestion means that we must 'look for the camel' (or the sheep, goat, donkey, cow and horse) as a way of seeing life in the Sahara as many Saharans have long experienced it.

Scenes from a Pastoral Life

The first signs that you are approaching a nomadic camp in the Sahara, long before you can see tents or people, are camel tracks and dung. The camels themselves may be out of sight; they are usually left to graze independently at quite a distance from the camp. Once you meet the camels themselves – which in the Sahara are all of the one-humped variety and more properly called 'dromedaries' – you will know whose camp it is. You will recognise their brand mark or perhaps even the camels themselves. Adult animals tend to be known individually by all those living nearby or even further away, as a particularly beautiful, fast or resilient camel's fame might spread far and wide. Once you approach the camp, tracks of other animals appear: goats, a few half-tamed donkeys, sometimes sheep, perhaps a dog, more rarely cattle. If in countless orientalist paintings and tourist brochures, camels are a symbol of the great 'empty' spaces of the desert, in the desert itself, they are a sign of human presence and activity.

Camps are usually established near good pasture, but 'good pasture' is a complex and highly contextual notion. It means not just available biomass but accessible and nourishing plants near sufficient water supplies. What is 'sufficient' varies from species to species, from season to season and from one flock to another: when grazing on fresh grass, camels, for instance, do not need to be watered, but they have delicate stomachs and do need regular salt cures; goats eat anything but need to be watered daily, as do cows. Moreover, animals and their herders do not necessarily agree among themselves about what constitutes 'good pasture'. Cows herded by Fulani pastoralists, for instance, do not feed in the same way as Tuareg or Arab cows, but even within the same linguistic or even family group, tastes vary. In marginal environments, calves learn from their mothers how to graze efficiently. Herders watch their animals attentively, and if they recognise a mother cow that strikes them as a particularly good and clever feeder, they will encourage her to have more calves than the others. Over time, one herd of the same type of animal can therefore develop a substantially different feeding pattern from another.

Lactating animals are kept near the camp, as they have to be milked once or twice daily; vulnerable young animals are kept there too, for protection and to stop them from suckling at will. As young animals are rarely slaughtered, for humans to have access to milk literally means sharing with them, which in turn requires careful management of both baby and mother animals. Adult camels like to roam far and wide; adult males have to be kept apart from each other to avoid fights and often also must be separated from the female herd. Individual families therefore might have their animals – and hence also their human members – scattered over large distances, some guarded by adolescent boys several days' walk away, others by the camp's women within walking distance, yet others away with adult men on a caravan or to be sold elsewhere.

Each herd will also contain animals that belong to others – cousins settled in the city or busy elsewhere, friends, clients or patrons. Sometimes this is so because these animals – cattle or horses, for instance – require a different kind of pasture. Very often, however, it is a way of spreading risk, of avoiding local droughts or diseases, or indeed conflict and raids, and of creating and maintaining ties with others. Herding is hard work, but it also constantly produces wealth, in the form of calves, kids, baby camels, milk and sometimes meat, that can sustain many a poor relative in times of need. Pastoralists have over time developed complex layers of ownership and use rights, of mutual aid, loans, of deferred payment of debts, of bride-wealth and fines.

The herds you see in a camp hence already tell a story of great social complexity and far-reaching alliances.

Herding is hard work, and in the past, those who could left it to slaves. Those who could not sent their pre-adolescent or adolescent boys. This is still the case in many regions today. Among the Tubu of northern Niger and Chad, for instance, children familiarise themselves with livestock from birth: first as babies attached to their mothers' backs while they tend to their flocks, then as toddlers, looking after sheep and goats, milking them and practicing handling them the way they see their fathers and older brothers handle camels. As older children, they start helping with the arduous task of watering the herd using a *dalū*, or animal-powered pulley well. During the dry season, encampments congregate near these pastoral wells. A dalū consists of a deep shaft, sometimes encased in wood or, more recently, cement. Over it is posed a simple wellhead with a bucket on a cord wrapped around a pulley. The cord is attached to an animal – a donkey or a camel – which is walked away from the well, thereby pulling out the bucket. The full bucket is emptied into a nearby trough.

Young children, girls and boys, start walking or sometimes riding the animal from the age of six. They usually ride bareback, with somewhat sore behinds, on their notoriously stubborn charges, and it always seems a minor miracle when the animal actually does what it is told to do. Older children are in charge of receiving the bucket and emptying it into the trough, which is quite as unpleasant as working a shadūf, as described in the preceding chapter, or even more so since the surroundings of the well tend to be muddy and odorous, trampled by thousands of animal hoofs, covered in dung and infested with flies and other insects. Pulley wells are easily identified on satellite images by the circle of devastated, overgrazed and torn-up soil around them.

The oldest children are in charge of managing the animals, which is the worst task of all: by the time they get to the well, the animals, whether camels or cows, tend to be crazy with thirst. It is true that camels can go for a long time without water, but when they finally smell it, it is almost impossible to hold them back. Yet they *have* to be held back, if only to avoid injury and fights with other animals. In the dry season, remote wells can attract hundreds if not thousands of animals belonging to people of different backgrounds, languages, herding traditions and even countries: managing a well is therefore hard physical labour and requires a flair for diplomacy.

At the onset of puberty, Tubu boys are sent out to guard larger herds, often at a distance of several days' walk from the camp. This means that boys as young as eleven might spend weeks at a time in total isolation, perhaps with a brother or cousin, living pretty much off whatever food they can find. At night, they sleep on a simple woven mat, perhaps in the shade of an acacia tree. They drink water from rock pools or small springs, collected in the calabash which forms their only equipment; they eat berries, *dūm* palm nuts and wild grains and drink milk – sometimes directly from the udder, fighting off the baby camel – if they are lucky enough to be herding animals with young. The privileged among them have an electric torch and a pouch of dried dates should they fall on hard times. Their job is to know where the animals are, all of them and always, even at night; they sleep lightly and acquire the skill of knowing instinctively what their charges might do, when and where.

They also have to protect the herd from predators (human or non-human) and to prevent the intrusion of 'foreign' male camels looking for a fight. Given that adult camels can reach a height of 2,4 metres at the shoulder, bite, fight, sometimes attempt to crush their opponent by lying on them and generally fight dirty, this is a dangerous if not impossible task. Similarly, it is virtually impossible to make an adult camel go to a place where he does not want to go, and herders acknowledge that their animals usually know better than anybody else what is good for them in any case. We should therefore perhaps replace the term 'herding', with its association of an omniscient shepherd managing dumb beasts, with the circumlocution the Tubu themselves use: the children are 'behind their camels', 'stuck to their bottoms' or 'following them around'. After years spent in the company of camels, Tubu adolescents know each individual animal's personality and characteristics intimately.

Among most Saharan pastoralists, women and older girls are mostly in charge of smaller livestock that can be kept close to the camp and need to be milked every day. Younger girls might stay in the tent, churning butter. Others take out the livestock during the day and return in the evening, penning them in enclosures made of thorny branches. Goats rarely attract the kind of poetic notice that camels, horses or even cows might, yet they are crucial for pastoral life. With their milk, they supply much daily food; they can be sacrificed when needs must, providing meat for all; along with tough desert-going sheep, they are more easily and frequently sold for meat than camels. Most importantly, perhaps, goats breed quickly. Camels take four years until they reach maturity, and an average pregnancy lasts fifteen months (camel mothers can slow down their gestation period when they feel that conditions are not right for giving birth). The onset of maturity in goats, on the other hand, is after six to eight months, and gestation lasts barely five months.

It is easy to do the maths here and to understand the crucial role played by goats – and hence by the women who raise them – in keeping the family afloat during periods of drought and disaster, which in fragile desert environments are always just around the corner. In moments of crisis, Tuareg camps often shrink – men leave with their camels to look for pasture elsewhere or on their own to see if they can find other sources of income. But the women, at the heart of the camp, always stay behind to ensure family continuity. Indeed, among many Tuareg groups, it is women who own the tents that make up the camp, while their husbands are mere guests under their tent-flap – an arrangement that becomes painfully obvious on divorce, when a grown man might find himself sleeping out in the open or meekly returning to his mother's tent.

Domestic Revolutions

This close connection between human and animal welfare is clearly very old in the Sahara and predates the arrival of camels by millennia. There is still some debate over whether cows were domesticated independently in the eastern Sahara around the eighth century BCE, but we can be sure that by 6000 BCE, sheep, goats and cattle were herded throughout the area. Donkeys were domesticated from native wild asses in what is now southern Egypt between the fifth and the fourth millennia BCE. Independent genetic mutations for greater lactose tolerance in adult humans appeared in East Africa at roughly the same time, indicating regular consumption of dairy products.

The story of human social evolution used to be told as follows: when *Homo sapiens* first emerged 300,000 years ago on the African continent, they lived in small bands of nomadic hunter-gatherers. At some undetermined point in time, they started to herd the animals they hunted as a way of keeping food for later. Then, 13,000 years ago, the Neolithic Revolution began in the region we now call the Middle East: sedentary agriculture, cities and states emerged, irreversibly replacing more mobile livelihoods, changing the landscape and altering society beyond recognition. Those innovations spread irresistibly outwards, conquering the globe, until we found ourselves in our current predicament. All other forms of livelihood, including pastoral nomadism, have been displaced and destroyed or survive as mere vestiges of an earlier age.

This story is wrong on several counts. For one, most livestock seem to have been domesticated at the same time as or just after the domestication of plants. This means that we should think of nomadic pastoralism not as the predecessor of agriculture but rather as its structural counterpart: while some people settled down to grow food, others became more mobile than ever before to keep herds away from fields and gardens. Moreover, this is anything but a unilinear story of 'improvement', as people seem to have dabbled with different livelihoods over time, toying with agriculture and husbandry in bad years and reverting to hunting and gathering when natural resources were more plentiful.

Even in this revised version, this story makes little sense on the African continent. In the northeastern Sahara, livestock imported from the East – including goats and sheep but especially cattle – were adopted, rapidly and enthusiastically, by local groups of more or less mobile hunters, foragers and fisherfolk about 8,000 years ago – 5,000 years after they were first domesticated among their Middle Eastern neighbours. From there, domesticated animals spread out and down across the continent, reaching West Africa 4,000 years later and the southern tip by the beginning of the first millennium. Yet the adoption of livestock did not entail the adoption of the whole 'Middle

Eastern package'. The people who then lived in the northeastern Sahara clearly liked the cows and, to a lesser extent, goats and sheep, but they had no interest whatsoever in domesticating plants or settling down to sedentary agriculture – at least not for another couple of millennia.

In fact, this particularly Saharan 'Neolithic revolution', far from increasing sedentism (and cities and states and whatever else is supposed to come with it), made people *more* rather than *less* mobile. They gradually abandoned good places for hunting, fishing and gathering in order to follow their cattle to pasture. This also meant that they produced less rather than more pottery as time went on, presumably privileging vessels that were easier to carry but did not survive in the archaeological record (such as woven baskets or skin bags). This reverses the usual assumption of archaeological research that the presence of more artefacts somehow indicates evolutionary 'progress'. Until the beginning of the first centuries CE, and in many regions not until much later, pastoralism rather than agriculture remained the dominant productive strategy and cultural form, not because people did not know better but because mobile husbandry must have appeared to be the most suitable, fulfilling and meaningful way to make a living.

This brief outline raises a number of questions. First, is 'domestication' even the right term to describe what happened in the Sahara 8,000 years ago? An animal is usually said to have been domesticated when it has changed genetically, whether that is seen in a reduction in size or in different muscularity, bone density or brain size. These are also the genetic changes that can be observed in humans as they settle to become permanent agriculturalists: they grow smaller and weaker and their brain size decreases in their own process of self-domestication (or are they in fact, as some suggest, domesticated by the plants and animals whose every need they now serve?). But these processes take much longer and might never even occur in an animal and presumably also human population that is tame but not penned – that has no house in which *domestication* might take place. Moreover, if we focus only on genetic changes, we might miss other significant developments: the mutual, though often unequal, transformation of human-animal, human-human and animal-animal relations. The most important cultural change might happen not when cows change their shape but when humans start thinking differently about cows – and cows about humans.

Second, if prehistoric Saharans were keen to adopt domesticated animals from the Near East, why did they have no interest in domestic plants? Some explain this apparent oddity with reference to environmental uncertainties – even in the then much wetter and greener Sahara, conditions changed dramatically from one year to the next, and mobility was the only viable response. Others point to the abundance of wild resources, which meant that pastoralists could complement their livelihoods with hunting and gathering wild seeds, as many still do today. The real answer might be found in an overarching preference for mobility: livestock made it possible for people who already valued their mobility to increase and sustain it over time. Rather than dismissing this as yet another sign of 'African exceptionalism', recent research suggests that this 'African pathway to food production' might in fact have been quite as common, if not more so, in world history as the Near Eastern one. If we stop and think about what long-term settlement without plumbing or municipal rubbish collection actually implies, we might understand why.

The third problem with this simplified narrative of

domestication and progress is the question of why people in the Sahara adopted animals so enthusiastically. Was it really just a matter of food security? And if this were the case, why did people suddenly feel the need to store a surplus if they hadn't for millennia? Some archaeologists suggest that what this was the emergence of private property in goods that are, as pointed out at the beginning of this chapter, movable and partible and increase on their own account, an early version of the spirit of capitalism. Others say that on the contrary, early accumulation is proof of the deeply engrained human tendency to throw large parties, to feast and to binge. These are mostly speculations, and rather anachronistic ones to boot; what we do know is that the relationship of herders to their animals was never merely utilitarian. From their earliest occurrence in the Sahara, cattle were depicted with great care and detail, and as we saw earlier, they seem to have been buried ceremonially well before people were accorded this treatment. Indeed, traces of ritual activity involving cattle or their depictions predate genetic domestication, and the lovingly painted images of cows leave no doubt that their herders found them beautiful.

Such a reading corresponds to the uses of livestock by contemporary nomadic pastoralists. Until recently, animals were rarely slaughtered for meat but instead were used in complex exchange relations and crucial social transactions as bride-wealth, compensation payments and gifts or to cure disease, temper divine anger and appease conflict. Even today, marriage among many Saharan pastoralist groups involves the exchange and redistribution of cattle, while potentially mortal conflicts after accidents and homicides can be averted through the payment of compensation money, which in northern Chad, for instance, continues to be calculated in livestock because livestock are alive in a way that money is not. Although we should be extremely cautious when projecting contemporary realities back onto a distant past, there is no reason to think that prehistoric Saharan pastoralists thought of their animals primarily as food.

At some point in the distant past, then, Saharan human societies transformed to include cattle and other ungulates in their own regionally specific variant of the 'Neolithic revolution'. This had profound implications for their degree of mobility and for the way in which they could establish relations over distance, among humans, animals and particular places, in a form of complexity that had little use for settled agriculture, cities and states. Livestock allowed early pastoralists to broaden their horizons geographically, socially, spiritually and aesthetically, thereby making life in the Sahara as we know it today possible. And this was even before the currently most important of Saharan domesticated beasts – the one-humped dromedary, more familiarly called 'camel' – made her first appearance in the region.

Nomadic War Machines

'Ah! Now I know / that nothing has a higher price than a faithful *mehari* [riding camel] / whose hump is erect and whose flanks are taut / Like a closely woven mat'. Thus spoke the Tuareg poet Kourman, who died in the late 1980s in northern Niger near the mining town of Arlit. 'When I put on his saddle / he knows what I want / ... / his frisky step puts my veil in disarray'.[2] While we can only speculate about the affection of prehistoric Saharan pastoralists for their cows, there can be little doubt about the strong ties between contemporary Saharan pastoralists and their camels. Camels, as everybody knows, are perfect desert animals: when feeding on fresh grass, they can go without water altogether for months at a time, storing surplus calories in their 'erect hump'. Otherwise they need to be watered only every three to four days, as they can absorb huge quantities of water in record time. They are heat- and cold-resistant, important qualities in an environment where temperatures can vary by as much as 40°C in a single day. They can carry heavy loads on their 'taut flanks' and walk up to 60 kilometres per day with their 'frisky step'. They turn salty water into sweet milk. As noted in the poem, they are intelligent animals and can pretty much fend for themselves. They seal their nostrils against sandstorms and protect their eyes with three sets of eyelids and two layers of eyelashes.

Camels were domesticated around 2000 BCE, long after cattle, sheep and goats, so we can infer that their domestication might have been intentional rather than just the result of an accidental entanglement of human and beast. The wild ancestor of one-humped camels was native to the mangrove forests of the South Arabian coast – which explains their constant need for salt. They were probably introduced to the eastern Sahara sometime in the first millennium BCE and then spread slowly west, reaching the western Sahara by the fourth century CE. As they need to be watered less frequently than any other domestic livestock, camels opened up pastures and routes that had been inaccessible to humans until then. Islamic folklore indeed hesitates regarding whether camels are God's special creatures – they are said to naturally observe the Quranic incest taboo – or, on the contrary, are fathered by demons, as they are so perfectly adapted to life in the bādiya that their owners themselves seem to acquire jinn-like qualities.

More soberly, there can be little doubt that it was only with the introduction of camels that the Sahara as we know and imagine it today – criss-crossed by traders and home to oasis agriculture – could come into existence. Without camels, oasis dwellers would have no contact with the outside world and hence nothing to eat; conversely, oases tend to be situated at the extreme points of a distance that a loaded camel can travel before it needs a break or indeed a replacement. Camels have long been bred for specific purposes: some are good hill climbers, others excel in sandy environments; some love the heat, others the cold, becoming an integral part of local ecosystems. Some are for riding, others for carrying loads, some for milk, others for breeding only. And then there are those that are quite simply beautiful, the object of praise poetry and song, of legends and much envy – as in the poem quoted above. The English word 'camel' is in fact a rather clumsy translation for dozens of words in local languages that describe animals according to age, sex, appearance, specialisation and race – akin, perhaps, to the complex vocabulary found among contemporary horse lovers or the proverbially abundant arctic vocabulary describing ice, snow – and reindeer.

Although without camels, life in the Sahara as we know it today would not have been possible, camels never just existed on their own, and 'pure' camel pastoralism was, for the most part, a myth. Although al-Qasum ag Himi, the Tuareg poet quoted in the epigraph to this chapter, clearly denigrated a diet of 'crushed millet', historians estimated that in the late nineteenth century, Tuareg pastoralists living in and near the Nigerien Aïr imported 7,500 tonnes of millet *each year* for human consumption, each and every grain carried on camelback. Most pastoralists owned mixed herds and sometimes even tried their own hand at agriculture. Take, for instance, the Arbā'a, Arabic-speaking pastoral nomads who live in and around the qsar of Laghouat, 400 kilometres south of Algiers. Traditionally, the Arbā'a had large herds of sheep and camels, with a few horses and goats. They owned houses and silos in Laghouat or had well-established relationships with local sedentists who would look after the Arbā'a's stores of grain. In exchange, the Arbā'a took care of the sedentists' herds.

We have detailed information about one Arbā'a family in the late nineteenth century thanks to a family budget that the amateur sociologist Auguste Geoffroy established for them in 1885.[3] According to him, a typical year for this family went something like this: in January, they could be found in the Sahara proper near Ouargla, about 200 kilometres south of Laghouat, where pasture would be abundant after the autumn rains. February and March were lambing season, and the whole family, including the smallest children, were busy day and night, looking after the newborns and their mothers. As soon as the lambs were old enough to make the trip, the whole family and their herds moved north, back to Laghouat. There they spent April and May in their family home in the qsar, sorting through stores, catching up with friends, looking after the garden and harvesting the grain that they had sown, alongside their cousins, earlier in the year.

In the hottest months, June and July, they travelled to the agricultural lands further north. If they needed extra money, they could find temporary employment in the cereal harvest; all took their herds to graze the stubble once the harvest had been brought in. These were the distant descendants of the 'badū' whom, 500 years earlier, Ibn Khaldūn had watched herding their sheep from the window of his study as he drafted his *Muqaddima*. The Arbā'a sold sheep and wool, alongside dates brought up from Ouargla, cheese, butter, and blankets woven by the women during the winter months, at local markets. They used the money thus earned to lay in supplies of cereals, tea and sugar, cotton cloth, perfumes and those kitchen utensils and tools they couldn't make themselves for the rest of the year. By September, they started moving south again, stopping in Laghouat to store surplus grain in their silos and to sow their seeds in a different spot to avoid soil exhaustion in the collectively held fields. Slowly, they returned to their winter pastures, which had had time to recover in the months of their absence. From there, the whole cycle started again, year after year.

Geoffroy's budget leaves no doubt that the Arbā'a were prosperous. They ate well of a variety of foods, dressed with distinction and imported materials, and had enough money left at the end of the year to participate in lavish festivals, give generous gifts to the local Sufi order and shrines and help their poorer relatives. As Geoffroy, ever the Victorian moraliser, noted with much regret, they could have saved a good tenth of their annual income if they had not been quite so given to socialising, feasting, poetry, keeping beautiful horses and other pleasures. Far from the 'restless wanderers' of orientalist fiction, the Arbā'a were in fact substantial property owners with a highly diversified economy who could rely on large family networks giving them access to collectively owned lands and help in times of need. Most importantly, perhaps, although Geoffroy studied them as part of a larger research project on late-nineteenth-century 'working-class families', they were in fact nothing of the kind but rather the only recently dethroned overlords of the central Algerian steppe.

Let us now fast forward almost a hundred years to the 1970s and cross the Sahara south to the Damergu in central Niger, a region inhabited by, among others, sedentary Hausa farmers and nomadic Tuareg-speaking pastoralists. For several centuries until the French colonial conquest, the area was dominated by elite Tuareg families who, like the Arbā'a, combined different economic activities, including livestock herding, salt mining and everything in between. They thereby controlled and taxed a multi-lingual, multi-racial and multi-occupational multitude of people who were linked to their overlords through a mind-boggling variety of different forms of dependence, ranging from outright servility to sporadic gifts given as tribute. Political relations within this system were never stable, as people individually attempted to better their position and to move into or out of the area of Tuareg influence. Yet the whole system was held together through their domination, expressed in military superiority and maintained by their incessant movement from one client's camp, mine or village to the next.

In pre-colonial times, at moments when pastures were abundant, these elite families would draw people into the Sahara, expanding their herds, buying and raiding slaves and incorporating them into their own families, settling dependent Hausa agriculturalists further north, attracting salt miners and creating new oases. As people from different backgrounds were integrated into the system, the proportion of 'Tuareg', and thus of 'nomads', would go up, although people of course often maintained their own languages and cultures to the extent that they could. Conversely, during moments of drought, these elite groups would shed as many people as possible – freeing the enslaved, letting clients fend for themselves, allowing Hausa farmers to return south, sending miners on their way, encouraging non-Tuareg wives to spend time with their natal families – and the number of 'Tuareg' would dwindle to a few elite families who, if things really turned bad, could seek shelter with their Hausa 'clients' further south.

The system would therefore work like a gigantic pump, bringing people into the desert (through force or persuasion) or shedding them. As a result, as the French geographer Denis Retaillé noted with the Tuareg in mind, 'even within so-called

Shifting Sands

nomadic societies, sedentists usually constitute the majority'.[4] We can nonetheless describe societies such as these as nomadic, he said, because political power lies with those who can command movement, which in turn means that elite nomadic families can arrange everybody else's life in ways that suit them best. This also explains the importance of camels: although they might in fact be less fertile than sheep and goats and produce less milk and meat than cows, camels – and especially the fast riding camels that Kourman celebrated in his poem – give elite groups the advantage of range and speed. The way in which, in endless novels, films, photographs and tourist brochures, white male dominant pastoralists and their beautiful sleek riding camels have come to stand for Saharan societies as a whole is therefore not just the result of an external fascination with the exotic but also a reflection of local power relations.

Once we recognise this close connection between political power and mobility, it becomes obvious that neither a nomadic nor a sedentary way of life is set it stone (as no political order is ever fixed once and for all, whatever its ideologues might claim). Whole groups might move up and down the ladder according to the whims of animal and human reproduction, climate and conflict. On an individual level, sedentists might dream of leaving the back-breaking labour of irrigation behind and moving towards a nomadic existence – if only they can acquire the means to do so. Nomads, on the other hand, might 'drop out' at either the top or the bottom. They might become so wealthy that they decide to live a more settled existence, letting others look after their herds; conversely, they might lose so much of their herds to drought, theft or disease that all forms of pastoral mobility become meaningless – in which case they have to start again from the (sedentary) bottom of the pile.

The Permanent Crisis of Pastoralism

In the 1970s and again in the 1980s, the Sahel was subject to severe region-wide drought. Although drought itself was not uncommon in the region, it was followed this time by a famine that seemed to confirm what everybody in the development-struck 1970s already knew: that nomadic pastoralism was dying out. Many were the anthropologists, historians and sociologists who at that time argued that this was not the case; that it was national boundaries and the misrecognition and dismantling of region-wide complex nomadic societies, with their roots in colonial policy, that had caused famine, not the alleged incompatibility of pastoralism and modernity. Nobody much listened to them because their arguments went against the grain of the evolutionary schemes sketched above in which pastoral nomadism is nothing but an anachronistic remnant of prehistoric times, the droughts just the last straw that broke a long-suffering camel's back. These evolutionary schemes are still with us, and when I teach classes on Saharan pastoralism, I always struggle to get students to talk about nomads in anything other than a somewhat nostalgic past tense.

The realities are different and infinitely more complex. By the 1990s, as international media attention turned away from the Sahel, livestock herds there had recovered almost completely. Many of the pastoralists who had settled out of necessity in the 1980s returned to their former occupation, often leaving parts of their families behind in the new settlement sites, just in case. Livestock markets boomed. Development programmes focussed on improving the viability of Saharan pasture by boring pastoral wells and attempting to make basic social services, such as education and health care, available to nomads. This image of recovery and continuity, however, hid profound changes in social and economic relations. During the drought, pastoralists had been forced to sell their animals, often at miserably low prices. The buyers were those who had access to ready money and humanitarian aid: primarily local civil servants and employees of NGOs but also livestock and grain traders and a few wealthy farmers. Many of these, ignorant of animal husbandry or reluctant to take up the hard life of the desert, started to employ their animals' former owners as salaried shepherds. By 1990, probably half of the animals in the Nigerien Sahara were herded by salaried shepherds, which led the French anthropologist André Bourgeot to speak of the emergence of a 'lumpen-nomadariat' throughout the Sahel.[5]

Eventually, however, funds ran out, boreholes resulted in overgrazing, and more generous rainfall made it possible for pastoralists to return to pastures too remote to be within the purview of resource-poor Sahelian states. Women had patiently built up their herds of sheep and goats and could now use them to invest in larger livestock. Hired shepherds were often paid in livestock, which allowed them over time to build up their own herds; money earned in emigration often served the same purpose. By the 2000s, national herds everywhere were far larger than they had been in the 1960s, and numbers continue to rise. All herders, however, had learned without fault what their forefathers had long known: that nomadic pastoralism can only ever be one part of a more complex and diversified livelihood strategy. If, in the past, this meant investing in houses, gardens, fields and trade, today, it meant establishing relations with state officials and NGOs; breeding and selling animals for meat, often over vast distances; and encouraging parts of the family to be sedentary and others to emigrate temporarily, join the army or become trans-regional traders. Everybody locally can point to the well-stocked herds of Saharans who have 'made it' in the modern state apparatus. The vast camel herds owned by the late

Chadian president Idriss Déby – whose grazing rights nobody dared contest – were but an extreme example of this.

Twice a week, on Tuesdays and Thursdays, you can stand on the N'Gueli Bridge, which marks the border with Cameroon just west of the Chadian capital, N'Djamena, and watch for hours the incessant flow of cattle brought in from across the country and herded towards Ngaoundéré, 700 kilometres south and terminus of the Cameroon railways. The first animals arrive before dawn. They cautiously cross the bridge, while others swim, after some hesitation, across the river beneath it. The lowing of cattle and sounds of clashing horns are lost in the morning mist along with the low, guttural calls of the herdsmen who accompany them; the cattle look like one slowly swaying body as they move towards and across the bridge. Hours later, as the heat rises, the flow continues relentlessly. It is impossible to imagine that there could be quite so many cows on the sparse pastures that surround N'Djamena and stretch all the way north into the desert. Especially as these are particularly beautiful beasts: not the spotted and somewhat overfed Frisian cows of European pastures or advertisements but sleek, muscular, reddish-brown oxen with elegantly curving horns who have spent their lives outdoors and sometimes turn to look at you with liquid and intelligent eyes.

In 2020, Chad had, according to official statistics, an overall national cattle herd of more than 100 million head, up by 40 per cent from the pre-drought golden age of pastoralism in the late 1960s. The country has very few ranches, and the vast majority of cattle are raised by mobile herders. This means that pastoral skills are still very much in demand and that, despite official announcements of programmes intending to 'rationalise' meat production in the country, nomadic pastoralism is anything but dying. This will not change in the near future. Lagos alone, within easy reach of the Ngaoundéré railway, has a population on a par with that of the whole country of Chad, and the wealthy among them want to eat beef on a daily basis. In 2010, livestock trade within West Africa was worth an estimated 1 billion USD, twice as much as in 2000.

The cattle trade from the Sahelian countries is mirrored by the camel trade from the southern to the northern Sahara. Kanem, just north of Lake Chad, is an important departure point because it has rich pastures and because the trade here is organised by the local sultan, who is today officially a Chadian civil servant but nonetheless a descendant of a dynasty that once ruled a territory stretching as far north as Fazzān in southern Libya. The sultan, his acolytes and allied merchants buy camels from regional pastoralists. These animals are then taken north on foot, usually by hired conveyors. Conveyors, often members of Bourgeot's 'lumpen-nomadariat', carry as their sole equipment a blanket, some water and sometimes a satellite telephone. They cover the whole distance – roughly 1,700 kilometres – on foot, eating dried dates, drinking powdered milk which they carry with them and sleeping on the ground next to their animals, wrapped in their blankets against the biting Saharan cold. They usually take their time on the way up so that the animals will arrive in an acceptable state in Libya.

Just north of the Chadian border, as the terrain gets particularly arid, they are usually met by trucks carrying fodder and water, hired with their drivers by the financial backers of the caravan. On arrival, the Chadian conveyors might spend some time in Libya, visiting relatives and friends, perhaps even working temporarily on one of the many building sites in the Libyan south. They then invest their earnings in Libyan consumer goods and staples and return on the back of one of the many Libyan trucks that supply Chad's northernmost towns from the north. The whole trip usually takes them three to four months, most of which they will have spent walking through the desert wearing flip-flops. After five or six trips, they can hope to invest in their own herd back home, perhaps get married. If all goes well, the financial backers of these caravans can expect to recoup their initial investment up to thirty-fold.

Milk Better Than Millet

My friend Zahra was delighted. It was autumn in northern Mali, a time when, due to short and widely dispersed rains, pasture finally starts to be plentiful again after the long, dry, hot months of spring and summer. Milk was plentiful, and it was time to go and drink it. We left behind the bustle of Gao, a major town in northern Mali, and headed for the pastures where Zahra's family kept their cows. 'We' included all the women of the extended family, bunched together on the back of a battered Toyota pickup truck. After a few hours' drive, the cattle camp came into sight: a tent made of woven mats; a place to cook; somewhat dry-looking shrubs, cow-pads and flies everywhere. This was where we were going to spend the next few weeks, growing fat.

In the absence of reliable electricity and thus refrigerators, milk is difficult to keep. Although most pastoralists in the Sahara drink it slightly soured – in fact, it tends to turn as soon as it hits the pail, given the ambient heat and bacteria remaining there – this is to make it easier to digest rather than to keep it. People make a little cheese, but most of the milk needs to be drunk straight away, while the supply lasts. Which is never very long, as Saharan animals lactate only during the wet season, when they get enough moisture from pasture. Traditional notions of female beauty in many Saharan societies emphasise fatness, and an autumnal fattening camp among women thus made perfect sense.

In fact, there were few lactating cows. The pastures, quite far north, were too dry for them, and the family seemed to keep them mostly out of nostalgia and, much as their distant cousins in the Western Saharan refugee camps kept their camels, as an indication of who they were: an Arabic-speaking scholarly nomadic family proud of their Mauritanian ancestry. We ate biscuits smuggled in from nearby Algeria; slaughtered a goat, whose carcass was then stolen at night by an unidentified predator (I suspected the chronically underfed camp dog); played endless games of a fiendishly complicated version of Ludo; listened to the BBC in Arabic; and hung out. And this was indeed the point. Zahra's family had long stopped being full-time pastoralists – indeed, they probably never had been. Zahra's father had been a guard in the French colonial army, and most of her brothers, half-brothers, nephews and sons-in-law were traders or, from a legalistic point of view, smugglers. They lived scattered throughout northwest Africa, with relatives in town-houses in Mauritania, Morocco, Mali and Algeria. Only Zahra's aging mother still insisted on planting her tent in the courtyard to sleep, as she thought it was nothing short of crazy to trust one's life at night to the instability of a mud-brick house.

Still, in line with many people like them, to spread out their risk, the family invested their surplus money in livestock of different kinds – camels, cows, some sheep and goats – kept by different relatives in different parts of the country (or indeed in different countries, as they had aunts, uncles and cousins living in Mauritania and southern Algeria). This made some economic sense – livestock markets are booming both in North and in West Africa – but I never saw them actually sell an animal. Their main reason for investing in livestock was more intimate.

The term 'Arab' derives from the Arabic root meaning 'to roam freely'; until rather recently, it was used in local manuscripts in this sense, as a synonym of 'Bedouin', to refer to nomads rather than to people who speak Arabic or claim Arab descent. One might therefore become an Arab or 'repent' of one's nomadic lifeways and cease to be one, becoming instead a *hadārī*, a settled urbanite. To be an 'Arab' is thus a matter of both descent and achievement. And this was why time spent in a cattle camp mattered so much to Zahra and her family and why they declared the pastoral life superior to any other, however much its actual boredom might irk them. It proved beyond any possible doubt that they continued to be true Arabs, mobile pastoralists who had temporarily fallen on hard times but could continue their pastoral ways because they had managed to diversify.

PART TWO

ENDLESS MOVEMENT

4

TO BE FROM FAR AWAY

Happy is the slave who, until the moment of his last breath,
remains close to his master, with his wife and children.
He creates a reason for living, a knot of attachment
with his place and his people. He clears the way for his
offspring, who thusly have roots and will know in the
days to come to take advantage of their origin ... for the
worst and the greatest solitude is to be from nowhere.

Mohammed Ennaji, 1994[1]

In November 2017, under the captivating title 'People for Sale',
CNN published 'an exclusive' segment 'on how migrants are
being sold by smugglers' in Libya. First we hear a gruff voice
over a black screen, speaking in Arabic. Then the scene is set
in writing: 'Unknown location, Libya, August, 2017'. The first
shaky footage appears, taken on a mobile phone and showing
three young Black men in a dark courtyard. One has a brown
hand on his shoulder, pushing him forward. The Arabic voice
continues, reciting figures, while the English commentary
explains the scene: 'A man addressing an unseen crowd. Big
strong boys for farm-work, he says, 400, 700, 800. The numbers
roll in. These men are sold, for 1,200 Libyan pounds [*sic*], 400
dollars apiece. You are watching an auction of human beings'.[2]

We then see other young Black men inside the house, reclining on mattresses on the floor. The video cuts to a car driving around Tripoli in daylight, and we finally meet the reporter: Nima Elbagir, a Sudanese journalist raised and educated in Britain. She and her team are searching for another auction in an unnamed town in northern Libya. Night falls again, the car stops at a house, the door opens, and we get a few glimpses of scenes similar to those described above. Quickly, the journalists are asked to leave.

We are then taken to Tariq al-Sika Migrant Detention Centre in Tripoli. The centre has all the exterior trappings of a prison: bars, controlled entry, guards. Inside, the paint is peeling off the walls. We see dozens of Black men, mostly sitting on the floor on mats or mattresses, waiting. Nima again: 'These men are migrants with dreams of being smuggled to Europe by sea... . It is hard to believe that these are the lucky ones, rescued from warehouses like the one in which we witnessed the auction. They are sold when these warehouses are overcrowded or if they run out of money to pay their smugglers'.

The camera zooms in on one of the migrants, a young man from Nigeria, against the backdrop of his and many others' complaining 'No food, no water'. 'Victory', says Nima, 'was a slave'. Answering Nima's direct question, Victory confirms that he has been 'sold', his words subtitled for the ease of viewers unaccustomed to Nigerian English. He and other migrants point to their ankles and forearms, exhibiting traces of beating. We then meet our first Libyan: the 'supervisor' of the detention centre, working, Nima says, 'with no international support'. He is first shown talking to two young migrant women, one of whom is in tears. He turns to the camera and says in English, 'I am suffering for them. I am suffering for them. What I have seen here daily, believe me, it makes me really feel pain for them'. He says that the Libyan authorities have no evidence of slave auctions. 'But we now do', concludes Nima. 'CNN has delivered this evidence to the Libyan authorities, who have promised to launch an investigation so that scenes like this are returned to the past'.

The history of the Sahara is a history of migration. Some of these migrations are ancient, others fairly recent, and some took place within living memory. Some were related to conquest, and we can track the linguistic and political changes to which they led in written history; others were less visible, concerning small groups of people or one individual at a time. Countless others were forced, incorporating people mostly from the southern edge of the Sahara into its midst through slavery, marriage or other forms of forced labour. Others still shape the Sahara today and play their part in the unequal access to mobility that informs the contemporary world.

Victory and the other migrants whom Nima encountered in Tripoli are part of this history. They are migrants, or 'adventurers', as they are referred to locally, who crossed the Sahara on their own accord, perhaps with Libya as their final destination, and got caught on the way. Yet the video portrays them primarily as hapless foreigners, 'people out of place' who do not really belong and would do best to return home. This assumption clearly does not correspond to their own aspirations. It also makes short shrift of a long and complex history of Saharan populations relying on newcomers from north and south and their integration – often on unequal terms – into local societies. This deeper history of population movement into and across the Sahara made the region multi-lingual, multi-racial and cosmopolitan long before any of these categories ever attracted analytical attention. We will explore these issues in this chapter, asking at the end how and why, from a simple fact of life, migration has more recently been turned into a 'problem'.

The CNN coverage of migrants held hostage in Libya summons a host of related histories and ideas. 'The past' Nima refers to, and which makes for the symbolic potency of the video, is one not of unhampered migration but of slavery – in the Sahara but also in the US. In fact, the two are amalgamated, and some of the images provided – such as the zoom on the migrants' wrists and ankles, as if showing traces of shackles – make more sense in an American than in a Saharan context. It is true that historically, slavery was at the heart of most Saharan societies as far back as we know. Although it has been legally abolished since the early twentieth century, its legacy continues to shape contemporary social relations. Yet slavery in the Sahara was never just the same as its American counterpart; rather, it was a historical and social phenomenon that must be understood on its own terms. To note this does not amount to an apology for enslavement or for the idea that Islamic or African slavery was somehow 'benign' when compared to its American counterpart, but it is a crucial intellectual exercise if we want to fully understand Saharan history and contemporary discrimination and struggles.

One of the most glaring differences between American and Saharan slavery has to do with race. CNN's rendering of events in Libya strongly associated the idea of slavery with racism. Racial distinctions matter in the contemporary Sahara and have clearly mattered across the region at least since the seventeenth century. As in the Americas, they are deeply entangled with the history of slavery. But there are important differences. 'Race' is a historically constituted category (there is nothing 'natural' about it) that cannot be simply generalised globally and projected onto the deep past. To do so is to naturalise it and on some level to accept its assumptions. Instead, we need to understand how it works from the inside out in a given context and see it as what it is: a form of *political* domination.

The CNN video went 'viral' immediately after its release. It inspired street protests throughout the world and was discussed by leaders of the United Nations and the European Union. It resulted in the UN sanctioning a handful of 'human traffickers' but also in increased financial and technical EU support for the notorious Libyan Coast Guard and Port Security and the Libyan General Administration for Coastal Security, both responsible for the internment and subsequent mistreatment of migrants, thereby further deteriorating the situation of migrants in Libya.[3] The unspoken assumptions about the articulation of migration, slavery and race that underpin the video therefore warrant further scrutiny. They demand that we pick up Saharan history where we left it, in the first centuries CE.

A World of Strangers

Anybody looking for 'history' (*tārīkh*) in the Sahara will quickly be redirected towards genealogies (*tawārīkh*, the plural of tārīkh). At least this is what happened to me as I set out to collect historical material in southern Algeria and northern Mali in the late 2000s. I went about this in the usual way, by looking for local archives and documents and asking to talk to the elderly. This seemed appropriate, as most people agreed that as a researcher, 'writing history' was the most legitimate thing I could possibly do – and that 'history' would be known by the old or consigned to a written document somewhere. The Algerian south is replete with private manuscript collections, which, although they are less well known than their famous Timbuktu equivalents, often hold thousands of volumes, so there was theoretically no shortage of material to look at. Yet as everybody who has ever tried to do the same knows, the matter is not as easy as identifying a knowledgeable person and knocking on his or her door. Both interviews and access to manuscript documents need preparation, patience and carefully chosen introductions.

During my first stay in the Algerian south, after I spent many hours waiting, attending religious celebrations and family festivities, washing up huge greasy containers of couscous and sorting through lentils and lettuce, one of my contacts finally came through. 'We can go tomorrow', said my friend Jamal, critically examining me from my (carefully veiled) head to toe. 'He is ready to meet you'. 'He' was a well-known and well-respected Kunta elder who lived in the nearby qsar of Zawiyat Kunta. The Kunta are a prominent religious family who own many *zawāyā* (singular *zāwiya*, religious strongholds) and libraries and whose members are scattered throughout southern Algeria, northern Mali and Mauritania. They used to be instrumental in trans-Saharan and Saharan trade and privileged representatives of the Qādiriyya Sufi order in the region. Many of the still best-known Saharan Islamic scholars were Kunta, and their current descendants still wield much influence. I met the current shaykh with some trepidation. He had granted me a favour in Jamal's name which I hoped I would not blow.

And this was what the shaykh told me: 'In the name of God. As to the Kunta, their father is Sīdi Muhammad al-Kuntī. And from him descend the Kunta who are in the Tuwāt and those who are in Morocco and those who are here. And those who are here are the children of al-Wāfī and the descendants of al-Shaykh al-Kabīr who is the son of Ahmad son of Abī Bakr son of Sīdi Muhammad son of Habīb Allāh son of al-Wāfī son of Sīdi 'Amar al-Shaykh son of Sīdi Ahmad al-Bakkāy who is buried in Walāta son of Sīdi Muhammad al-Kuntī who is the father of all the Kunta. And he is the son of 'Alī son of Yahya son of Yahya also son of Ward son of Yahas son of Tamīm son of Sā'id son of Shākir son of 'Uqba son of Nāfi' al-Qurayshī the companion [of the Prophet] who conquered all of the Maghreb until he arrived in a place where animals die because of the sun. Then he returned to Ifriqiyya [present-day Tunisia] where he built [the city of] Qayrawān. He died near this city'. It was the exact same text that I would find, several months later, in a manuscript held at the state-run manuscript centre in Timbuktu, but I didn't know this then, of course. I finally held the truth, from the great man himself, and could make nothing of it.

One thing that the shaykh's recital pointed out very clearly is that the history of the Sahara is primarily a history of migration. While this is true everywhere, North African and Saharan populations stand out for their genetic heterogeneity, particularly when compared, for instance, to the peoples of sub-Saharan Africa or Europe (where genetic diversity is also much higher than we might think). This heterogeneity can be found across the region, even in the smallest out-of-the-way places where people look the same and insist on their shared origin, telling a story of constant mobility and exchange. Most Saharans recognise this and attach little value to the idea of local roots. What matters instead are prestigious origins: family lines that stretch back via putative ancestors to the many centres of the Islamic world. And since these are all situated outside the Sahara, external origins are best.

Local history reflects this attachment to prestigious external origins. Most is recounted or written in the form of genealogies of the kind that Shaykh al-Kuntī recited to me and clearly had recited to many others before me: so-and-so begat so-and-so, who begat so-and-so, and so on. These genealogies are not just about people but also take us on a journey across space, through places that hold as much (and perhaps even more) resonance for listeners as the ancestors themselves. Shaykh al-Kuntī's genealogy mentions the Tuwāt and Morocco but also Walāta in contemporary southern Mauritania and Qayrawān in Tunisia. Genealogies are thus maps of a sort, recounting the gradual trajectories of ancestors until they arrived at their current destination. While they speak of the past, they also describe the world as it is experienced by contemporary family members, who might return to their ancestors' tombs for pilgrimage or simply to visit distant relatives who still live there. They imbue the physical world with historical sense, creating dense emotional landscapes.

And so genealogies inscribe local places and people into a history of the world. Shaykh al-Kuntī made his family descend from 'Uqba b. Nāfi' al-Qurayshī, 'the companion [of the Prophet] who conquered all of the Maghreb until he arrived in a place where animals die because of the sun'. The real historical 'Uqba may or may not have achieved these feats and may or may not have been the ancestor of the Kunta, but the claim made here is clear: the contemporary Kunta not only belong to the same extended family as the Prophet Muhammad but also descend from the first Islamic conqueror of the Sahara, which makes them the legitimate masters of all living creatures in the land, including anybody else who might have lived there before. Their current high status is thus the direct result of their ancestors' prowess, inscribing them into Islamic and therefore world history.

Which is perhaps where my initial disappointment really lay. As a Western-trained scholar, I wanted *local* history: the particularities of everyday life that made the place and the people I wanted to write about different from all others. As a religious scholar and leader of a prestigious zāwiya, Shaykh al-Kuntī wanted to tell me how much local, and therefore his own, history corresponded to the universal model of Islamic history, indeed was part and parcel of it. From his point of view, it was in fact this exact correspondence to a universally recognised model that granted his current family the special status that they still enjoy throughout the region today. As a sharifian (descendant of the Prophet) friend of mine put it later, 'Our history and the history of the Prophet Muhammad and his friends and companions are just the same'.

These genealogies pretend to be exhaustive but in reality leave out the vast majority of people who live locally. They only ever mention people considered to be worthwhile because they are of prestigious origin or because today, they are important enough to make such claims. All others – especially the descendants of populations locally classified as 'slave descendants' – are quite simply left out. The only way for outsiders to be integrated into 'history', then, is either to found a prestigious lineage or to attach themselves to one that already exists. In this way, names and group labels might tell us little about actual population movement; instead, they stake out the categories through which political influence is negotiated and through which individuals can act in a historically meaningful way.

Even more blatant is the omission of women (a familiar feature also of classical European historical narratives). Almost all the genealogies that make up Saharan history of this kind are unilateral, which means that they trace descendants through only one line, which most commonly (although there are some notable exceptions in the Sahara) is the male line: grandfathers beget fathers beget sons and so on. It suffices to imagine a family tree to see that in this way, in the parents' generation, half of the family is ignored, and as we ascend the branches, more and more family members are left out. It follows that unilateral genealogies, whether they are genetically 'true' or not, inevitably obscure the vast majority of the biological ancestors of any given person.

In purely technical terms, of course, this is quite necessary. Genealogies that take into account both the female and the male line at every generation very quickly become unmanageable and, in regions with low population density where marital alliances routinely cross family and linguistic boundaries, quite useless as tools of social distinction. This does not mean that connections through women are of no importance – quite the contrary, in fact, as women tend to be in charge of most of the daily labour of maintaining kin connections and arranging marriages. Genealogies are only the public representation, hiding the messy realities of human reproduction and everyday care through which the neat picture of genealogical order is constantly upset and disturbed. In a sense, these connections are quite simply too important, too specific and hence potentially too explosive to be made public. This, then, is another way of explaining my frustration when confronted by the shaykh's genealogy: he gave me the public version, whereas I wanted the women's gossip – on which all locally specific history really turns.

A Desert as Big as the World

Like all forms of history-making, genealogies offer a specific and very partial insight into people's relations and their place in the world. And, like all forms of history-making, they tell us more about how people today envisage their past – and their contemporary – place in the world than about the realities of that past. Take, for instance, the so-called Arab conquest of North Africa in the second half of the seventh century. This was the moment when some of the large categories used for people in the region to this day first emerged, in particular the distinction between 'Arabs' (descendants of the conquerors) and 'Berbers' (descendants of the people who were there before them).

As it is recounted in history books, the story goes something like this: in the seventh century, united and enthused by the new religion of Islam, a strong militarist polity emerged in Arabia and then went on to conquer the regions now known as the Middle East and the North African parts of the Byzantine empire. By 642, Islamic rule was established in Egypt; by 670, the Islamic armies, led by 'Uqba b. Nāfiʿ, Shaykh al-Kuntī's putative ancestor, founded Qayrawān in present-day Tunisia and reached Tangiers in present-day Morocco in 682.

The Islamic army brought with it not only a new religion but also a new way of thinking about people, dividing them into believers and unbelievers but also, increasingly, into Arabs and non-Arabs. They used the elaborate genealogies that might already have existed in the pre-Islamic Arab peninsula as a way of deciding who was who. Who, therefore, was entitled to a military salary and booty. Who, on the other hand, was defined as a conquered local and might be lawfully reduced to slavery or forced to pay tribute. As the conquest proceeded, those distinctions became increasingly complicated. It is in the nature of victorious armies to absorb others on their way; much as Napoleon's army in Russia counted as many Germans and Poles as French, the army that carried out the 'Arab' conquest of North Africa and then Spain was probably a motley crowd, but one in which soldiers had good reasons to invent an Arab identity and origin for themselves.

From the point of view of the conquering army, the multitude of different peoples who then lived in North Africa fell into two categories: on the one hand, 'Africans' (*afāriq*), Latin-speaking city dwellers, many of whom were Christians and Jews and therefore fell into the Islamic legal category of *dhimmīs*, people to be taxed and protected; on the other hand, *al-barbar* (a word that has given us the contemporary term 'Berber' but originated as the Arabic equivalent of the Roman and Greek 'barbarians'), who lived in the countryside and whose status was not defined in Islamic law and was therefore much more flexible. The al-barbar of the Arab conquest included both settled populations and nomads. They probably all spoke related languages but had been understood to constitute many different peoples (Numidians, Gaetulians, Libyans, Mauri) until then. It is therefore barely an exaggeration to claim, as does the historian Ramzi Rouighi, that there were no 'Berbers' in North Africa until the Arabs invented and popularised this category.[4]

These 'Berbers' were interesting to the conquering Arabs primarily as military foes, recruits to the army or potential slaves, and these three points of contact shaped the way the category 'Berber' was constructed. It was, from the start, a gendered category inasmuch as the first two options were open only to men; women were mostly integrated into Arab families as slaves, concubines or wives – or indeed all three. Military service required an act of submission to a named Arab patron whose client, or *mawālī*, the 'Berber' soldier thereby became, eventually adopting his patron's name and genealogy. The resulting inferior status clearly irked Berber soldiers so much that they rose in revolt in 742. Although they were successful in their revolt and subsequently established a number of independent Berber polities in North Africa, Arab identity continued to be a prized good. Although most inhabitants of North Africa continued to speak Berber for the next millennium or so, manuscripts with do-it-yourself Arab genealogies could be freely acquired on local markets for centuries to come.

This means that the massive demographic shift that we can observe at that time – from 'Berbers' to 'Arabs' – probably had little to do with actual population replacement. According to the fourteenth-century historian Ibn 'Idhārī, the Arab army sent to conquer the Maghrib contained only 50,000 people, while the later 'invasions' of nomadic Arabs regrouped under the loose label of 'Banū Hilāl' in the eleventh century probably counted no more than 150,000 – many of whom were 'Arab' only inasmuch as they were mobile (as noted above, the Arabic root *'araba* means to 'move around', and in many historical documents, the term 'Arab' is thus equivalent to Ibn Khaldūn's 'badū'). By the time Ibn 'Idhārī's contemporary Ibn Khaldūn was writing his monumental history of the world, he could claim for his Berber patrons genealogies quite as noble as those of their Arab predecessors, although both the language within which he did so (Arabic) and the broader historical and cultural framework (Quranic history and genealogies) had been brought by the conquerors centuries earlier.

The category of 'Berber', then, was initially political and designated a relationship based simultaneously on cultural rejection, alliance, enmity, rivalry and intimacy. Replacement was never total: many local groups hedged their bets, retaining both a Berber and an Arab identity. This compromise was facilitated in areas that historically had reckoned descent matrilineally, as is still the case today with a few Tuareg groups, where one could be Arab by one's father and Berber by one's mother. Today, many Berbers prefer to label themselves 'Imazighen', or free men, thereby underlining both the political nature of their claim and, less consciously perhaps, its deep roots in regional patterns of inequality. There can be little doubt that historically, the Imazighen were those 'Berbers' whom the Arab conquest had failed to reduce to slavery – and who, like everybody else at that time, probably defined themselves as 'free' primarily in opposition to the people they themselves had managed to enslave.

Similar principles were at work in later moments of identity formation that led to the configuration of Saharan peoples and languages as they are today. We need to keep two things in mind. First, 'ethnic' ascriptions throughout the region are closely tied both to language and to unilateral descent, which means that people can often claim multiple identities, as multilingualism is the norm and intermarriage between different linguistic groups frequent (and as, despite their exclusion from public genealogies, mothers matter greatly, and genealogies can be reworked over time). Nonetheless, we can roughly divide the Sahara from west to east along linguistic lines, from Hassaniya Arabic speakers in the west (Mauritania, Western Sahara, southern Morocco, northwestern Mali) via Tamacheq Berber speakers in the centre (northeastern Mali, southern Algeria, northwestern Niger) and Tubu speakers and others closely related to them in the eastern Sahara (northeastern Niger, northern Chad, southern Libya, northwestern Sudan).

Interspersed among these large linguistic groups associated primarily with pastoral nomadism and living in close symbiosis with them are groups of sedentists, often but not always also distinguished by their language. Prominent here are Haalpulaaren and Soninke in the west, Songhay and Hausa in the Central Sahara, and the Kanuri and Kanembu further east. Together, these more sedentary populations have probably always accounted for the majority of Saharan populations. They have also all been associated with state- and empire-building projects just south of the Sahara: the Kanembu with the Kanem-Bornu empire (which was founded in the eighth century and is among the oldest continuous state formations on the African continent), the Songhay with the Songhay empire (fifteenth and sixteenth centuries), and the Haalpulaaren with the wave of jihads that swept the Sahel from the eighteenth century onwards.

This history suggests that categorical distinctions here were quite as flexible as those between Arabs and Berbers further north since, in a context of imperial expansion, the adoption of an 'ethnic' identity associated with an empire might be primarily a political choice, something which can therefore change over the course of one's life and according to that empire's military fortunes. The Tubu and Kanembu languages, for instance, are closely related and mutually comprehensible; whether one counted as one or the other was certainly a matter of family but also of livelihood (pastoralism versus agriculture) and, perhaps primarily, of one's attitude towards the Kanem empire.

Second, all of these linguistic groups are divided horizontally into status groups, ranging from 'noble' at the top via free tribute-paying dependents and freed slaves to slaves and artisans at the bottom. For day-to-day life, these status distinctions are much more important than 'ethnic' or linguistic differentiations. They tend to be legitimised through narratives of past conquest that mirror those of the 'Arab' conquest sketched above. Winners take all, and losers pay tribute; some might even be reduced to slavery. Over time, past conquest tends to be rephrased as an ongoing relationship of protection by which the 'weak' pay tribute in exchange for protection from 'nobles': the sword-yielding, mehari-riding, turban-wearing, light-skinned desert warriors of popular lore and Tuareg and Arabic poetry.

Much of this is of course ideological. Being born to a courageous father (who might in fact just be a thug) in no way guarantees courage in children; the vicissitudes of real life, the hazards of birth and the rapid economic and political changes in the Saharan environment meant that descent, here no more than elsewhere, was a poor indicator of personal quality or even of power and wealth. Status distinctions, like genealogies, were thus negotiable over time, always contested and inherently dynamic. Moreover, for any economic system to function, nobility had to be a minority pursuit: somebody, after all, had to carry out the mundane tasks of caring for flocks and children, trading for essential goods, hauling water and tending gardens. Historically, most Saharans were thus subordinate to others in one way or another and however they might chafe at this. The most extreme form of subordination was slavery.

Slavery as an Institution

In 2008, the southern Saharan country of Niger briefly came to international attention. The court of the Economic Community of West African States (ECOWAS) ruled that the Nigerien government owed its citizen Hadijatou Mani 10 million F CFA (17,000 USD) in compensation for its failure to uphold her human rights and to protect her against enslavement. Although slavery as a legal category had long been officially abolished throughout the country, Hadijatou Mani's mother had been considered a slave in her local community and had passed her alleged status on to her daughter. In 1996, at the age of twelve, Hadijatou was sold, for the equivalent of 400 USD, to al-Hājj Souleymane Naroua, the forty-six-year-old local 'chief' of the village where she had lived all of her life. For years, she had to be sexually available to her master and carry out domestic chores for him and his four wives. After Hadijatou had borne him several children, Naroua emancipated her. Naroua clearly thought that, according to his interpretation of Islamic law, Hadijatou would now automatically become his wife as an *umm walad*, a mother of his legitimate children, and continue to form part of his household.

Hadijatou, however, wanted to leave and took the case to a local court. The court ruled in her favour: Hadijatou could not legally be Naroua's former slave, as slavery and hence also the *walā*, the legal tie between a master and a former slave, had been abolished in Niger. Nor could she be his wife, as Naroua had never paid bride-wealth for her. Encouraged by this ruling, Hadijatou contracted marriage with somebody else. She was promptly sued by Naroua in a higher court for bigamy. Hadijatou, her brother and her husband were sentenced to jail; Naroua claimed her last child as rightfully his (in addition to all the others). We can discern, somewhere behind these simple statements of fact, Hadijatou's yearning, not so much for an abstract right to 'freedom' but rather for the very concrete right to have a family and to know that her children were safely her own.

With the help of international anti-slavery movements, Hadijatou took the case to the Niger supreme court and eventually to the ECOWAS court – with the result that, in addition to her financial compensation, her previous conviction was overturned. She was now legally allowed to marry and keep her younger children, although her older children claimed by their father were lost to her forever. She has since been active in national and international abolition movements, receiving in 2009, from the hands of Michelle Obama and Hillary Clinton, the US State Department's International Women of Courage Award. She has been severely (and unfairly) criticised by some Nigeriens who think that she has heaped shame on her own country, motivated merely by a search for personal gain. In any case, one might wonder what kind of financial compensation could ever make up for a life of slavery in Niger or elsewhere.

It is easy to tell this story as a victory of the downtrodden (which it was) and as another step in the inexorable march towards progress in even the most 'backward' places. The realities are, however, as always more complex. Slavery had been abolished throughout the French empire in 1848, then again in 1905 in French West Africa, in 1922 in Morocco, in 1960 in (freshly independent) Niger and in 1981 in Mauritania. In 2003, thirteen years after Hadijatou was sold into slavery, the practice was criminalised in Niger. In 2007, Mauritania followed suit and then in 2012, under international pressure, went even further, declaring slavery a 'crime against humanity'. Nonetheless, many people in both countries and elsewhere in the Sahara continue to live in conditions of extreme dependency, and many more labour under the stigma of their putative slave descent. Legal abolition, then, is clearly not enough: true emancipation requires a profound change in social, political and economic relations. And despite much lip service paid to abolitionism by the powerful, from French colonial officers of the distant past to contemporary politicians today, nobody in charge really seems to want this to happen anytime soon.

Talking about slavery is a tricky business. It is used both as an analytical and descriptive category and as a way of politically mobilising for a practice to be stopped. Labelling a practice slavery, as CNN did, can be a way of attracting international attention. This might be salutary, as it might help effect change on the ground, but also risks making short shrift of local complexities in favour of international moral certainties. In Libya, the real culprit of migrant suffering is not some form of cultural atavism but policies of the EU that work towards criminalising all forms of migration on its southern borders; in Niger, the persistence of slavery or slave-like relations of exploitations similarly is not about backwardness or ignorance. Rather, it is the result of an economic, social and political situation rooted in global inequalities and that leave little choice to the poor but to put up with and sometimes even seek out relations of extreme dependency and exploitation. Legal abolition can do little to remedy these problems; indeed, a cynic might say that it is a cheap way of never having to address them head-on (something that Sahelian countries are unable to do on their own in any case).

Slavery is never just one thing, nor is it the same everywhere. It is an institution that could be found, to some degree, in most known human societies. Slavery is one possible answer to the old question of how to make people work for you for less, how to make them surrender their own lives in order to further somebody else's wealth, prestige or glory: a question that is not limited to slavery alone but traverses all systems of exploitation, including those that make it possible for the contemporary world to (mal)function as it does today. Particular situations of slavery are, moreover, always historically specific, as they are the result of an ongoing struggle between masters and slaves. The first thing one must try to do when approaching Saharan slavery is therefore to try to understand it on its own terms and as a dynamic historical process.

One of the reasons slavery is such a slippery category is that one of the advantages of slavery – from the masters' point of view – is the versatility of those enslaved: they can be set to do any kind of work or perform any kind of function that suits their master. This versatility derives from what the historical sociologist Orlando Patterson called 'social death': the enslaved are first and foremost, he argued, people violently taken out of their social context and stripped of their identity, of the ties that turn them from mere generic bodies into individual persons.[5] Once this process has been accomplished – by taking slaves away from their homes and families, stripping them of their language and culture, renaming them and often also marking their bodies in distinctive ways – they can function as social beings only through their master. It is this existential dependence that makes them different from victims of other forms of exploitation.

The Western historical tradition deriving from Roman law tends to think of slaves first and foremost as 'property'. This is because property is a central idiom within contemporary Western legal systems, but property is too specific and culturally variable a category to define slaves everywhere. In most African societies, where status traditionally depended on relations to people rather than to things ('wealth in people' rather than 'wealth in things'), slaves were instead archetypical strangers: people who had no kin ties that could protect them and therefore had to accept total submission to their masters in exchange for some form of attachment. This was particularly important in an area where access to all vital resources – water, land, protection, herds, other people – was managed through personal relations and ties of patronage. 'For', as the historian Mohamed Ennadji noted in the epigraph to this chapter, 'the worst and the greatest solitude is to be from nowhere'. Genealogies are the most concise expression of this principle. In a world where everybody is from somewhere else, to be from nowhere has to be avoided at all costs, including that of one's freedom.[6]

From the point of view of the slavers, slavery promised to solve a number of structural problems in the Sahara: first, how to obtain labour when, as we saw in chapter 2, the establishment of even the smallest settlement required a tremendous amount of work, often with returns insufficient to feed local populations. If you cannot make enough people, why not steal them? Second, how to obtain followers whose loyalty was beyond doubt in a world where everybody depended on everybody else. As we shall see, historically, every attempt to establish a strong state in the area also involved the creation of a 'slave army' whose allegiance could be counted on in all situations. Third, how to acquire sons who really would belong only to their father in a way that would make the promise of patrilineal genealogies – men begetting men without female meddling – almost a reality. What influential man has not, at some point in his life, dreamt of a wife without in-laws?

As a result, slaves were crucial not so much for production – as in the plantation capitalism of the Atlantic – as for reproduction in the biological (producing children), the political (producing military power) and the social senses of the term (allowing elite groups to have sufficient leisure to engage in elite pursuits and, literally, to be masters). It should not come as a surprise that throughout the long history of Saharan slavery, women slaves were much higher priced than men and that men were used for military and prestige purposes quite as much as for hard labour. Women served as concubines, producing children who were recognised as fully legitimate, on a par – at least theoretically – with their brothers and sisters born to free mothers. They also acted as wet nurses and were in charge of the arduous tasks of day-to-day domestic labour. In an inherently mobile and centrifugal society where great value was (and is) placed on male mobility, this freed elite women to engage in the daily labour of cultural reproduction, to spend the hot hours of the day drinking tea, receiving visitors, transmitting cultural and historical lore (including patrilineal genealogies) and negotiating potential marital alliances: to reproduce, in other words, the local social order.

This shaped the ways slaves could negotiate their position. If they were not employed as domestics, concubines or soldiers, many were left to live independently, in settlements or nomadic camps, as long as they paid tribute to their masters. They probably led a life not all that different from those of their freed or free counterparts of lower status, who also usually owed tribute to some kind of overlord. The big difference was their inability to securely build their own social ties and families – to live under their own rather than their master's name. Like Hadijatou, slaves in the past knew well that the day might come when, needing money, their master might seize and sell their children, spouses or siblings, a knowledge that made every one of their projects, every plan, accomplishment and birth, uncertain and infused with bitterness.

This became painfully clear in the 1930s in Niger to an unnamed enslaved woman – let's call her Zahra – who somewhat miraculously left traces in the French colonial archives. Zahra had lived for more than twenty years in her master's household, without any signs of rebellion, alongside her younger brothers. She had even borne her master a child. One day, however, her master suddenly decided to sell her youngest brother, a boy of fifteen, to a group of passing Arab herders despite her desperate pleas. Had her brother been sold locally, Zahra might have put up with it, visiting him whenever possible. But she could not bear to see him carried away to an uncertain fate in the desert. She immediately set out after him on foot, leaving her two-year-old child behind.

When she finally, footsore and tired, managed to catch up with him, she went to find the local French commander. As noted above, slavery had long been officially abolished throughout the French empire but was in fact tolerated, as French colonial officers were quite as frightened as the local elites of 'hordes' of newly liberated and landless slaves roaming the countryside (land reform never seemed to be an option to them).

But when faced with an individual complaint, the French officer had to act. He went to see the Arabs and brought back Zahra's brother, freeing her into the bargain. She had kept her brother and earned her own freedom – at the cost of losing her child.

Slavery in the Sahara, then, was not just about labour and property but also about the right to socially reproduce, which in turn was central to the achievement of full personhood. It was therefore heavily gendered, and its legacy continues to impact women more than men. Most importantly, perhaps, slavery was at the heart of the cultural and social reproduction of elite families in a way that made exploitation deeply intimate (as slave women gave birth to their own masters) and muddled easy distinctions between Black and white, subordinates and kin, care and exploitation in ways that still haunt Saharan societies today.

Complications of Race

In 1614, Saʿīd b. Ibrāhīm al-Jirārī, a trader from the Draʿa valley in what is now southern Morocco, asked the renowned Timbuktu scholar Ahmad Bābā (whose life is described in more detail in chapter 7) about 'Black' captives from the Niger Bend whom he had recently acquired and who claimed to be Muslim. According to Islamic law, it is absolutely not permissible to enslave a fellow Muslim. Should he believe his captives and set them free immediately? Ahmad Bābā answered with a resounding yes. He then expounded, at length, the long history of voluntary conversion to Islam and indeed the high quality of Islamic scholarship in the southwestern Sahara and Sahel. These captives very likely were Muslim, he argued, and in any case, it was the trader's responsibility to verify their claim. If any doubt remained, then he should free them rather than risk his soul for the love of profit.

Ahmad Bābā's answer to al-Jirārī's question is a famous text in Saharan history because it is the only one that addresses questions of slavery and race head-on. There can be no doubt that throughout the Sahara, there was a close connection between slavery and racial hierarchies. Colour terms more generally were and still are used routinely not only to distinguish different sets of humans but also to rank them. This vocabulary ranges from 'white' (*bīdānī* in Hassaniya) to 'black' (*sūdānī*) or 'blue' but also contains people identified as 'red' or even 'green'. Yet racial distinctions were worked out somewhat differently than in Europe, mostly because, as mentioned earlier, in patrilineal systems, children's status followed that of their father regardless of who their mother was – at least in theory. The Moroccan historian Chouki El Hamel hence famously (and controversially) defines 'Blackness' in Morocco not as a matter of appearance, but as 'a lack of Arab lineage'.[7]

While El Hamel is right to a certain extent, Ahmad Bābā's response tells us that things were a little more complicated. Ahmad Bābā wrote at a time when power relations in the Sahara were shifting in favour of northern populations, who, it seems, increasingly started to think of themselves as 'white' as opposed to everybody else, whom they thereby defined as 'Black'. He had witnessed the 1594 Moroccan conquest of his hometown of Timbuktu (on which more in chapter 7), an event that was symptomatic of this shift and the growing inability of Sahelian states to protect their populations against northern raiders. The association, throughout the region, of darker skin with slavery was clearly not the result of this – it was already present in Quranic texts, and older documents – but probably took on an additional edge, and the limits of the category of 'Blackness' extended to people who had never thought of themselves in these terms.

Given that it was impossible to justify racial slavery with

reference to sharī'a, the only way this emerging racial order could be legitimised in legal terms was through an association of Blackness with unbelief. 'Blacks', or so the story went, historically converted only under duress, and they therefore could be enslaved regardless of their current faith (histories of conquest again); in other words, they might be Muslim, but not quite Muslim enough. This was exactly the kind of prejudice that Ahmad Bābā sought to dispel, not by denying the validity of slavery but by pushing the boundaries of enslaveability further south – probably to little avail.

This suspicion is confirmed by subsequent events. Half a century later, the Moroccan sultan Mawlay Ismā'īl, great state- and empire-builder of his time, wanted a slave army in order to avoid the many disparate loyalties and entanglements that came with his usually tribal regiments. His agents quickly found that his project was either unrealistic (there weren't enough slaves in Morocco at that time) or unaffordable (the ones whom they could find were too expensive). Instead, they recruited everybody who they considered looked the part. Mawlay Ismā'īl's so-called slave army was ultimately largely made up of harātīn, landless but free agriculturalists who had been settled for generations in southern Morocco, where they might indeed have been indigenous. Their enslavement was clearly illegal and based exclusively on their local classification as 'Black'. For a brief moment in time, 'Blackness' alone became a justification for enslavement (although the new recruits' actual skin colour varied considerably, from yellowish to red to 'liver' to black, as per the recruitment register). Even then, the replacement of genealogical by racial principles was not total: Mawlay Ismā'īl's henchmen left dark-skinned members of the elite – to which, incidentally, Mawlay Ismā'īl, born to an enslaved mother, himself belonged – well alone.

*

Genealogical definitions of status and race were never completely displaced by categories based on observable characteristics; rather, they intersected with each other and with other types of hierarchical distinctions, such as age, gender, wealth and lifestyle, to create particular Saharan forms of racialisation. These, in turn, are exceedingly complex. In contemporary Mauritania and northern Mali, for instance, 'bīdānī' means a high-status Arabic speaker regardless of his or her skin colour, whereas the root whence it derived (*abyad*) can in a different context be purely descriptive of hue. In everyday conversation, there is another, parallel hierarchy of colour terms which is more concerned with hue and evaluates beauty rather than status. A person can thus be 'white' in terms of status but be considered 'black' (*kahal*) because of his or her skin tone, and vice versa. Too much time spent out in the pastures might turn you kahal with sunburn, to the point where you might *look* like a sūdānī, but it will not turn you into a sūdānī if your high status is recognised by all. The same logic applies to the use of whitening cream: it might make you 'beautiful', according to local bīdānī standards, but not noble.

Women might fuss over newborn babies, pinch their noses, pull their hair to straighten it, and predict their future colour by looking at wrists and behind the ears. This is a racist practice by any standard and one that acknowledges the influence of both the father and the mother on a child's appearance. Indeed, many women locally suggested that I, with my light European skin, would be able to produce beautiful babies despite my 'ugly' (i.e., dark blond) hair and obvious inability to transmit Arab or Tuareg excellence. None of this would shed doubt on the publicly ascribed racial identity of the child: a son or daughter of an Arab is an Arab. Conversely, Black men in Tunisia's south might marry 'foreign' (i.e., Algerian or urban Tunisian) white women and produce lighter-skinned children. People might locally praise their children's beauty and envy their lighter skin tones and wavy hair; this, however, changes nothing about their categorical Blackness, at least not as long as they stay with people who know them.

When Barack Obama was elected US president in 2009, I was in northern Mali minding cows with a bīdānī friend. As we listened to the news on BBC Arabic radio, she was highly concerned: what had the world come to if the strongest country in the world was to be governed by a 'slave'? What she meant, of course, was 'a person of slave descent', but to her mind, any history of slavery tainted descendants several generations down the line, making them notoriously irresponsible and unable to rule. Much as the CNN reporter in Tripoli was to do ten years later, she wholeheartedly imposed her own understanding of slavery on realities that had little to do with it.

Later reports that Obama was in fact the son of a Swahili immigrant and that he was therefore probably of 'noble' descent somewhat reassured her. It did leave her wondering, though, why anybody had classified him as 'Black' in the first place when he was clearly no Blacker than she was herself. Objectively speaking, my friend was right: there was no more reason to think that Obama was Black than that he was white – unless, of course, one situates him in the US context, marked by a long history of brutal racial discrimination and the legacy of the 'one-drop' rule and where far-flung origins from Yemen and prestigious Islamic credentials – as she assumed any Swahili would have – counted for nothing.

A similar clash of perceptions occurs in the Saharan regions of contemporary North African countries on a daily basis. Most civil servants in the south are from the Mediterranean coast and have no idea of the subtle distinctions in local colour variations. Many simply consider everybody darker than themselves inferior and do not hesitate to label them 'Black' or (supreme irony) 'African', thereby (usually) never getting anything done at all. More spectacularly, when Khadidja Benhamou from Adrar in the south of the country was elected Miss Algeria in 2019, her election was met with a wave of racist comments on social media claiming that she was 'too Black' to represent her country. Others defended her, exhorting their fellow nationals to practise racial tolerance and celebrating Algeria's racial diversity. From a Saharan point of view, all of these comments, good or bad, racist or anti-racist, clearly missed the point, as Khadidja Benhamou was in fact white: of impeccable Arab descent in her father's line.

Southern Segregation

Here as elsewhere, then, class, race, gender, and categories of belonging intersect in complicated ways. The historically specific ways in which they did so in the Sahara as opposed to the Atlantic world goes some way towards explaining the great paradox of trans-Saharan slavery: if roughly as many sub-Saharan Africans were taken to the Sahara and North Africa as to the New World (as many historians think today, although numbers are notoriously difficult if not impossible to establish), why are there so few recognisable communities of colour in contemporary North Africa? None of the North African states produce statistics in this regard. 'Blacks' are estimated to represent 15 per cent of the overall population of Tunisia, a percentage that is probably higher in Morocco, Algeria and Libya (in the US, people who self-classify as Black constitute 13 per cent of the overall population). Yet until recently, they seemed much less visible, both on the national stage and internationally, than their North American counterparts.

Some of this invisibility clearly has to do with the much larger historical time frame of the trans-Saharan slave trade, stretching from Roman times to the early twentieth century. Also important is the weight of genealogical models and the high degree of incorporation, especially of female slaves, into dominant families. But there is a more general point here. As pointed out above, not only is 'race' a social rather than a 'natural' category, but the very idea of sorting people into mutually exclusive groups is the result of a particular vision of the world. This vision is different from genealogical ordering principles, as genealogies potentially stretch infinitely far – on some level, we are all related, although this does not make us all equal. Both visions have long coexisted in the Sahara, and the predominance of one over the other is the result of power relations. Racial discrimination, in other words, does not in itself create minority groups – something else has to intervene to keep people segregated over time as a group or to make their physical appearance and common exploitation more relevant to them than other potential grounds for solidarity or exclusion.

Despite its long history as a commercial hub between West and East, the Sahara to the south and the Mediterranean to the north, Tunisia has long been considered the most 'homogeneous' of the North African nations. The first Tunisian president after independence in 1956, Habib Bourguiba, forcibly put forward an idea of 'Tunisianness' as based on one shared language (Arabic), one shared religion (Islam) and, less explicitly, one shared 'Arab' ethnicity. Subsequent authoritarian governments continued this policy, thereby, superficially at least, turning it into reality; by the early 2000s, there were hardly any Jews or Berber speakers left in the country. Black Tunisians never disappeared but remained relegated to the globally poor countryside of the Tunisian south and were rendered invisible in the national media, history books and school curricula.

In late 2010 and 2011, this suddenly changed. Massive street protests succeeded in ousting the Tunisian president Ben Ali. Among the many placards being waved on 22 November 2011 outside the Bardo palace, where a newly elected assembly was busy drafting a new constitution for a new Tunisia, a few, mostly handwritten signs demanded an end to racial discrimination. This was the beginning of the Tunisian Black movement. Animated by people such as Maha Abdelhamid, born in Gabès in the south of the country and at that time studying for her doctoral degree in geography; the flight attendant Saadia Mosbah, sister to the famous Tunisian singer Slah Mosbah; and Houda Mzioudet, a well-known journalist, they advocated for the inclusion in the constitution of a law against racial discrimination. Although their demands were not heeded at the time, an anti-discrimination law was passed in 2018 – the first of its kind in the Arab world. A year later, 23 January was declared a national holiday to commemorate the official abolition of slavery in Ottoman Tunisia in 1846 – two years before slavery was abolished in France.

Black Tunisian activists had two principal goals: first, the official recognition of Black Tunisians as a minority, alongside and in similar terms to other minorities that started to emerge in the public scene at that time, and second, the official recognition of Tunisia's legacy of slavery. Their models and inspirations were mostly drawn from the other side of the Atlantic, the US very prominently (Saadia's association was called Mnemty, 'my dream', a direct invocation of Martin Luther King Jr.). This does not mean that their struggle did not make sense in Tunisian terms; rather, to inscribe the discrimination they had suffered all their lives into a global movement opened up new ways towards emancipation and international solidarity. They were, moreover, not just speaking for a putative Tunisian Black community. Many Tunisians, whether routinely classified as Black or white, felt that it was time to break the long-standing taboo on any kind of difference from the state-endorsed model of Islamic, Arab or white 'Tunisianness' and that this was a necessary precondition for any meaningful democratisation of the country, or merely for a life in which one could breathe and walk freely. Many of these aspirations were crushed in May 2024, when prominent members of the Tunisian Black movement, Saadia Mosbah among them, were arrested on charges of 'terrorist' activity.

Black Tunisians, however, were rather different from the other 'minorities' that emerged in the public sphere in post-2011 Tunisia: they did not share a religious difference (like Tunisian Jews) or a particular language and culture (like Tunisian Berbers). They had never constituted an interest group in and of themselves; struggles for social and racial mobility had been individual or functioned through the ties of patronage that still mediated political relationships in the rural south. Nor was the appeal to the legacy of slavery in any sense straightforward. Although objectively, here as elsewhere in the Sahara, it is difficult to disentangle contemporary Tunisian racism from an association of darker skin with enslavement – words used to insult Blacks tend to refer to their supposed slave status rather than their appearance – many Black Tunisians claim free origins and do not wish to endorse an additional stigma that brands them both as 'lowly' and as intrinsically foreign to the Tunisian nation.

After the revolution, many people of slave descent hence preferred individual strategies to collective protest. For instance, they petitioned local judges to change their patronym, which in many cases still bore traces of their ancestors' slave status (labelling them 'abīd so-and-so, according to the genealogical ordering principles by which freed slaves were integrated into their former masters' lineage). Slavery in Tunisia, as in the Maghreb as a whole, had been a multi-coloured affair, and, as the Tunisian historian M'hamed Oualdi points out, the legacy of slavery in Tunisia concerns probably quite as many whites as Blacks.[8] Yet for whites, it has been much easier to avoid the stigma of servile descent, and they now have little desire to rock the boat.

Urban university-educated activists from the north and Black rural Tunisians from the south often found it hard to see eye to eye, moreover. In 2016, Al Jazeera broadcast a documentary in which it claimed that school buses in the southern Tunisian town of Sidi Makhlouf near Medenine were segregated: one for Black children, the other for white. 'The bus for whites carried an advert for yoghurt, the bus for Blacks also an advert for chocolate yoghurt', as a resident explained. 'They have two buses to prevent mixed marriages'. Black Tunisian activists flocked to the city to protest segregation, but to little avail. Yes, local children took different buses to school, local residents said, but this was quite simply because they lived in different parts of town in a different, perhaps more insidious form of segregation. To many inhabitants of the Black part of town, school buses mattered less than the absence of paved roads, functional plumbing, basic health care and job opportunities, which set their district apart from nearby white neighbourhoods. Yet most locals did not want to protest openly because although they experience racism on a daily basis, they did not feel that it would be wise to upset their white neighbours and sometime employers, landlords and patrons.[9]

Although many local Black Tunisians probably wish for the kind of emancipation proposed by northern activists, they know that this is a possibility only if they can see a way out of their fundamental economic dependence and precarity. This usually means moving away from places where everybody knows who they are, giving men a clear advantage over women, whose freedom of movement tends to be more limited. This echoes the long history of the abolition of slavery throughout the area (and elsewhere) and partly explains its constant repetition: if 'freedom' does not also translate into a redistribution of economic opportunity, land, wealth and political influence, it probably won't last. 'Hunger', as Rossi noted with regards to Niger, 'revives respect for hierarchy'.[10]

On 21 February 2023, the Tunisian president Kaïs Saïed made headlines by declaring that 'hordes of illegal immigrants' had 'swarmed Tunisia', where they were engaging in 'violence, crime and unacceptable behaviour'. Their presence, he said, was part of a 'conspiracy' to 'transform Tunisia's demographic make-up' and to turn the country into 'merely an African country that does no longer belong to the Muslim-Arab world'.[11] His statement led to an immediate increase of violence, not only against sub-Saharan migrants resident in Tunisia but also against anybody identified as 'African' – in other words, as 'Black', including Black Tunisians. More insidiously, tens of thousands of sub-Saharan migrants lost their jobs overnight or were thrown out of their lodgings, as their employers or landlords feared government reprisals.

In the last thirty years, Tunisia has turned from a country where 'migration' always referred to 'emigration' – Tunisians travelling to Europe, mostly to France – into a country that attracts immigrants in its own right. West Africans especially have settled in Tunis and other large cities on the coast, either to continue their studies – Tunisia has liberalised its higher education sector, attracting French-speaking students from throughout the continent – or to work as waiters and dish-washers in restaurants, on building sites or in the agricultural sector for men and as cleaners and childminders for women. Migrants have settled in poorer parts of the capital, where they frequent local markets and have set up their own football teams, churches, hairdressers, restaurants and cultural associations. They and the labour they provide are crucial for the Tunisian economy, although this has never been recognised officially. Tunisian labour law restricts the legal employment of foreign nationals to those (rare) cases where no comparable skill can be found nationally, making it very difficult for migrant workers to obtain an official work permit.

Kaïs Saïed's xenophobia is part of a global trend, and there is nothing particularly Tunisian about his racism: he resembles right-wing populist leaders everywhere, from Donald Trump to Viktor Orbán via Silvio Berlusconi to Jair Bolsonaro. Com-mentators were quick to point out the direct transfer of the idea of the 'great replacement' (of originally 'white' populations by 'Blacks') from France's infamous right-wing politician Éric Zemmour (himself of North African origin) to the southern shore of the Mediterranean. Zemmour took the term from the French essayist (and one-time gay icon) Renaud Camus, who coined it in 2010, but the idea itself has long historical ante-cedents stretching back to the late nineteenth century and is currently extremely popular among far-right groups worldwide.

Others point to the influence of EU policies (which are dis-cussed in more detail in chapter 9), that, since the 2000s, have aimed at the externalisation of EU borders to third countries, also in North Africa. These policies, with their rhetorical emphasis on 'floods of Black migrants' set to 'swamp the European continent', are inherently racist. As in Libya, where we started, they have certainly contributed to the difficult situation in which many sub-Saharan migrants settled in Tunisia find themselves, if only by redefining them as 'transit migrants' (i.e., necessarily on their way to Europe, which is in fact only the case for about 10 per cent) and therefore rendering questions about their long-term position in Tunisian society apparently irrelevant.

But Kaïs Saïed's statements also participate in a long history both of northwest African migrations (the number of people classified as 'Black' residing in Tunisia has probably changed little over time) and distinctively Saharan racial hierarchies. After all, he explicitly opposed 'African immigration' in the name of the 'Muslim-Arab' identity of Tunisia, as if any of these categories were mutually exclusive. As we've already seen, this echoes a long-standing prejudice in the region claiming an irreducible contradiction between Blackness and Islam, but it also echoes contemporary media portrayals of Black migrants as inherently 'foreign' to North Africa. It endorses a fiction that somehow describes North Africa as not Africa and Arabs as not (also) African, and it puts forward a vision of history shaped by the eternal opposition between 'Arabs' and 'natives', however else one might like to define them (as 'Berbers' or 'Blacks').

As we have seen throughout this chapter, these categories can only poorly account for the past, nor can they explain the present. While they have mattered throughout Saharan history, they are precisely that: historical categories that have changed over time and are context-dependent rather than globally valid explanatory schemes – as was assumed in the CNN video with which this chapter began. The Sahara used to be a place where movement and migration were the norm. This does not mean that societies were egalitarian or colour-blind in any sense or that the slavery and racism that were rampant then were somehow 'nicer' than their contemporary legacies or avatars. It does mean, however, that we must understand all attempts at human classification and hierarchisation – in the region and elsewhere – as historically specific languages of power, obfuscating the complexities of the long history of migration that has, over millennia, made northwest Africa what it is today.

5

SAINTS ON TRUCKS

And much I mused on legends quaint and old
Which whilome won the hearts of all on Earth
Toward their brightness, ev'n as flame draws air;
But had their being in the heart of Man
...
Imperial Eldorado roof'd with gold:
Shadows to which, despite all shocks of Change,
All on-set of capricious Accident,
Men clung with yearning Hope which would not die.

Alfred Lord Tennyson, *Timbuctoo*, 1829

It is very cold in al-Khalīl, and there is not much to eat. Even water has to be brought by large tankers that cross the border from Algeria to Mali and carry it over the 15 kilometres that separate the town – if that is what it is – from its Algerian twin, Bordj Badji Mokhtar. The nearest cities on the Malian side, Gao, Timbuktu and Kidal, are all more than a day's drive away on unforgiving mud tracks that carefully circumvent all human settlement and where teenage drivers practice at night with no headlights. The Sahara is far from pretty here – no rolling dunes or palm gardens, just a vast flat plain with no protection against the constant wind and sand-storms, the beating sun and the emptiness of a distant horizon.

Men spend their days huddled near their trucks or shops, their faces covered with indigo veils, wearing thick leather jackets and Algerian army boots over their long shirts and baggy trousers, playing cards, boasting, shivering, smoking and drinking tea: life is fast in al-Khalīl, but the days are long and are best described, in Spanish-inflected Algerian Arabic, as utter *miseria*. The few women in al-Khalīl are always hungry, with the exception of local Tuareg women married to Khalīlīs whose husbands have bought them generators so that they can watch Jackie Chan videos. There are few children, all smoking incessantly.

As the evening draws in, people gradually get up, stretch, adjust their veils and begin to load cars and trucks, fill tanks and check their satellite phones. Customers arrive from the other side of the border: a bad-tempered Algerian soldier, haggling over a car, kneading his cap between his sinewy hands and twitching fearfully at every sound behind him; several well-nourished and rosy-cheeked Algerian traders crossing over from Bordj with 'good business' and a pronounced interest in such improbable items as the latest Mauritanian fashion in Moroccan upholstery for the wife back home; a small and skinny Mauritanian, bent with age and moral doubt, waiting for the appointed time to carry some camels across the border and meanwhile trying to find food and to maintain control over his teenage apprentice; the pony-tailed drug-smuggling neighbour from Chad haggling over a second-hand satellite phone and inviting people for dinner; a group of rather nervous youths from Gao, waving their AK-47s while looking for a spare tire; West African migrants, grey with fatigue and visibly bearing traces of repeated stints in Algerian prisons.

Although al-Khalīl is marked on no map, every child in the area knows it: it is *'āsima ta'l-frūd*, the capital of illegal trade in the northern Malian desert, and when I visited it in 2009, it was booming. Its oldest permanent house was built in 1993; at that time, the building served as a store for arms for the separatist rebellion of the early 1990s. Fifteen years later, al-Khalīl had developed into almost a town, with shops, restaurants, hostels and call centres. Its scattered habitations – several hundred of them, with at times a score of inhabitants in each – stretched far into the surrounding plain; at its outskirts, *coināt*, or 'corners' of future buildings, staked out claims to further construction sites as far as the eye could see. All construction materials were imported from nearby Algeria, and manual labour was usually provided by sub-Saharan migrants.

Al-Khalīl exists because of its close connection to Bordj Badji Mokhtar: it is primarily a transhipment point for smuggled goods of all kinds. Flour, pasta and petrol come down from Algeria on small jeeps, in antique trucks or even on the backs of camels and donkeys. Livestock and cigarettes come up from Mali, the former on the hoof or on the backs of trucks, the latter on relatively new Toyotas. Veils, perfumes, jewellery, incense and furniture arrive from southern Morocco and Mauritania, places at the forefront of feminine fashion with harbours wide open to Chinese imports. These commodities are often traded by women, who travel themselves, in jeeps, or who send their drivers. Narcotics arrive from Mauritania via the Western Sahara or from the Gulf of Guinea and travel around the southern tip of Algeria through Niger and Chad to Egypt and thence to Israel and Europe.

The mere mention of trans-Saharan trade evokes images of tremendous riches lost in the hazards of arid lands; of camels loaded with gold, cloth, ivory and ostrich feathers; of half-starved slaves dragging themselves across the desert, brutally driven on by ruthless merchants. These images can be traced a long way back through European literature, even – or rather especially – to times when direct knowledge of the West and North African interior was scarce. They durably stoked imperial fantasies of Africa's unlimited riches and were so resilient that less dramatic descriptions of trans-Saharan trade were discredited rather than being allowed to imperil the myth. These images speak of a world very different from al-Khalīl. Yet both describe trans-Saharan trade, and both were and still are causes of endless fascination to European observers – so much so, in fact, that it is a rather arduous task to peel away the layers of romantic fantasies that have come to cover what little knowledge we possess of actually occurring trans-Saharan trade then and now.

Once we have reckoned with the imagined version of Saharan trade, we can look to the reality by grappling with the technical constraints faced by anyone wanting to carry goods into, out of or across the desert, whether these constraints are geographical, ecological, political, institutional or more prosaic matters of managing the workers and animals necessary for organised caravans. The Sahara was never an empty space. Moving through it has always required careful negotiation with local pastoralists and oasis dwellers. The people best placed to carry out such movement had at least some claim to being locals themselves, either because they were regional pastoralists or because they had married into locally influential families.

As even the briefest description of al-Khalīl indicates, many of these constraints have changed as Saharan trade was transferred from camels to trucks in the mid-twentieth century, but the profound imbrication of local economic and social life remains. Khalīlī traders work the roads so that they can fund their families and herds elsewhere, send their children to school and keep their wives and sisters housed and clothed, their brothers studying or running shops in town, their fathers provided with health care. Primary school children in northern Mali today explain proudly that their fathers are *ashāb al-frūd*, smugglers, and therefore in their eyes heroes, echoing generations of Saharan children who grew up with the knowledge that their dads were out there, facing impossible journeys and bringing back exotic riches – or perhaps just the millet, wheat and dates needed to spend the dry season in relative comfort.

From this perspective, al-Khalīl is not in fact the marginal desert outpost it seems to be at first sight, inhabited by shady characters and stock figures of a semi-criminal underworld. It is instead at the heart of local economies and societies, and they and their values, aspirations and categories should be the starting point of analysis. This, however, is easier said than done.

Gold and Spice and All Things Nice

In 1824, the French Geographical Society promised a cash prize of 10,000 francs for the first European traveller to reach the fabled city of Timbuktu and to come back alive. This was the high point of a more general 'Timbuctoo craze' which had swept Western Europe since the founding of the British Association for Promoting the Discovery of the Interior Parts of Africa (more commonly known as the African Association) in 1788. People then imagined Timbuktu as a great desert metropolis, the hub of a trans-continental trade in gold, other luxury items and slaves, worth millions of pounds. Popular published accounts that claimed to be based on first-hand reports by former slaves spoke of a city as large as Paris, situated next to a forest abundant in timber and (yes) elephants, with a salubrious climate and fertile soil that could feed an urban population counted in hundreds of thousands.

Many explorers had taken up the challenge of reaching

Timbuktu even before the price was set. They included the ruthless and exceedingly trigger-happy Scottish medic Mungo Park, who actually passed, on a boat and unbeknownst to him, a few kilometres south of Timbuktu before he was killed by locals (probably for good reason); the Englishman Dixon Denham and the Scot Hugh Clapperton, who returned from an overland journey from Tripoli alive but so angry with each other that they never spoke again; and finally, after the prize money had been put on the table, the Scotsman Alexander Gordon Laing, who reached Timbuktu in 1826 just weeks before he was killed by his own guide (again, presumably for good reason). The prize finally, and against all expectations, went to the Frenchman René Caillié, son of a humble baker. Caillié, who had spent a lonely childhood reading *Robinson Crusoe*, had self-funded his trip by working in an indigo factory and then spent two years learning Arabic with Hassaniya-speaking tribesmen on the north side of the Senegal River. He travelled disguised as a Muslim convert and, in clear distinction to others who had insisted that 'true Europeans' wore waistcoats and breeches wherever they went, was generally well treated on his journey.

His arrival in Timbuktu, however, proved to be a disappointment:

> I looked around and found that the sight before me, did not answer my expectations. I had formed a totally differ-ent idea of the grandeur and wealth of Timbuctoo. The city presented, at first view, nothing but a mass of ill-looking houses, built of earth. Nothing was to be seen in all direc-tions but immense plains of quicksand of a yellowish white colour. The sky was pale red as far as the horizon: all nature wore a dreary aspect, and the most profound silence pre-vailed; not even the warbling of a bird was to be heard... .

Timbuctoo and its environs present the most monotonous
and barren scene I ever beheld.[1]

As to the fabled trans-Saharan trade in gold, spice and all things
nice, it was much like the elephants: Caillié saw nothing of it. As
he presented his rather sober account of the city on his return,
the British public was therefore (for once) unanimous: Caillié
could be nothing but an inveterate liar. It took years for his
account to be vindicated, and Caillié concluded his memoirs
with the statement that the many 'unjust attacks' that he was
subjected to after his return were more painful to him than anything he had ever suffered in the 'interior of Africa'.

There is a long-standing debate among historians and archaeologists about when trans-Saharan trade started, exactly. Was
it brought by 'the Arabs'? By 'Islam'? Linked to Roman influence? Was it even older than that? The intensity of these debates
is often linked less to the empirical evidence available than to
larger overarching agendas. The persistence with which French
historians tried to link the introduction of the camel, and hence
the beginnings of trans-Saharan trade, to Roman influence, for
instance, was rooted in these scholars' image of the non-Ro-
man Maghrib and Sahara as incapable of their own historical
development as well as their own self-identification with imperial Rome. Although contemporary historians do not share this
imperial agenda, to phrase the question in terms of origins pre-
supposes, on the one hand, that we can identify a time before
trade and, on the other, that 'trade' constitutes a unitary object,
whether it is local, regional, Saharan or trans-Saharan, and
that it encompasses all other possible forms of exchange. Both
assumptions need to be questioned.

Some trans-Saharan exchange, whether on camelback or not,

clearly did take place in Roman times. Herodotus's fifth-century BCE description of a trans-Saharan trade from the Nile valley to the Niger Bend has long been dismissed as fanciful, placing, as it does, various Saharan people always at a neat ten days' travel from each other. However, this curious fact might in fact bear witness to its authenticity, reflecting Saharan travellers' practice of journeying in stages and lay-overs filtered through Herodotus's overly tidy mind. Roman artefacts have been found in the Sahara, as in the fourth-century tomb of Tin Hinan in the Ahaggar, mentioned in chapter 1, and a nearby cache of Roman coins. They, and first-century CE remnants of chickens in Mali, indicate that *some* form of exchange did take place in late antiquity, but such remnants are too rare to prove large-scale regular patterns of commerce and tell us nothing about the terms of exchange: were they gifts, tribute, curious exotica? In any case, such finds differ radically from the abundance of mundane Roman artefacts found among the Garamantes in what is now Libya (as described in chapter 1) – a difference that should caution us against treating 'trans-Saharan' trade as a phenomenon that would have been homogeneous across the Sahara and hence have a single starting point.

But does an absence of Roman artefacts further south really indicate an absence of Saharan trade in antiquity? It might just be that by focussing on Rome (and hence on north-south exchange), we are defining trade too narrowly. Cotton, for instance, was cultivated in the first century CE in the Egyptian oases of Kharga and Dakhla and in the Fazzān by the Garamantes alongside millet and sorghum, first domesticated south of the Sahara. Archaeologists long assumed that the cotton had come from India via the Nile valley and been produced for consumption in Egypt. Recent DNA analysis points rather to independent domestication in Lower Nubia (contemporary

Sudan), whence it might have been imported to the northern Sahara as a package with drought-resistant sub-Saharan African cereals. Production probably flowed into a Sahara-centred network that had little to do with the Roman world, much as it seems that the Garamantes produced cotton primarily for trade with the south.

We therefore need to distinguish carefully between *Saharan* and *trans*-Saharan trade: trade that crosses the region and therefore becomes visible in archaeological sites and historical sources produced beyond it and trade that functions and establishes economic sub-regions within it. Indeed, given the structural interdependence between regional economies sketched out thus far, it is difficult to imagine life in the Sahara prior to trade, or at least prior to some form of exchange over distance. By the time Arab geographers provided the first written accounts of Saharan caravans in the centuries after the 'Arab conquest' of North Africa, these already seemed to describe a system that was well in place, with regional salt caravans, for instance, obtaining 'enormous profits, fat gains, and abundant benefits'.[2]

This famous ninth-century quotation by Ibn Hawqal notwithstanding, most of these external chroniclers were interested primarily not in the regional salt trade but either in truly *trans*-Saharan caravans, bringing goods to North African cities, or in those that dealt in goods that might be of interest to North African merchants: slaves or low-bulk, high-value luxury items such as ivory and gold. They, like much later European consular reports on which most historical research on trans-Saharan trade continues to be based, can tell us much about *trans*-Saharan trade and its fluctuations over time, but they speak only indirectly about the *Saharan* trade that went on invisibly under its surface. Seen from the Sahara itself, however, trans-Saharan trade was probably primarily an epiphenomenon of Saharan trade, which in turn was essential to local livelihoods: the tip of the iceberg, to use a somewhat inappropriate metaphor.

To start with trans-Saharan trade, then, without considering its regional underpinnings is to put the cart before the horse, or perhaps rather the camel on top of the packsaddle. This means that we need to rethink the models we have inherited from centuries of more or less fantastical accounts that compare desert to overseas travel – the kind of accounts that led nineteenth-century explorers on their wild goose chase to a Timbuktu that never was and blinded them to the Timbuktu Caillié found: a regional trading hub in salt, millet and goatskins. In particular, we need to discard large-scale mental maps of vertical and historically immutable trade routes that supposedly 'opened up' sub-Saharan Africa to northern traders and that still figure in most history books. Instead, we should consider the nitty-gritty realities of Saharan logistics: how do you actually get things across vast distances in a hyper-arid environment that is anything but homogeneous and empty? To answer this question, we must consider the three crucial elements of any Saharan journey: camels (how to carry goods), caravans (how to organise travel) and security (how to come back alive).

How to Organise a Caravan

Until the motorisation of trans-Saharan trade in the mid-twentieth century, all trans-Saharan trade had to rely on pack animals, which usually meant camels. A variety of other animals were used, but, as described in chapter 3, it was camels that made such far-ranging travel possible in the first place. Yet even a camel cannot go without water forever and needs to rest now and then. The welfare of camels, as the main source of wealth for nomadic populations, is and probably always was taken very seriously. Ideally, camels should be able to feed on the way, and most trade routes were dependent on the availability of pasture and water. In the seventeenth century, the Moroccan scholar Abū Sālim ʿAbd Allāh b. Muhammad al-ʿAyyāshī, on his way to Mecca from his native Sijilmāsa in present-day southern Morocco, watched impatiently but helplessly as his whole caravan repeatedly ground to a halt or went on long detours so that the animals could eat their fill.

Pasture is notoriously variable with time. A substantial caravan depletes resources in a way that makes it unwise for others to follow suit immediately. Navigation in the Sahara is therefore not so much a matter of knowing one 'route' as of knowing how to interpret the signs that indicate the best direction to take at that particular moment and with the number and state of animals at hand. In the mid-nineteenth century, as French colonial officers started to move towards the Sahara from what is now Algeria, they had to learn this lesson the hard way. Not only did all their attempts to reroute or 'capture' trans-Saharan trade fail miserably, but their establishment of a fixed 'supply route' from northern Algeria to the French colonial outposts in the Sahara resulted in hecatombs of camels. Those beasts that survived refused to continue, as, according to the colonial archives, 'numerous dead camels from the preceding convoys were lying on the road ... smelling very bad'.[3] Things improved only as the French army decided to delegate transport to pastoral nomads and to imitate pre-existing regional patterns of exchange.

Due to variations in pasture and the nature of the terrain, camels tend to be trained as regional specialists and often find it difficult to cope with unfamiliar pasture and ground. In his 1848 description of a trans-Saharan caravan, the Shaʿanbī trader Sīdī al-Hājj Muhammad recounted losing many of his camels as he crossed the Ahaggar Mountains, today in the country's south, as his animals, used to the plains of the north, slipped, twisted their ankles and fell into ravines; on the way back, he claimed, they lost two-thirds of the camels he had bought in what is now central Niger, as these animals could cope with neither the rocks nor the unfamiliar climate.[4] Also, camels need a lot of rest. After Ibn Battūta bought the camels necessary for his Saharan crossing in the fourteenth century, he was obliged to put them out to pasture for four months before he could start his journey, no matter how much the world-famous globetrotter chafed under his enforced leisure. It was an exceptional camel that crossed the whole of the Sahara in a straight line; trade proceeded mostly in stages, with frequent changes of pack animals at known way stations.[5]

Ibn Battūta not only was stung in his camel deal (having tired camels fobbed off on him) but was probably also unusual in that he had bought his own camels. Camels need to be looked after carefully, and the people best placed to do this were nomadic pastoralists who had known the animals from birth. More regionally rooted traders, especially if they were urbanites, preferred to hire rather than buy camels as a way of ensuring that the camels' owners – who tended to travel with their beasts – would still feel responsible for them and look after them well. Even in cases where urban traders owned their own camels, they needed nomadic pastoralists to look after them, as they could hardly keep them in their garden or in stables, or indeed dirty their hands with their care during the arduous trans-Saharan treks.

Elite urban travellers such as Ibn Battūta hardly ever mention the many workers who necessarily accompanied long-distance car-avans: the guides, camel-herds, cooks, scouts, grooms and slaves who made up the main body of the caravan and kept it moving. Ibn Battūta did, however, tell the story of an urban trader who throughout the journey and against everybody's better advice entertained himself by playing with snakes. Until the day, that is, when he was bitten so badly that his life was saved only by the intervention of one of the 'camel people' (*jammālūn*), who slaughtered a camel and told the merchant to leave his hand in the beast's belly overnight until the poisoned flesh rotted away. We can only guess what the jammālūn thought about *him*.

Similarly, al-'Ayyāshī, the seventeenth-century Moroccan scholar and pilgrim mentioned above, barely mentioned the role of the jammālūn in his own travels. Yet we know from his account that he spent many a pleasant afternoon on his journey debating the finer points of Islamic law and vying with his companions in the composition of impromptu poems – while, we presume, others were looking after him and his beasts (al-'Ayyāshī alone had brought three horses, which needed to be watered and fed daily).[6]

Camels in caravans were used as pack animals, and humans usually walked – unless, like Ibn Battūta and al-'Ayyāshī, they were wealthy enough to bring horses. For everybody else, the chores to be carried out after a long day's walk were endless: unload the camels, rub them down, haul water for them if there was a well and take them to pasture, organise camp, cook dinner (usually some variety of couscous, dried meat and dried dates), repair packsaddles and ties, stand guard. Then roll up in one's burnous for the night, hoping that it will provide enough protection from the biting Saharan cold. Tents were a luxury granted only to caravan leaders and the wealthy and powerful, but everybody, even the humblest of the jammālūn, was very careful to take good care of their shoes and to always have a spare pair.

Who, then were these jammālūn who made up the bulk of the caravan? Most were probably recruited from among local pastoralists, some of whom had made it their special business to work on caravans. Sīdī al-Hājj Muhammad, quoted above, was one of them. They often travelled with their sons to teach them their trade from a very early age. Others were lower-status pastoralists who saw trade as a way up and out. Others were slaves and had no say in the matter. Yet others, especially in the eastern Sahara, belonged to the local elites and worked in close collaboration with Sahelian sultans. Take, for instance, the *khabīr* ʿAlī, the foremost caravan leader of mid-nineteenth-century Darfur, who had successfully married into wealth and power and become probably the richest and most influential man in his hometown of Kubayh near al-Faschir, the starting point of the forty-day road to Egypt.[7] Or Chegguen, the Tuareg khabīr who guided Sīdī al-Hājj Muhammad's caravan south and whose reputation was such that the mere mention of his name tripled the size of the caravan as they passed through the Tidikelt. 'At night, if not one single star shines in the sky, he knows where he is, by simply inspecting a tuft of grass on the ground or the texture, smell or taste of the soil'.[8] Travelers like Ibn Battūta and al-ʿAyyāshī paid for the services of such a man in pure gold in addition to the many presents and trading opportunities that his profession and exceptional skill drew his way.

Given its many complications and dangers, Saharan travel was mostly a collective undertaking. Hence the best-known institution of desert travel: the caravan, which comes, in the Islamic tradition, with the highest possible authority: 'One rider is a devil', the Prophet Muhammad is reported to have said; 'two riders are two devils, three: a caravan'. Despite this long and noble pedigree, the English term 'caravan' – which has multiple translations in Arabic according to size, composition and range – can hide a wide variety of empirical realities, from a group of three or four companions and their animals via the smallish but socially diverse trading caravan with which Ibn Battūta travelled to the kind of oversized travelling fair that was the annual pilgrimage caravan to Mecca, which, Ibn Battūta claimed (probably with some exaggeration) could contain as many as 12,000 camels.

In the nineteenth century, Sīdī al-Hājj Muhammad watched as the annual Western Sahara pilgrimage caravan travelled past In Salah on its way back from Mecca with 2,000 camels, 'a river of men growing larger everywhere it passes'. Here it was met by a motley crowd of locals, either family members and friends eager to greet the travellers or traders wanting to exchange provisions for the many precious items that the caravan brought back with it from the east: perfumes, incense, cloths, jewellery, holy water, spices, books.... 'The two crowds intermingled in an indescribable disorder.... Family and friends called to each other at the top of their voices; all Muslim names sounded across the chants of the pilgrims and the screams of women and children who were suffocated in the dust, rolled in the reflux of this tumultuous sea.... Frightened camels threw their riders to the ground, and, with their lowing and their senseless rushing about, added to the confusion and noise'.[9]

We know quite a lot about these larger caravans because writers external to the Sahara – those most likely to leave a written account of their journey (not because Saharans couldn't write but because they did not think to write down what was obvious to them) – usually travelled with them rather than with smaller outfits. They were organised in a strictly hierarchical fashion, with a caravan leader whose word nobody dared contest and who was responsible for the welfare of everyone under his care; in the nineteenth-century northern Sahara, he was assisted by *shuwāsh* ('sergeants'; this is an Ottoman term) who executed his orders; a *khūja* (scribe) or qadi who solved disputes and recorded sales; an imam to lead the congregation of travellers in prayers; one or several *shuwāf*, look-outs; and, in large caravans, a *dalīl*, in charge of selling off goods belonging to anybody who had died on the journey, taken by sickness, fatigue, the bite of a snake or the sting of a scorpion, or been lost in a sandstorm. We can think of these large caravans as complex social and economic institutions akin to the transatlantic commercial sailing ships of seventeenth- and eighteenth-century Europe.

As spectacular as they were, such large caravans were not, in fact, very practicable: just imagine the complexities of watering camels in the evening, an occasion when conflict typically broke out among the different travellers, already tired from their long day. Nor could they stop if somebody got lost and a few camels ran away or were rustled at night. Large caravans were therefore usually subdivided into smaller sections, often organised according to the travellers' origins; camels had to walk in smaller groups anyway, for reasons of pasture, but also so that they would not bump into each other and so that any accident befalling one camel would not bring the whole caravan to a halt. The only reason people travelled in such large numbers was security, and in many cases, smaller caravans came together to form a larger one to cross areas considered particularly dangerous and then split up again after a few days.

This brings us to the third and final element essential to trans-Saharan trade: safety. Any traveller facing the long journey across the desert had to consider the very real question of how they would arrive at their destination and return alive. Whoever they were, the jammālūn recommended themselves to wealthy travellers such as Ibn Battūta and al-ʿAyyāshī not only by their skills as guides, caravan managers and camel-herds but also by their ability to offer protection on the way, or at least to know whom to pay off in order to acquire such protection. This was not always easy in a Sahara that for most of its history was politically fragmented, divided into different and always shifting areas of influence. Chegguen, for instance, was not only Tuareg, with close and long-standing connections to the leader of the Ahaggar, whom he was known to pay off regularly and lavishly, but had also married three wives, one in Metlili, one in In Salah, and one in the Ahaggar, which 'put him in necessary contact with traders from southern Algeria, Tuwāt and Morocco, and granted him protection from the Tuareg, which is indispensable'.[10]

Travellers who failed to obtain protection could easily find themselves in an uncomfortable position. In 1964, guided by local antelope hunters, the French naturalist Théodore Monod found in the eastern Mauritania *majābat al-kubrā* (literally, 'the greatest crossing', a Saharan 'empty space' half the size of France) the remnants of what people then thought of as a 'capsized caravan', dating from the twelfth century and loaded with 2,085 copper bars and thousands of cowrie shells. Monod speculated that these goods had been carefully hidden for future retrieval, either by caravaneers who had run into problems with their camels, or who feared attack, or else by raiders themselves.

Centuries later, Sīdī al-Hājj Muhammad's account was similarly peppered with references to potential raids: he and his companions avoided certain good pastures and wells for fear of attacks; didn't light fires or smoke in certain places; kept the camels in camp, feeding them on dates rather than sending them out to pasture, for fear of rustlers; imagined a spy in every Tuareg they met on their way south; killed one of three shepherds whom they spotted stealthily trying to approach their camp at night; and paid good money to Chegguen's Tuareg chief for his protection – so much, in fact, that the chief decided to accompany them in person in order to better keep an eye on their trade goods, in which he now had a personal interest. Nor did Sīdī al-Ḥājj Muhammad ever fail to mention the many graveyards that surround their stopping places, offering a final resting place to all those who were less lucky then he – careless shepherds, pilgrims and caravaneers alike.

Even those who had paid for protection were not always exempt from further demands. The North African traveller al-Tūnsī described at length how, when traveling through Borkou in what is now northern Chad in the early nineteenth century with a large Arab caravan, he duly followed his local guide's advice and sought out the local 'sultan' in order to hand over the customary fee of passage. This, however, was not enough; the sultan 'hung around, prowling through our tents, looking like a mischievous imp; he stuck his nose into every bag. Everything that he saw and that was to his taste, ropes, even the smallest begging bowl, he snatched it and made himself a present of it'. The sultan was followed by his people, 'a troop of ogres and devils escaped from hell' who proceeded to relieve the caravan of all remaining valuables: 'They scour the caravan. Every spear they like, they take it; everything they ask for, we have to give it to them. By the end, we had nothing left of any value'.[11] But at least they were still alive.

We can grant al-Tūnsī his fair share of prejudice and romantic exaggeration (although he had spent many years at the court of the Waddaï sultan in eastern Chad and was thus no stranger to the region), but the basic phenomenon he described was clearly real: the Sahara was most definitely not a no man's land. All parts of it were controlled by somebody, and these somebodies had to be paid in order to secure safe passage. This was easier for outsiders to the region if they grouped together and travelled under the protection of known local guides. In many cases, it was probably mostly a matter of paying those most likely to attack the caravan in the first place for 'protection' against their own aggression. While their caravan was being 'inspected', some of al-Tūnsī's fellow travellers were busy negotiating with the 'troop of ogres and devils escaped from hell' for a loan of fresh pack animals and camel-herds to take them and their wares safely to their final destination – for, we can surmise, a good price.

Trans-Saharan Traders

Given the dangers and discomforts of the journey, it should come as no surprise that many traders preferred to deploy intermediaries. In the first years of the twentieth century, a French colonial officer noted, deeply impressed, the complex networks that made it possible for Jewish traders based in Tripoli to order goods directly from Europe and then send them across the Sahara with the help of merchants from Ghadames (now in Libya), who in turn relied on agents or associates in Ghat (Libya), Agadez, Zinder (both in Niger), Kano and Sokoto (Nigeria). 'I met one of [the Ghadamsi associates] in Iferouane [northern Niger], travelling with a parasol. He was able to offer me candles of transparent wax, perfumed pastes, and he very willingly gave me all the general information I asked him for, while resisting approximate statistics; he was going to Kano.'[12]

Many of these regional intermediaries also traded on their own account. Indeed, while we can easily see why external traders and other travellers would need help locally, the reverse is not the case: local jammālūn and their close associates were clearly very capable of going where they liked when they liked, and there can be no doubt that they did so routinely. Think back, for instance, to the Arbāʿa pastoral nomads described in chapter 3, whose pastures straddled the southern agricultural lands of the Tell and the extreme north of the Sahara. They were in no way professional traders, but in the late nineteenth century, one-third of their annual income derived in one way or another from regional transport and exchange as they took dates to the north and cereals and manufactured goods south while always also finding room in their saddlebags for 'perfume, knick-knacks, jewellery, coffee, tobacco, cloths, ostrich feathers, incense and musk' which they peddled through the oases on their way north or south.[13]

As locals, the Arbāʿa did not have to worry about their own security; as pastoralists, they had all the transport animals they needed and knew exactly which routes to take that particular year. Camels held no mystery for them, and as their journeys were quite simply part of their seasonal migration, they did not even have to factor in transport costs but could count everything they earned as profit. We can thus imagine the Sahara as crossed not so much by unvarying vertical trade routes as by innumerable travellers, some alone, some in small groups, some in large caravans; some primarily trading, others visiting family, on pilgrimage, or searching for good pasture; some local, some from nearby, some external traders to the area, some all three all at once (think back to the flexibility of genealogical ties and identities); all carrying a few goods from one part of the Sahara to another.

At the other extreme from Ibn Battūta's or al-ʿAyyāshī's urban travel companions, we find people like this Tubu pastoralist from central Niger, described in the 1950s by the French military officer Jean Chapelle:

A Tubu from Gouré [in central Niger] leaves his camp with two goats and one pack-camel to go to Bornu [in northern Nigeria] at harvest time, i.e. in October. Here, he exchanges his two goats against one camel-load of millet. He returns to his camp, leaves some of the millet behind, and carries on to Kawar with all of his pack animals, and perhaps with another one or two camels or donkeys hired from somebody else. He again takes two goats, some butter, a few skins... . He gets to Kawar [in northern Niger] in December, where he exchanges his millet and goats against two loads of salt or two to three loads of dates... . He then goes back south, leaving the best part of the dates in his camp, and returns to Bornu. Here, he exchanges his salt and the rest of the dates against four loads or 480 kg of millet, two or three pieces of cloth, a few kitchen utensils, some knick-knack for his wife, a little bit of money to pay his taxes. Having left in October with two goats, he will return to his camp in February or March with the necessary provision of millet and dates, and almost everything that is needed in his tent. He will have travelled 2,000 km, and he will have to wait for the good pasture of the rainy season for his animals to recover, before he will be able to travel again.[14]

These concrete cases have a few implications for correcting the gilded image of trans-Saharan trade. Most Saharan trade was probably not in luxury items but in staples, the kind of thing that the Arbāʿa and Tubu were carrying: cereals, dates, salt, cloth, dried meat, skins. We can thus think of the famous goods of trans-Saharan trade – gold, spices, ivory, even slaves – as convenient add-ons to more permanent and vital patterns of exchange. When times were right – say, when fashion in London and Paris required women to adorn their heads with ostrich feathers or when there was in increased demand for slaves in the Sahara, as happened in the nineteenth century – these add-ons might yield considerable profits, so much so that even traders from further afield might be persuaded to dabble in trans-Saharan trade. But times weren't always right, and such trans-Saharan ventures might easily collapse, leaving the more regular but much less glamourous exchange of staples to carry on regardless.

Saharan fashion and culinary habits bear witness to this close integration of local economic life and regional and trans-regional trade. Take, for instance, the stereotypical 'Tuareg' as he appears in tourist brochures: dressed in long cotton robes, with an indigo turban veiling his face; armed with a *takuba*, the Tuareg sword; his wife proudly displaying her silver jewellery and also dressed in an indigo veil perfumed with sandalwood, her eyes made-up with kohl. To welcome their foreign visitors, they might offer sweet tea and perhaps even prepare a couscous or a *taguella*, a galette made from semolina and cooked in the sand, and serve a few dates while you are waiting.

In the mid-nineteenth century, the French traveller Duvey-rier estimated that at least twenty yards of cotton cloth were needed to make a full Tuareg outfit. Cloth was mostly imported from North Africa at the time, with the most sought-after material woven in Egypt or, for truly precious stuff, imported from as far away as India. The best indigo veils, those that earned the Tuareg the nickname 'the blue men' (as they stained skin, thus protecting it from the sun), were made in Kano in what is now northern Nigeria. By the late nineteenth century, most other cloth worn in the Sahara was probably produced in Lancashire mills. By then, takubas were mass-produced (alongside America's legendary Bowie knife) in Sheffield, where certain factories specialised in catering to North and West African markets. Although jewellery was made locally with great skill by Tuareg smiths, the raw material was usually provided by European-minted silver coins. Sandalwood and kohl were imported from the east.

Similar logics persist today. Tea and sugar are both imported, of course, one from China and the other mostly from the Caribbean. The couscous or the wheat used to make the traditional Tuareg galette is of North African manufacture, although it was probably initially grown in Ukraine; millet, the other staple cereal in the region, is imported from the Sahel; dates are exchanged with oasis dwellers. In other words, even the most stereotypically 'traditional' manifestations of 'Tuareg culture' rely on imports. This has been the case for at least one and a half centuries and probably for much longer. Although some of the elements of 'tradition' are more recent than one might initially think – tea, for instance, was introduced to the area only in the late nineteenth century – the readiness and skilfulness with which new imports are adopted and adapted locally might be much older. Mutatis mutandis, we can perhaps already observe this ability to incorporate external goods into local fashion in the Garamantian infatuation with Roman wine and bath houses, described in chapter 1.

As a result, most traders were probably somewhere in between the two extreme cases outlined above, the 'foreign' traders with external financial backing carrying transparent wax candles and the local pastoralist with his two goats. That is, they were of regional origin but able to travel far; they traded in staples but also occasionally tried their hand at trading in luxury items; they might rely on external financial backers but probably invested most of their profits in local assets, oasis gardens and livestock; and they could accomplish all this mostly by tapping into regional trade routes and alliances that already existed.

The most common way of gaining access to regional networks was through marriage. Successful traders were those who could count on local allies, that is, who had married into influential families who could provide the knowledge, skills, connections and security necessary for commercial transactions. In the fourteenth century, Ibn Battūta noted that the best way of obtaining protection from 'nomadic Berbers' was by getting married 'to one of their women', but this in turn implied a long-term commitment to a particular region, as local women refused to leave their natal regions. 'In this respect', he concluded, 'the women are more important than the men'.[15] From the inside out, Saharan trade then looked less like a solitary quest for (male) adventure than like an – arguably much harder – exercise in domestic diplomacy. This truth struck me as I was conducting interviews with members of one of the most prominent southern Algerian trading families today, the Zijlāwī. I had made friends with Zayda, one of the daughters of the family and an important trader in her own right, in Adrar, the administrative capital of the Tuwāt. Knowing my interest in the history of Saharan trade, she sent me to visit her stepmother Maryam in the family fief in Aoulef, a couple of hundred kilometres further south.

Aoulef is a medium-size town on the main road that leads from In Salah to Adrar. It has a rather modern and Algerian feel, with a high school, several middle schools, various regional administrations, shops, a market and regular public transport. Yet in addition to the cluster of modern concrete buildings, the town centre is dominated by two large buildings: the local zāwiya, of recent construction, financed by the Zijlāwī and led by their son-in-law Shaykh Bāy, and the even larger *qasba* Zijlāwī, made up of a cluster of individual houses ranging from mud-brick huts to large, comfortable concrete villas. Indeed, my request that the bus driver let me down at the Zijlāwīs' house was the cause of great hilarity: 'Shūfi dār Zijlāwī' (Look, this is the Zijlāwīs' house), he said, pointing to the whole of Aoulef, then including with a vast sweep of his arm the whole world.

I nevertheless managed to find Maryam, who was staying on her own in a spacious villa. Surprised at my unexpected arrival, she rapidly composed herself (she was clearly used to surprise visitors from all kinds of strange places and with dubious claims of 'relatedness'). Once we had settled down to tea on colourful rugs and cushions in her living room, she told me the story – almost a fairy tale – of the Zijlāwīs' rise to wealth. This telling was accompanied by family photographs, arranged in several large albums: her daughters, cousins and only surviving son (the other had died on a trip to Niger); brothers, nieces and nephews in Aoulef for the *'īd*, in Niamey in bathing suits sitting next to a large swimming pool, in end-of-year photographs from expensive private schools in Niamey, and in four-by-fours on travels through the desert.

Tālib Sālim, the first Zijlāwī, Maryam told me, arrived in Aoulef from the Wād Sūf near the contemporary Tunisian border in the late nineteenth century. He had already been married in the Wād Sūf and brought with him his three sons. In Aoulef, he took another three wives: one from a family of leading nomadic pastoralists who could furnish him with transport and security and two from the local leading religious family, cousins of the Kunta shaykh encountered in chapter 4, who provided the blessing for his enterprise to prosper. His sons and grandsons contracted similar marital alliances as they gradually pushed south and set up shops and houses first in what is now northern Mali and then in central Niger. Thus, the family's fortunes began through a history of judicious marriages.

Maryam still remembers with a certain bitterness how her own husband, Mustafā, Tālib Sālim's grandson, left by himself to settle in Gao, saying that the Sudan was not for women and children, only to then take a second wife in Gao. The second wife, Lalla 'Ā'isha, did not know about the existence of the first; otherwise, at least according to her daughter, she would have refused to marry him. After all, she was from a reputed sharifian family of Moroccan descent. Her father was perhaps the most influential trader in the region. Her uncle was qadi of nearby Goundam. Mustafā had more to gain from the alliance than she did, as he well knew and as she constantly reminded him. And gain he did: much if not most of the family's success and ongoing popularity in the area stemmed from the good relations they established with their in-laws, who still provide many political and social dignitaries in northern Mali. As bitter as she might be about her husband's second marriage, Maryam knew this well and kept an open house for the many Malian and Nigerien relatives who might drop in on surprise visits. After all, marriage produces in-laws, but it also produces children – and one never knows what they might do, or indeed who they might be.

Saints on Trucks

Hammū Zafzaf was a rather small man, tanned by the sun, with a pointy white beard, his eyes sparkling with energy and intelligence; he seemed not even vaguely astonished when I told him that having sought him in vain in Kidal in northern Mal, I had come to Tit (800 kilometres and an arduous Saharan crossing further north) with the express purpose of looking him up. He received me in his large mud-brick house, which was spartanly furnished; despite his legendary wealth, Zafzaf clearly did not indulge in conspicuous consumption but preferred to invest in gardens, water and livestock herded by his in-laws back in Kidal.

Zafzaf had been a trans-Saharan trader like the Zijlāwīs. At an early age, when he could barely hold on to the camel's saddle, he had followed his father to Kidal, where his father, who had married locally, owned a shop, livestock and extensive gardens. Zafzaf fondly remembers his childhood, spent helping either in his father's shop or in the lush pastures of northern Mali with his new family, far from the austerities of his native oasis town. Throughout the following decades, Zafzaf accompanied his father's goods up and down the Sahara, earning his nickname: 'the one who is back before you even knew that he had left'. He married once in Tit and twice in Kidal, thereby acquiring large families, abundant herds and well-watered gardens in both locations. Hammū Zafzaf's life hence corresponds to a set pattern of trans-Saharan success. Yet it also spans a time when the first trans-Saharan trucks made their appearance, changing the logistics of Saharan trade forever.

The first motorised vehicles had crossed the Sahara in the 1920s, before Zafzaf was even born. A convergence of imperial ambitions, the allure of exploration, the spirit of sporting challenge, technological progress, industrial interests and a desire for publicity culminated in the Citroën Mission of 1922–1923 and the Algérie-Niger Mission of 1924. By 1926, two state-owned French companies ran weekly or bi-weekly bus services from Béchar to Gao and Algiers to Tamanrasset. Prices, however, remained prohibitive, and Saharan traders such as Zafzaf's father mostly stood by and watched as the first trans-Saharan trucks laboured slowly over rough terrain, loaded with French military personnel and the occasional tourist – if they didn't employ themselves in one of the many camel teams that accompanied those trucks, carrying petrol and supplies and making sure that the trucks had at least a chance of making it to their destination.

This changed as the Second World War suddenly turned the Sahara, for a brief moment, into a region of global strategic interest. French West Africa, which remained loyal to the Vichy government, improved trans-Saharan transport in order to bypass the British maritime blockade, mapping out desert tracks and equipping way stations with supplies. French Central Africa, whose governor had sided with General de Gaulle's Free France, chose as its first military target fascist Italian garrisons in Kufra in southern Libya, sending the famous Colonne Leclerc north from Cameroon. In order to get there, however, they needed to first improve trans-Saharan connections and equipment in northern Chad. In 1940, the French military detachment stationed in Faya-Largeau, northern Chad's largest military post, had no viable motor vehicles and relied entirely on animal transport. By 1941, the Colonne Leclerc, with assistance from the British in Cairo, had at its disposal 650 American-built trucks in working order; in 1942, when they had mostly moved on to Libya, this number had risen to 1,500.[16] The imperatives and follies of warfare suddenly made calculations of costs and benefits, which until then had prohibited sustained investment in motorised trans-Saharan trade, seem irrelevant.

As a result, for a few years, isolated desert outposts such as Kidal or Faya suddenly boomed, turned from imperial backwaters into glittering cosmopolitan market towns where everything (and everybody) seemed available and commercial fortunes could be made overnight. Not only was the army that won the first military battle for Free France recruited from throughout Central Africa, but the organisational feat hat underpinned the Colonne Leclerc was in fact possible for the French officers – most of whom knew little of the local terrain – only with the help of experienced and internationally well-connected intermediaries. Some of these were international traders, Syrian,

Greek and Armenian, while others were Libyans who had been settled in Faya since the 1900s.

None of this cosmopolitan glory was to last. As soon as the war came to an end in 1945, global attention shifted once more away from the Sahara. Military budgets ran dry. As the world's most powerful armies left the region, they forgot to tidy up, leaving behind vast amounts of military equipment, trucks, jeeps, unfinished roadworks, spare parts and trained drivers and mechanics. The golden age of trans-Saharan trucks could begin. In northern Mali, Zafzaf's father was the first Algerian trader to invest in a truck. But he wasn't the only one for long.

The Akacem are originally from Metlili near Ghardaïa and belong to the Bani Brahim, a sedentary section of the Shaʻanba, camel nomads who long furnished guides and camel drovers to traders based in the trading hub of the Mzab. Sīdī al-Hājj Muhammad, whose mid-nineteenth-century account of desert travel is quoted at length above, had been a Metlili Shaʻanbī. With the French colonial conquest, many of the Akacems' nomadic cousins enrolled in the French army. Familiar with their relatives' tastes and needs and aware of the supply needs of the French army and the ready cash offered in exchange, the Akacem set up shops near French garrisons. Al-Hājj Ahmad's father, the first Akacem in this story, was among them. By 1934, Al-Hājj Ahmad had stepped into his father's shoes and, as soon as it became available, started to rent space from the French company that then held the monopoly on motorised transport in the oasis. Yet his capital was never quite sufficient to buy his own trucks.

With the Second World War, he too invested in laid-off Italian army trucks and put them to work on the many roads that then connected southern Algeria with French West Africa and beyond to Nigeria and Ghana. He was soon not only among the most important traders but also one of the wealthiest landowners in the area. In 1952, he started organising annual pilgrimages by bus to Mecca and often travelled with them, establishing contacts in Tripoli, Benghazi, Alexandria, Cairo, Suez, Jeddah, Mecca and Medina, to the great concern of the French colonial administration. In his house back in Tuwāt, local elites met daily to listen to Nasser's Egyptian radio spreading the news of triumphant Arab nationalism.

By the late 1950s, members of al-Hājj Ahmad's extended family had built houses and shops in Gao and Niamey, whence they travelled to Timbuktu, Bamako, Maradi in southern Niger, Ouagadougou, and even Kano in northern Nigeria as well as Lomé and Accra. In southern Algeria, al-Hājj Ahmad was said to be able to make and unmake political careers; he had bought the monopoly for truck transport between El Menia and Adrar, while his brother had received an exclusive concession from the nascent Compagnie des pétroles algériens to supply research stations and digging sites and to provide transport for oil prospectors. As the war of independence broke out in Algeria in 1954, the brothers became indispensable allies of the Algerian Armée de Libération Nationale (ALN); during the war, the late Algerian president Abdelaziz Bouteflika even sought refuge in one of the family's houses in Gao.

As a result, the Akacem family managed to maintain their strong position in independent Algeria, although their trading ventures and transport infrastructure suffered from war-time changes and confiscations, the rapid devaluation of land and economic reform in the 1970s. By then, however, the younger generation of the family was well established in administrative posts throughout the country, leaving the tiresome work of trans-Saharan trade to others, perhaps their own distant in-laws.

Meanwhile, the older generation, among them al-Hājj Ahmad himself, had retired to their abundant oasis gardens in Metlili in central Algeria.

Contemporary Trade

Trans-Saharan trucks remain the most economic and popular means of transport between the southern and northern Sahara even today – at least, this was the case until the official closure of the border between Mali and Algeria in 2011. Travelling at a leisurely average speed of perhaps 30 kilometres per hour, trucks take between five days and a week to get from Adrar or Taman-rasset in southern Algeria to Gao in northern Mali during the dry season and up to three times as long during the rainy season in August. Truck drivers are known to all (we met one of them, Ghali, in the introduction), their whereabouts never a secret, and even small children can identify the make of trucks and sometimes even individual vehicles from afar by the sounds of their engines.

At the discretion of the driver, trucks carry family visitors, trans-border peddlers, shepherds and Sahelian labour migrants to Algeria. Women travel to visit members of their extended families on both sides of the border, sometimes with babies on their laps. They have their reserved seats in the cab and their own privileged position in the complicated hierarchy that governs truck society. Messages and letters are passed on, petrol bartered against food along the way and goods dropped off in known depots; everybody has his or her own family to supply somewhere along the road and 20 tonnes of dates to distribute. The trucks' conveniently large beds and tanks provide room not only for hitch-hikers but also for various more or less legal trade goods, including petrol.

Some trucks, especially those owned by Algerian business-men, make for Gao in a relatively straight line; others can be seen in the most improbable places somewhere between Algeria and Mali, peddling dates, petrol and exported Algerian goods against livestock among the local nomadic population. Such trucks move slowly but constantly, with little food and rest; this rhythm changes only in the event of a flat tire or more serious breakdowns, repaired with few or no matching tools and spare parts and much physical force and ingenuity. All truck drivers know each other and the strengths and weaknesses of their machines; they tend to stop in fixed spots at times when they know that they are likely to meet and invariably share at least the three customary glasses of tea. Drivers invite each other for lunch and dinner, and some food is always offered to women travelling on other trucks.

Smaller four-by-fours ply the same route, but at a somewhat less leisurely rhythm, carrying pasta, semolina, flour and pow-dered milk. All of these exports are technically illegal, but without them, as all traders and customs officials readily admit, the people of northern Mali would probably starve. (Indeed, border closures during the 2011 and 2012 war and the subse-quent construction of a wall along Algeria's southern borders have been disastrous to local livelihoods.) Neither Timbuktu nor Kidal in northern Mali is directly accessible by paved road, and travel by car – let alone by truck – from Kidal to the Malian capital, Bamako, takes at least three days. Moreover, basic food and petrol in Algeria used to be and partly still are heavily sub-sidised, making them incomparably cheaper than their Sahelian alternatives.

Trans-border trade in staples remains relatively democratic: anybody with a four-by-four, some initial capital and enough cousins along the road can become a carrier or else trade on his own account, and deals with Malian custom officials used to be commonplace and cheap. By all accounts, the same used to be true of cigarette and petrol smuggling, which became a mainstay of the local economy in the 1980s. Cigarettes, either Chinese counterfeit or real semi-official imports, were unloaded in the major harbours on the Gulf of Guinea, from where they were carried north overland. They were redistributed in Burkina Faso, crossed the Maghrib and the Mediterranean and were sold throughout Western Europe. Traders returned home with staples and imported consumer goods.

Trade of this kind has an ambiguous status in local perception: it is seen as an inherently honourable occupation that makes it possible to exploit the region's perhaps most important 'natural' resource, the Algerian and Libyan borders, while strengthening family ties and relations. Yet where it leads to profound social changes and a questioning of regional hierarchies – as when young men suddenly have 'too much' cash at their personal disposal or formerly low-status men start marrying 'noble' girls regardless of their parents' opinion – some families consider it to be morally tainted, not for what it is but for what it allows to happen. A similar sociocentric logic is at work in the moral judgement applied to other types of commerce that flourish in the border area today: arms and drug trafficking and trade in stolen cars.

Everybody locally agrees that the gun, car and drug trades are firmly in the hands of large-scale centralised organisations locally referred to as 'mafias'. Recruitment to these 'mafias' is made on an individual basis, irrespective of social origin. Payment is also made on an individual basis, in cars, not cash: after three or more successful return trips, the driver owns the car, either to keep it and start his own business smuggling cigarettes or staples or to sell it and continue with the mafia. Drivers tend to start their jobs as apprentices when they are adolescents, hoping to move through the ranks as they grow older and eventually to become small-scale patrons themselves. In most cases, however, they fail, either by dropping out of the business altogether or by dying or being maimed in accidents or shoot-outs with customs officials.

This means that most drivers are very young, often barely in their twenties. Stories they tell at night around campfires in the smuggling outpost of al-Khalīl (where we began this chapter) speak of heroism, nomadic excellence, honour and personal autonomy. They dwell on car chases and shoot-outs with the Algerian gendarmes; on feats of extraordinarily fast driving on treacherous desert tracks on starless nights; on the tremendous fortunes they will gain fast, the beautiful girls they will then court, the pockets overflowing with money. Yet drivers usually know as well as anybody else that despite the rare individual success stories known to all, these claims to personal autonomy are largely illusory, that they are 'the stupidest people in the world', as one put it in a thoughtful moment, who 'just risk their lives to make other people rich'. Still, as most other avenues for social mobility or just towards a decent livelihood have closed in the region, jobs as drug runners are pretty much irresistible to all those who have the necessary skills (and protective family networks) to undertake them.

For, as different as this kind of trade might look from age-old images of trans-Saharan trade, some of the basic structural constraints that have shaped transregional mobility for centuries are still in place. Most prominent is the need for security. The raiders of old have been replaced partly by Algerian security forces, who give chase to smugglers' cars and appropriate their loads and equipment, and partly by the many armed groups that have flourished in the region since the 2010s and who all levy 'road taxes', making the region difficult to navigate to all but locals. Drivers not only need to be able to drive fast and without headlights through often dangerous terrain, but they also need to know how to navigate complicated social terrain should they be caught. Successful smuggling requires social ties on both sides of the border, if only as a safety net when things go wrong (as they often do). As in the past, these social ties tend to be those of kinship; therefore, beyond tales of male heroism, women continue to be crucial for Saharan exchanges of all kind.

Take, for instance, the Ahl Sidi, northern Malian Arabs with close ties to Mauritania. When I spent time with them in the 2000s, the family was held together by a group of adult sisters whom marriage and the Sahel droughts of the 1970s and 1980s had scattered across the Western Sahara. The oldest sister was a successful tradeswoman, dealing mostly in cloth, in Nouakchott, the capital of Mauritania, and keeping an open house for those of her brothers desirous to pursue their education in Arabic. Her mother still lived in Gao, where she taught the Quran to the youngest girls of the family with the help of her stepdaughter, who also managed the family's local affairs in northern Mali. Two more sisters were settled in Adrar and in Bordj Badji Mokhtar in southern Algeria, where they had first moved as refugees and then stayed.

The men of the family continuously peddled between their sisters' houses: one owned a truck, another a *garāj* in al-Khalīl; the younger brothers worked as drivers for others, including, for the youngest among them, for the 'mafia'. This, however, they – or at least their older sisters – saw as an essentially temporary arrangement. They were hoping to earn enough money to buy their own trucks and then to invest both in livestock (herded by a cousin nearby) and in less risky forms of trade. This, they hoped, would eventually grant them the status they wanted: wealthy, well-established and thoroughly respected trans-border citizens – the kind who had, for centuries, been at the heart of the regional economy and society.

6

QADIS ON CAMELBACK

It is quite possible that all throughout the North
African past, one was always somebody's puritan or
heretic, much like one was always their nomad or
sedentist. And perhaps even their 'Arab' or 'Berber'.

Jacques Berque, 1954

The heat of the day finally abates and conversation picks up
again as our pickup truck speeds along the one straight, long
road. We pull into Talmin as the sun is setting over the dunes
that stretch as far as the eye can see. The qsar is hardly visible in
the evening light, its crumbling mud-brick buildings blending
into the surrounding dunes that are gradually reclaiming this
fragile outpost of human life. Nobody lives here anymore; the
qsar's former inhabitants have all moved to the modern village
that we saw on the main road before turning into the sandy
track that led us here. Over there, they have access to running
water and a primary school and, most importantly, the road
itself. They return periodically to visit their old houses, digging
them out from under the sand that piles up inside and blocks
doorways and gives the impression that somehow, the old qsar
was built for people smaller and nimbler than we are. The next
day, our host, Abdelmalek, will take us to his own family home,

built from mud brick many years ago. It still contains his grand-father's collection of manuscripts, mostly letters, contracts and other administrative documents, written neatly in locally pro-duced ink on small scrolls that were then rolled up tightly and stored in woven baskets hung from the rafters that hold up the low ceiling.

For now, however, we are heading to the centre of the qsar. It is already bustling with people, perhaps 200 of them, all men, all clad in white turbans and robes, in an atmosphere of quiet anticipation and excitement. Here and there, groups of men start humming and stop again. When it finally starts, the *ahellil* seems to come from nowhere. First there was small talk, chatter, greetings, movement; then suddenly everybody is intent on the same chant, ebbing and flowing, with a few drums beating to keep the rhythm, an occasional flute and rhythmic clapping of hands. It is pitch dark by now, no moon, no electricity, just stars and the flicker of burning cigarettes. Polyphonies develop, disappear. I recognise words, phrases I have heard elsewhere: religious invocations in Arabic, words repeated. Others remain totally obscure to me.

The night wears on. The chanting never seems to stop. When people step away from the circle of singers for a break, others seamlessly replace them. Most have put brown woollen burnouses over their white gandouras, with a pointed hood to protect them from the cold that gradually creeps in. Still no women in sight, although elsewhere they are regular partici-pants and indeed have their own version of the ahellil, called *tagerrabt*. At about 3 a.m., a bowl of food – *harīra*, thick chick-pea-and-lentil soup – materialises. There is a faint odour of marijuana. Somebody has lent me a burnous, too, and nobody seems to notice or perhaps rather show any interest in my pres-ence. I finally fall asleep, crouched next to a mud-brick wall on a pile of sand that is ice-cold to the touch. When I wake up in the early morning, I can see the first sunbeams outlining the dunes to the east of the qsar. The chanting is still going on, a little more quietly but unabated. As the sun rises, one after another, the men get up, pray, shake out their burnouses, thank each other and praise God, and disappear. By midday, Talmin is once more deserted.

In 2008, the 'ahellil of the Gourara' was inscribed on the UNESCO Representative List of Intangible Cultural Heritage as a 'Berber musical and poetic genre'. It had come to prominence in Algeria as a 'Berber tradition' in the late 1970s as northern Berber-speaking authors travelled south and were struck by its poetic beauty and richness. The first published version of texts was penned by the prominent Berber activist Mouloud Mammeri in 1984.[1] At that time, Berber activists were struggling against proponents of nation-wide Arabisation who tended to be associated – wrongly or rightly – with Islam. Their aim was to reclaim a place for their language and literature in independent Algeria and to prove that it had even deeper roots than the country's Islamisation and concomitant Arabisation. 'Islamisation' in this reading was seen as an external process that had imposed an alien religion and language on prior cultural and social relations, which, with careful restoration work, could still be salvaged. Mammeri therefore presented the ahellil as somehow prior to, and outside, Islam, an understanding that is clearly reflected in the UNESCO description. Yet, as pointed out by the anthropologist Rachid Bellil, for the performers themselves, the ahellil is above all else a religious duty and a spiritual experience.[2]

Both interpretations have their place in Algerian national politics and history, but what makes the ahellil transcend them is its sheer beauty. Only when it is heard – any online search will yield a selection – can a listener begin to understand how it is that it, and other practices like it, cannot be easily so contained. In fact, the categories put forward in the debates sketched above ('Berber', 'Arab', 'indigenous', 'foreign', 'religion', 'art') bear a promise of simplicity that they cannot fulfil. The realities they point to are so entangled that to pull them apart would be to destroy whatever they purport to describe and whatever we are trying to understand.

Much like the ahellil, Islam in the Sahara was never an artificial layer superimposed on local realities. It participated and still participates in every aspect of local societies and culture. At the same time, Islam is one and, like all other revealed religions, derives its spiritual appeal and claim to absolute truth from its universality. Trying to understand Islam in a region such as the Sahara – in which Islam is central to virtually all aspects of social and cultural life but which itself has long been marginal to the centres of Islamic learning and statehood – requires a careful balancing act between these two poles, the locally and historically particular and the universal, the many and the one. It also demands peeling away the many stereotypes that have been used to describe Saharan – or even 'African' – Islam for so long that these stereotypes have in some places become part of the thing itself.

To achieve this, we first must take a closer look at standard narratives of the 'Islamisation' of the Sahara and, through it, of the Sahel. Many of these stereotypes are currently revived in media coverage of 'radical Islam' in the area, and we can suspect that they are as incorrect with reference to the past as they are incapable of explaining the present. As matters of faith are difficult to assess retrospectively, we will then examine the cluster of institutions that in the region go under the name 'zāwiya' – their social, economic and political impact and their continuing relevance. This will also be the occasion to pick up the historical narrative from the 'Arab conquest' of the Sahara from the eighth to eleventh centuries as a way of tracing the historical genesis of the categories today used to (mis)interpret Islam in the region and their long-standing close entanglement both with local economies and with international politics.

Veni, Vidi, Vici

According to the traditional telling, the Sahara had always constituted a barrier to human exchange until North Africa was conquered by Arab troops from the East, first in the eighth century and then again from the tenth to the thirteenth centuries. Unlike their Phoenician, Greek, Roman and Byzantine imperial predecessors, these 'Arabs' knew how to deal with deserts and were exceptional camel- and horsemen. This allowed them to go further into the Sahara, a region that had been of little interest to earlier imperial armies. Although they never established a lasting hold on it, they opened the first trans-Saharan trade routes – or rather, their advance, and subsequent political rivalries in the Maghrib, pushed North Africans further and further into the desert until they had no choice but to become trans-Saharan traders. These traders were usually Muslim (with a few scattered Jews); wherever they travelled, the new faith travelled, too. Later missionaries followed their lead and succeeded, from the eighth century onwards, in converting the rulers of powerful states and empires in the Sahel belt to Islam – Kanem and Songhay from the ninth and eleventh centuries onwards, respectively – although their populations often remained recalcitrant to the new faith. Other rulers refused to convert but granted Muslim traders access to their markets and courts.

Our explorations of population histories and trade in chapters 4 and 5 showed that many if not all components of this narrative need to be questioned, not because they are in themselves wrong but because their simplicity hides more complex historical entanglements. As a rhetorical device, this story has nonetheless durably shaped the way in which 'Saharan Islam' is perceived by external observers as well as by Saharans themselves. It implies that geographically, Islam spread first along trade route corridors; that it was inherently urban, associated with a particular type of person, with trade and mobility; and that it was always opposed to a dimly perceived 'heathen' hinterland, to non-Muslims who were often more numerous and certainly militarily more powerful but who rarely figure in Islamic historiography as anything but a vague menace.

This narrative makes a number of important points. Islam was imposed not through conquest but through conversion; it was first adopted by a select few, who had to accommodate to living with the non-converted. Political power often remained in the hands of non-Muslims. This led to repeated conflicts and to categorical oppositions between particular groups, some strongly identified with Islam, some less so. In such a context, accusing others of lesser faith or orthodoxy was ordinary practice and infused most political endeavours, however worldly their stakes might have been. In some areas, the traders' missionary zeal was probably limited by their desire to trade in slaves, which meant that they needed to maintain a sizeable non-Muslim (or 'not-quite-enough Muslim') population within reach of their raids. As a result, 'Islamisation' was never, indeed never could be, complete. Instead, it was an ongoing process that provided a template for local distinctions, oppositions, hierarchies and exclusions and fundamentally influenced region-wide notions of political legitimacy as something acquired through *jihād* and (more or less violent) missionary activities. In this sense, the Sahara is an eternal missionary frontier, although it has been mostly Muslim for more than a millennium.

Saharan Islamic scholars – like rural scholars elsewhere – were, from the start, struck by the gap between Islamic normative expectations and the realities of their own lives. When Islam first emerged in seventh-century Arabia, it did so in a desert society some of whose constraints would probably have been recognisable to many Saharans. Subsequently, however, Islamic law and scholarship became primarily urban focused. Islam required a central state and contained a strong practical prejudice in favour of sedentary and urban life. Its centres of scholarship were situated far beyond the Sahara. Although the Sahara came to develop its own university towns, of which Timbuktu is just one albeit the best-known example, the resulting sentiment of marginality durably structured Islamic thought and sentiment in the region. Saharan scholars were often widely travelled and produced highly sophisticated scholarship, yet they knew that few of their eastern and even northern colleagues would ever repay their visits.

Although this standard narrative is no doubt true, it also glosses over many internal complexities. For one, it is teleological and unidirectional. It assumes that once a new faith has spread, people will never turn back: they will see the light and convert others in turn. Although missionaries might wish this to be true, it rarely is. It further assumes that faith is a 'thing' that you can carry along in your saddlebag, unchanged, and that will transform a local situation while itself remaining pristine. In actual fact, Islamic missionaries, like the Saharan traders described in the previous chapter, had to live with and in local societies, becoming part of them – if they had not already belonged there anyway. Historically, the most vociferous and militant among them were in fact locals, and Arabic was rarely their first language. This most certainly required myriad arrangements from which the convert, the missionary and the faith itself emerged transformed.

This narrative also derives a major blind spot through its focus on men and assumption that 'religion' and 'conversion' occur in public spaces. A settlement is said to have become Islamic when archaeologists identify traces of a mosque, for instance. Yet we know that due to the mobility of men, much of the social life and the cultural transmission in the Sahara is and probably always has been in the hands of women. 'Islamisation' was perhaps a matter of household management and education as much as of public display. The two might not necessarily coincide, but we can easily imagine how fundamental changes in inheritance patterns, marital strategies and female literacy might have had more far-reaching consequences for local social life than public prayer. Also, if Islam really was imported by 'foreign' traders, then women – their spouses – were probably the first to have been converted. Conversely, women were in the best position to amend their new husband's religious practices and to control how the new faith was (or was not) transmitted to their children.

A narrative of conversion through trade also leans too heavily on the urban. It is true that even today, Islam tends to be associated primarily with city life. But cities are only ever part of the story, and they could only ever survive – in the Sahara even more than elsewhere – if they maintained close relations to their rural surroundings. However much urban scholars might have thought that all of their neighbours were irreligious barbarians, they still needed people to protect them, fund their scholarly endeavours and bring food to their tables. We therefore need to understand this emphasis on cities as rhetorical, as an ideal towards which many in the Sahara strove all their lives, with varying success. Much as the presence of Arabs created 'Berbers' in North Africa, it was only the presence of Muslim towns that could create the 'rural barbarians' that surrounded them – and vice versa.

Most importantly, this narrative of incremental north-south Islamisation is problematic because it feeds contemporary prejudice. It encourages the imagination of an ongoing gradient of orthodoxy running from the East to the West and the North to the South. In this narrative, local populations – however they might be defined, as 'Berbers', 'Africans', 'nomads' or simply 'Blacks' – pre-exist Islam, which is then added to them, as a foreign imposition, by people who will always somehow be more Muslim than they can ever be. This 'lesser Muslimhood' is sometimes seen to be a function of the date of conversion – as if to live in a region that became Muslim 'only' two centuries ago would somehow predispose one to be 'less' Muslim than if it had happened eight or twelve centuries ago. We saw in chapter 4 that this argument was initially made and promoted by slave traders. It was then picked up by French colonial officers, who distinguished between 'Black' (nice, syncretic, accommodating of foreign rule) and 'white' (fanatical, orthodox) Islam; we should therefore be wary of it, as we should be wary of contemporary reiterations of similar prejudice. Let us therefore approach the Islamic tradition from a different angle, through the eyes of a somewhat exceptional early-twentieth-century Egyptian traveller.

Rose Gardens in the Desert

Born in 1889, Ahmad Muhammad Hassanein Bey was a man of many talents. His grandfather had been the last admiral of the Egyptian navy before the British colonised Egypt in 1882. His father was a professor at the prestigious Islamic University al-Azhar. Ahmad himself, in keeping with the times, was sent to Balliol College at Oxford University in 1910 and returned with a BA in law and an impeccable British accent and manners. He then started his long and fruitful career in the Egyptian civil service as secretary to the commander in chief of the British forces in Cairo in the troubled years of the First World War. One of his missions was to negotiate with the Sanūsiyya Sufi order, based primarily in the formerly Ottoman and now nominally Italian province of Cyrenaica, which was making trouble in Egypt's western confines. His diplomatic skill enabled direct military confrontation to be avoided, and Hassanein Bey developed a lasting friendship with the Sanūsiyya's leader, Sayyid Idrīs al-Sanūsī (the future king of Libya). Ahmad fenced for Egypt in the 1920s Olympics in Antwerp, acted as tutor to the Egyptian prince Farouk, became his chamberlain and head of the royal household as Farouk acceded to the throne, and secretly married Farouk's mother – all while developing a somewhat dangerous passion for early aircraft.

In 1923, he decided to travel to Kufra, now in southern Libya, to chart the last of the until then unexplored (by European travellers) Sahara and to map out the eastern borders of Egypt, disputed in this final bout of European imperialism.[3] After an arduous desert trek marred by incessant sandstorms – 'It is as though some great monster of fabled size and unearthly power were puffing out these hurtling blasts of sand upon the travellers' heads' – he finally reached his destination, where he was received with great pomp by the local Sanūsī representative, Sayyid Idrīs's cousin Muhammad al-ʿAbīd. He was immediately ushered into the shaykh's house, whose spaces seemed more richly adorned than ever with gorgeous rugs, many-coloured cushions and stiffly embroidered brocades. On the walls hung [his] collection of clocks, barometers, and thermometers in which my host takes naive delight. The clocks, of which there are at least a dozen of assorted shapes and sizes, were all going strong, and when they struck the hour, they very much reminded me of Oxford, with the endless variety of tones coming from all the church towers of the University town.

Here he was served 'a feast fit for the gods, or for mortals fresh from the monotonous living of the desert – lamb, rice, vegetables, delicious bread, rich Badawi cakes, sweet vinegar, sour milk, followed by coffee, milk with almond pulp beaten in it, and finally the ceremonial three glasses of tea, flavoured with amber, rose-water, and mint.' Indeed, as he noted with some irony, 'of all the dangers I encountered in the desert, Muhammad al-'Abīd's hospitality was, I think, one of the greatest! He had to produce fifteen courses for late breakfasts and dinners, and I exhausted all my sodium bicarbonate and indigestion tablets'.

Most of these delicacies had been grown locally, as, during the twenty-odd years of their presence, the Sanūsiyya had transformed Kufra from an isolated desert outpost – the 'chief centre of brigandage in the Libyan desert' – to a prospering agricultural colony. They 'grow melons, grapes, bananas, marrows, and other vegetables of the more delicate kinds, all of which are a great treat after the monotonous fare of the desert. They also raise mint and roses, from which they make rose-water and mint essence, so essential in their ceremonies of hospitality. From a few olive trees some olive oil is produced in primitive presses.' Physical labour was carried out by slaves, the majority of the residents of the zāwiya, leaving the Sufi *ikhwān* (brothers) free to pursue their religious studies, writing, teaching, prayers and ritual incantations.

The Sanūsī-induced prosperity and relative peace in the area had attracted trans-regional merchants to the oases, who had built their lavish houses right next to the zāwiya. Of an afternoon, they relaxed on their Persian rugs and silken cushions, listening to the latest Egyptian songs on their wind-up gramophone. As Hassanein Bey's fellow traveller the vivacious, intrepid and somewhat dishonest British divorcee Rosita Forbes concluded,

> Apart from the beauty of the valley, the interest of Kufara to the ordinary traveller lies not in any startling features, natural or architectural, for there is nothing unusual in the group of villages with their salt lakes and palms, but in the fact that in this oasis some 600 kms. from the outskirts of civilization, surrounded by formidable natural barriers, there exists a self-sufficient, self-supporting community, educated and intelligent, utterly remote from, almost oblivious of, the existence of the outer world.[4]

This, then, was the Sanūsī zāwiya at Kufra, just a year before the Italian army destroyed most of it through aerial bombing in 1931 as part of its brutal territorial conquest of Cyrenaica and Fazzān – but that is a different story.

Earlier in his text, Hassanein Bey had described zāwiyas in rather more sober terms, pointing to their three main functions: education, hospitality and devotion. 'A zāwiya', he wrote, 'is a building of three rooms: a schoolroom in which the Badawī children are taught by the ikhwān; the second serves as a guest house in which travellers receive the usual three days' hospitality of Badawī custom; in the third the ikhwān live'. The term 'zāwiya' originally referred to a corner in the mosque earmarked for teaching. It was then gradually extended to refer to purpose-built centres of learning, trade, exchange and agriculture. They were often, but not always, associated with Sufi orders. From the fourteenth century onwards, some started to contain the tomb of a holy man whose *baraka*, or blessing, infused it beyond his death and attracted pilgrims (and the poor and needy) from far and wide. Some of these might choose to settle for good, and many zāwiyas gradually turned into towns of the kind described by Hassanein Bey in Kufra (although the gramophones clearly were a later addition). Yet others were urban from the start, providing shelter from the hustle and bustle of city life.

Zāwiyas were thus primarily places of spirituality and study, retreats from ordinary life, knots of settlement and religious life in a hostile environment, sanctified by the presence of holy men (or more rarely women), dead or alive, and religious teachers. In terms of architecture, imagine a small mud-brick building surmounted by a pointed dome, usually white-washed, gleaming in the sun, surrounded by lush gardens, in startling contrast to the monotonous brown that stretches to the horizon. Zāwiyas were protected spaces, set apart from the chaos of the outside world, where everybody could find shelter: people on the run from exploitative tax-men, weary Saharan travellers, rival pretenders to the throne and badū and peasants in times of famine. True to their calling as sanctuaries, they presented thick, unadorned walls to the outside in keeping both with the tradition of fortified settlements (qsūr) and with that of militarised spiritual outposts or guard towers (*ribāt*).

Hassanein Bey's visit to the Sanūsī zāwiya in Kufra occurred at the end of the splendours of the pre-colonial zāwiya tradition, but let us briefly turn the clock back by almost a millennium to take a closer look at its beginnings. In the eleventh century, the large empires that had shaped early Islamic history – the Abbasids in the East and the Umayyads in Andalusia – were crumbling. The Sahara had been briefly brought into their orbit, enough for most Saharans to have some notion of Islam and of a faraway caliph, but not enough to impose any form of Islamic rule through the area. Cairo at that time was governed by the Fatimids, an originally Berber-speaking Shi'a empire, while most of the Western Sahara was structured by large, Berber-speaking tribal federations who did pretty much as they pleased. They were visited occasionally by renegades and refugees from the imperial orders in the East or by less-than-orthodox Muslim proselytisers setting up small and often short-lived urban communities in their midst and with their support.

Most locals were probably satisfied with this state of affairs. But not all. In the early eleventh century, as he returned from his pilgrimage to Mecca – where his eyes had been opened to the many shortcomings of arrangements in his natal region – the Berber chief Yahya b. Ibrahīm al-Gūdalī stopped at the prestigious university of Qayrawān (in what is now Tunisia) to ask the leading shaykh to lend him a missionary for his people back home. Nobody wanted the job, but the shaykh recommended a student from a remote teaching institute in the Moroccan Sūs: 'Abdullāh b. Yāsīn – perhaps himself a convert to the new religion, who was ready to go and confront the recalcitrant Berber-speaking tribesmen he knew so well from his own childhood.

As is often the case when a zealous reformer returns home with inflexible new ideas, things didn't quite work out. A few years later, in 1040, we find Ibn Yāsīn with an even more southerly group of Berbers, the Lamtuna, who grazed their livestock in the Adrar in present-day Mauritania, establishing a ribāt. Some say that this 'ribāt' refers to a fortress, constructed on an island in the Senegal River, where Ibn Yāsīn and his followers practiced ascetic devotion and military discipline, thereby launching the fashion for armed religious orders that was soon to sweep both North Africa and Europe (think of the Knights Templars, for instance). Others argue that Ibn Yāsīn and his followers quite simply practiced ribāt, that is, guard duty on the frontier with the infidels – who in this case were not the Portuguese or Spanish Christians but insufficiently converted Berbers.

Whatever they were doing, they were doing it well. Two decades later, the Almoravids (*al-murābitūn*, those of the ribāt) had conquered all of the Western Sahara, had founded Marrakech just north of the Atlas Mountains and were poised to invade al-Andalus. Which they then did, successfully, in 1086, not even fifty years after Ibn Yāsīn had first emerged onto the local scene.

The Almoravids were very clearly Saharans, and critics – especially in hoity-toity al-Andalus, centre of learning, culture and refinement in the Islamic world – incessantly poked fun at their cultural difference: with them, inheritance was passed on in the female line, women had great political weight and, as with contemporary Tuareg, men rather than women veiled. This earned the Almoravids the surname *al-mulathimūn*, 'the veiled ones', as well as endless jokes hinting at Almoravid gender confusion. The veiled man riding a camel and swinging a whip on Abraham Cresques's fourteenth-century map, described in the introduction, was perhaps the Almoravid leader Abu Bakr. The same figure appears on many maps of that time, sometimes Black, sometimes white, indicating a general lack of consensus, at least in Europe, on the racial ascription of the Almoravids – though great certainty with regards to the veil and the whip.

Barely a century later, the Almoravids were swept away by another Berber tribal federation with their own holy man (Ibn Tūmart, avid reader of Plato's Republic), this time from the Central Atlas Mountains. The Almohads (from the Arabic *al-muwahhidūn*, 'those who proclaim the oneness of God', that is, fight all forms of idolatry) claimed that rulers were not just military chiefs but also divinely guided imams and therefore infallible; that they were caliphs, who owed no allegiance to the Abbasid caliphs (the Prophet Muhammad's successors and representatives) in the East; that they embodied both physical and spiritual perfection; and that they even counted among themselves a *mahdī*, a divinely guided successor of the Prophet whose appearance announces the end of times. They forced everybody in their realm – which was considerable, stretching, like that of their Almoravid predecessor, from central Spain to the southern Sahara and from Morocco to Tunis – to convert: Jews, Christians and Muslims. (At a time when forced conversions of Muslims and Jews to Christianity were also all the rage north of the Iberian frontier.) They translated the Quran into Berber, adding a few lines here and there. They minted their own – square – coins and rewrote Almoravid history.

What they did not do, however, was abolish the ribāt, which they instead co-opted from the Almoravids for their own imperial projects. The legacy of this institution therefore remained, both in the name *mrābut* ('marabout'), still given to members of religious lineages and other religious specialists throughout North and West Africa today, and in regional toponymy from contemporary Spain and Portugal (hence the many 'Arrábias' to be found in those countries) to Mauritania via the Moroccan capital, Rabat. With the end of imperial warfare, the military

aspects of those ribāts gradually abated, as did centralised political control. They turned into zāwiyas, places of spiritual retreat,
without essentially changing their function, location or architecture. Many others were built on the same model, mostly on
the individual impulse of a prospective saint. By the fourteenth
century, it was indeed difficult to be recognised as a holy man
of any clout *without* the establishment and visible success of a
zāwiya.

The Almohad empire collapsed in its turn in 1269, leaving the
political scene to smaller kingdoms until the Ottoman, Spanish
and to a lesser extent Moroccan empires appeared on the scene
five centuries later. But like the Almoravids, the Almohads had
developed political ideas and built an institutional framework
that continued to shape regional political thought and practice
until at least the fifteenth century – if not today. The contemporary Moroccan sultan, for instance, still bears the Almohad
titles of *amīr al-muʾminīn* (prince of the faithful) and (infallible)
imām and is alone in the (Sunni) Muslim world in doing so; some
of the political vocabulary forged in this period of intense imperial expansion resurfaces today in radical Islamist pamphlets,
programmes and names. Both ʿal-murābitūnʾ and ʿal-mulathimīnʾ
have been recycled as group names by Islamists currently fighting
in northern Mali, indicating both the importance and the malle-
ability of historical references throughout the region.

Nodes in a Network

What can this tell us about zāwiyas as institutions? Although
there is much debate among historians about what the ribāt
actually represented – a particular kind of fortress, a militarised
monastery, a state of mind, a commitment, another word for
jihād – there can be no doubt that it is linked to the notion of

a sacred duty to protect the 'frontiers' of the *dār al-Islām*, the region where Islamic law holds sway. Whatever else they might have been, ribāts were forward positions in a hostile world. As such, they carried particular spiritual worth: several *hadīth*s (reports of the sayings and doings of the Prophet) claim that a few days of guarding a ribāt is the equivalent of a life of prayer and fasting (a hadīth that was, incidentally, cited by Usama Bin Laden when describing the peace and fulfilment he felt in the early 1980s when fighting the Soviet invasion of Afghanistan). In the Sahara, however, ribāts and zāwiyas were situated almost everywhere: along the former Roman limes, along trade corridors, at the meeting points of different trade networks and ecological zones – much like the oasis towns we saw in chapter 3.

This can tell us a lot about the status of the Sahara within the Islamic imagination, as an eternal missionary frontier but also as a place of particular spiritual value. It also goes some way towards resolving the fundamental puzzle of Saharan settlements. In earlier chapters, I asked why anyone would ever have been reckless enough to set up an oasis in the middle of the desert, given the usually small returns, great costs and hard labour involved in such an undertaking. The zāwiya tradition provides one answer: for anybody animated by the desire to retreat from civilisation in order to better implant it elsewhere, a desert outpost in the middle of nowhere holds immediate appeal. Spirituality here provides the necessary spark, making oases feasible where purely economic rationality tells us that they are not.

This, however, is a two-way process. As much as certain strategic locations held a particular appeal for would-be founders of zāwiyas, zāwiyas (like medieval monasteries in Europe) durably structured space by organising markets and fairs, attracting people and their labour, building irrigation systems, assembling caravans, mediating conflicts, creating roads and imposing their peace and protection. Empires and princes came and went, but their ribāt-zāwiyas remained. In outlying areas (and much of the Sahara is 'outlying'), they gradually took on many of the functions more usually attributed to the state: looking after the needy, storing grain for times of famine, dispensing education and promoting the law, ensuring the safety of roads and markets, fixing prices and raising Islamic taxes for their own benefit. Most importantly, they connected Saharan localities to others, providing gateways (through education, travel, literacy, libraries and trade) to the wider world: gateways through which travellers, students and pilgrims might depart and others, imbued with sacred knowledge and carrying heavy loads of manuscripts, might enter – or return, transformed.

Some of these connections were mediated by what in English is most commonly (and somewhat misleadingly) called a 'Sufi order' or 'brotherhood'. In Arabic, the word is *tarīqa*, literally meaning 'path': a privileged way towards God and true knowledge through the heart as well as the mind – although, as noted above, at least in the Sahara, Sufi tarīqas quite literally cleared pathways of a more physical kind. These 'paths' became institutionalised in northwest Africa from the fourteenth century onwards, barely a century after the Almohads' demise. At their most basic, they were a group of initiates around a holy man who had had a revelation, often in a dream, of a particular addition to the common forms of devotion, usually in the form of a text to be recited (*dhikr*, literally 'remembering') or a special form of prayer. Engaging in dhikr brought the holy man closer to God, and his disciples with him. There is thus much overlap, throughout the region, between Sufi and saint (*walī*, literally, a 'friend' to God, or somebody 'close' to Him): similar images of proximity and access pervade them both; both channel God's baraka to a world that badly needs it.

These special forms of devotion were passed on from shaykh to disciple, horizontally to disciples who might travel on or vertically to descendants and initiates, in such a way that Sufi tarīqas came to mimic genealogical networks, stretching far and wide through the Sahara. And like genealogical networks, they operated on different scales. Many of the smaller Sufi tarīqas had only a local impact. Others were affiliated with tarīqas with global reach, such as Shādhiliyya, founded near Fez in the twelfth century by yet another Berber-speaking holy man with global ambitions, or the Qādiriyya, founded in Baghdad at the same time, which spread through northwest Africa from the sixteenth century. Like genealogies, tarīqa affiliations structured space in particular ways: a disciple of one of the major Sufi orders, equipped with an introduction letter from his shaykh, would know where to stay and whom to speak to wherever he went. The Sanūsī zāwiya in Kufra during Hassanein Bey's visit was thus a late representative of a long-standing phenomenon.

Fast forward to the twenty-first century, to the Moroccan city of Fez. This is clearly no outlying embattled frontier post but rather one of the most ancient and holiest cities in northern Morocco and its sometime imperial capital. Its historic quarter was recognised as a UNESCO World Heritage site in 1986 and still houses the world's oldest still functioning institution of higher education, the mosque-university of al-Qarawiyyin. Nearby, one building stands out even here, with its richly decorated façade and turquoise-and-gold minaret: Ahmad al-Tijānī's zāwiya, built under his own guidance in 1789 and today the main spiritual centre of the Tijāniyya Sufi order.

Inside the zāwiya, people congregate, pray and approach Ahmad al-Tijānī's sepulchre. Some insist that any wish made here in good faith and a true state of devotion will be granted.

Others just enjoy the peace and quiet offered by the zāwiya. Women relax in the spaces set aside for them, chat in low voices or find time for a little snooze as their children play on the carpet that covers the floors from wall to wall. Activities pick up every day after the afternoon prayer as people assemble for the daily *wadhīfa*, or 'duty'. The men sit cross-legged on the floor around the rectangular main prayer room, facing each other and the current shaykh in their midst, and start reciting. The women, in an adjacent room, follow the men's dhikr via a microphone.

The participants are an eclectic bunch: young and old, some dressed in flowing robes, some in nylon shirts and pants, some in track-suit bottoms and jumpers; some with tight-fitting white skull-caps, others wearing turbans or with their heads bare. All chant in unison, repeating sacred invocations of God and the Prophet, slowly passing simple rosaries through their fingers. The repertoire seems inexhaustible, but the rhythm and voices grow in intensity and urgency as the chant goes on for ten, twenty, thirty minutes. Finally, the chanting peters out. A large white tablecloth is spread on the floor for the shared meal that marks the end of the wadhīfa.

During Ramadan and the annual *mawlid* (the Prophet's birthday) celebration, the atmosphere changes radically. Outside the zāwiya, large buses release hundreds of weary sub-Saharan pilgrims onto the car park, dressed in their finery, their expectations high. They head to the already overcrowded zāwiya while the Moroccan caretakers do what they can to keep order inside. The fences staking out male and female spaces have been removed; the courtyard and kitchens of the zāwiya ring with voices in Arabic, Berber, Wolof and other West African languages as women prepare the generous helpings of food, sponsored by the city's wealthy families, that are dished out to all visitors. Outside, lavishly dressed Senegalese ladies indulge in a spot of shopping in local shops and restaurants whose owners have learned to cater to their tastes while Moroccan girls look on in awe of their beauty and elegance.

Pilgrims come, pray, eat, visit the current shaykh and his family, leave a donation and return to their lodgings in the many boarding houses and hotels that have sprung up around the zāwiya to cater for them specifically, filled with enthusiasm and the shaykh's baraka. Others sleep in the zāwiya itself in quarters prepared for this purpose. The cohabitation of Moroccan disciples, West African pilgrims, the inhabitants of the medina and other migrants is not always easy. But it is essential: in Morocco, the Tijāniyya is but one, rather small Sufi order among others in a crowded spiritual field. In Senegal, on the other hand, almost half of the country's Muslim population are Tijānī; that is, they recognise Tijānī shaykhs as their principle spiritual guides, supplement their prayer with a special Tijānī litany and make donations to Tijānī shaykhs.

These West African constituents are crucial for the tarīqa, both economically and politically. Pilgrims come with generous funds, and the shaykh's trans-Saharan influence grants him considerable clout with the Moroccan sultan, who is much concerned with his own trans-Saharan spiritual influence ('soft power' in the current parlance) and never omits to take a substantial Tijānī delegation along on state visits to West Africa. This does not mean that the Tijāniyya and others have put themselves entirely at the service of national governments. Many of their transnational connections are in fact difficult to control, even for the shaykhs themselves. Baraka is not state power, and acts in mysterious ways, successfully promoting its own particular form of trans-Saharan connectivity in the contemporary world.

The pilgrims who crowd the zāwiya and the streets adjacent

to it care little about international diplomacy. More than half of them are women of all ages: the elderly, sent their by their adult children as a present and a sign of their own success in life; the young, eager to travel and discover the world, for whom a pilgrimage is an ideal occasion to escape, at least partly, their family's tutelage and to engage in a little bit of trading on the side. Others hope that the pilgrimage and the brief proximity to the saint it affords will advance their own scholarly careers back home. They might stay on for further study, perhaps in one of the many Moroccan institutes of higher education that cater specifically to West African imams. Yet others are primarily economic migrants and seek shelter in the zāwiya from the harsh realities of their everyday struggle. Even West African Christians can therefore be found, sheltering under the awning of the zāwiya, in a moment of respite from the outside world. Whatever national governments might make of it, the zāwiya tradition, transformed to cater to the needs of contemporary adherents, continues to weave people on either side of the Sahara into tight networks of solidarity and spiritual brotherhood.

Striving for Completeness

Northern Mali, 2009, very early morning. My blanket has slipped, and the intense early-morning cold wakes me up far too early. All that can be seen of the sun is a vague promise of greyish light on the horizon. I grumble internally, wrap the blanket over my head Saharan style to protect myself against the biting wind, and fall back into a light slumber, which is then immediately pierced by small voices reciting, rather sleepily, '*Al-bā taht-hu wahidun, al-tā, fawq-hu ithnayn* ...' (One [dot] under the b, two over the t ...). In the faint suspicion of morning light, the children of the family I am staying with, seven girls aged five to ten, crouch on a small heap of sand near their great-grand-mother Dida's tent. Dida is sitting cross-legged in front of them, wrapped in the dark blue indigo veil she likes to wear in winter, leading the lesson with a steady, high-pitched voice. The girls sway to and fro, studiously bent over their chipped wooden boards, chewing their reeds in concentration. I fall asleep again, lulled by their voices. When I wake up to full sunlight, all traces of the school have disappeared; the girls have returned to their usual wild games, and Dida has retreated to dignified silence in her tent.

A thousand kilometres further north, evening, a few months earlier. Khadija has sent me to collect her youngest daughter, Asma, to prevent her from dawdling on the way home, as she is wont to do. I approach the small side entrance to the shaykh's mud-brick house. Piles of plastic sandals outside the door indicate that the lesson is still in full swing. Through the door come the same sounds, the same rhythms that would wake me months later in northern Mali: '*Al-bā taht-hu wahidun ...*', sung in a cacophony of innumerable young voices. Asma comes out and runs towards me; she loves me mostly because I give her ample opportunity to mock my classical Arabic, which sounds so different from the dialect she speaks at home.

At five years of age, Asma just started primary school. In the evenings, however, she is sent, along with all her classmates, to the shaykh's house. As Khadija explains, there is no redundancy here, as the two forms of education serve very different purposes: one makes you a functioning citizen of the Algerian state, the other a good, or rather a 'complete', person. For Khadija, the knowledge of the Quran is intimately bound up with moral worth, which is in turn literally incorporated into language: you can speak proper Arabic only if you know how to recite the Quran; you can be a complete person only if you 'carry' the Quran, God's word, within yourself. Conversely, even if you memorise the Quran in your youth and you then turn bad, you will forget it, as the words will quite simply wither on your tongue. So says Khadija before getting up to scold Asma's older siblings, who have once again switched from the Quran recitation channel to *Tom and Jerry*.

Quranic education is often portrayed, in Western media and folk perceptions, as mere mindless rote learning, especially in areas where, as in parts of the Sahara, Arabic is not the children's first language. From Khadija's point of view, this criticism clearly misses the point: Western-style education might be about what one knows, but Quranic education is about what one is. As such, it is addressed to the heart and the body as well as the mind and transforms the whole person. Even tiny babies are playfully taught to say *Bi-smi 'llāh* (In the name of God) before they eat and *Al-hamdu li-llāh* (Praise be to God) afterwards. Everyday speech is saturated with small pious phrases, literally invoking the sacred at any turn and involving it deeply in all social relations, to the point that Khadija is right: it is indeed difficult to speak Arabic correctly, from the local point of view, without at least oblique reference to a vast world of spirituality. From this point of view, questions of literal comprehension are neither here nor there.

Education was one of the main purposes of Saharan zāwiyas. In much of the Sahara, basic Quranic education for boys and girls was simply the norm and small Quranic schools a feature of even the smallest settlements. Although most students attended school for only a few years, leaving after they had acquired basic literacy and enough knowledge of the Quran to fulfil their religious duties, a few went further and enrolled in higher education in Islamic letters, grammar and law. This usually meant leaving their home qsar to travel to one of the prestigious zāwiyas of higher education, perhaps in the Algerian Tuwāt, home to Khadija and her family, or the Mauritanian Adrar. There they would meet students from throughout the region or even beyond: far from being the stereotypical barbarian hinterland of urban Islamic lore, some parts of the Sahara were exceptionally well provided with higher-level teaching institutes, attracting students from far and wide.

Once they had completed their curriculum, most students became teachers, scribes or qadis, locally in other Saharan settlements or encampments or even in the cities on the coast, where many scholarly families still bear the surname 'al-Tuwātī'. Those who wanted to pursue their studies further had to travel on to the centres of Islamic learning on the North African coast, or even as far as Cairo and Mecca. Many never returned, and all great centres of Islamic learning still contain recognisable northwest African communities. For those who didn't make it that far, the act of travelling could itself be an eye-opener: remember the seventeenth-century Moroccan scholar al-'Ayyāshī, who spent many days of his Saharan journey arguing the finer points of Islamic law with his colleagues. Travelling in such company was in itself an education.

Another option was to bring knowledge back in the form of manuscripts, leading to the constitution of manuscript libraries in places like Timbuktu, of course, but also, and less famously, scattered throughout Saharan qsūr and even nomadic encampments. In a context where every single sheet of paper had to be imported on camelback, manuscripts were precious possessions; many a zāwiya's account books still bear witness to the sad destiny of shaykhs who ruined themselves by travelling to far-flung markets to acquire them or neglected their other duties while lying in wait for caravans that might be able to sell them the one manuscript they had been hankering after for years.

Similarly, maintaining a group of people who spent some or all of their lives dedicated to study required a considerable and sustained investment to finance their education, to take a large number of adult men permanently out of the pool of productive labour and to create and fund the institutions that permitted them to pursue their calling. In the heartlands of Islam, these institutions – schools, libraries, scribes, courts – were usually funded or at least under the control of central states, although religious foundations (*awqāf*) also played an important role. In the Sahara, where states were few and far between and loath to spend any money on those whom they mostly considered to be 'barbarians', all of these institutions had to be paid for either privately – usually through endowments – or by local political institutions, most commonly local assemblies (whose role in irrigation was mentioned in chapter 2 and which will be discussed further in the next chapter).

The Algerian Tuwāt is, once more, an extreme example. From at least the late seventeenth century onwards, its inhabitants independently funded a large number of qadis and set up sharī'a courts. They even maintained a council of legal experts (*muftīs*) for hard cases. As the French colonial officers conquered the oases in the first years of the twentieth century, they noted with astonishment that there was 'a qadi in every qsar' (a judge in every village), many of which, as we know from other sources, at that time contained barely 200 inhabitants. And this was even without mentioning the many *tālibs*, or Quranic schoolteachers, found in even the smallest of settlements or the notaries drafting written contracts for even the most insignificant of local transactions, in the process filling the baskets with tightly rolled scrolls of the kind I saw hanging from the rafters in

Talmin. All of this in a context where people clearly knew each other intimately and most likely had other ways of managing affairs than the rather rigid categories of formal law and were living hundreds of kilometres from any state power that might enforce the law in any meaningful way.

This high density of Islamic legal professionals posed innumerable practical problems. Take, for instance, one example gleaned from a collection of legal questions put before the chief qadi of the Tuwāt in the eighteenth century. A qadi decides to move to a small qsar that until then had not had its own court. Initially pleased, the villagers provide him with a space to hold court and a house in which to live with his family. But they soon regret his arrival. Whereas before, life was quiet and peaceful and everyone, including women, could circulate freely in the qsar's narrow streets without having to worry that they might run into a stranger, now, the clamour of judicial disputes can be heard day and night, say the plaintiffs, and strangers travel daily to the qsar to have their cases heard. Worse, local custom obliges villagers to extend three days' hospitality – food and lodging – to all who come to see the judge. Instead of tending their gardens, they now spend their days looking after unwanted guests, who eat up all the food they had set aside for leaner times. If this goes on any longer, they say, perhaps somewhat melodramatically, it can end only in famine.[5]

This problem occurs only once in the hundreds of pages of jurisprudence produced by Tuwātī legal scholars, but we can surmise that it was of general concern: the law, if nothing else, is costly and attracts potentially troublesome outsiders. Why, then, did people go to all this trouble? One answer might be that the presence of a judge yielded practical benefits. Legal disputes were decided more quickly and efficiently; the resulting peace of

mind and more rational social organisation made it all worthwhile (this is roughly the argument that has come to justify the
existence of a highly legalised state apparatus in Europe). The
only problem with this answer is that it was quite clearly untrue.
Law did not simplify but rather complicated matters.

Take, for instance, the thorny issue of inheritance. Islamic
law grants each heir an equal share, with daughters receiving half
shares. Now place this in a context of small plots of land and
heightened mobility of both sons (as traders and scholars) and
daughters (as wives). You can easily imagine how, even within
two generations, this combination potentially threatens the survival of any form of viable oasis horticulture as tiny plots are
split up and land and water are passed on to absentee owners,
non-resident husbands or, worse, 'strangers' who married into
the family. This is of course an issue for agriculturally based
Muslim communities everywhere; in many cases, people have
found legal ruses to obviate at least the problems of female
inheritance. In the Tuwāt, fathers clearly encouraged daughters
to 'donate' their inheritance if they married out of the community, but not all did, and the law stood.

In the eighteenth century again, a local qadi is confronted
with the following case: a local landowner's son, let's call him
'Abd al-'Azīz, left his home qsar to become a trader in the *bilād
al-sūdān* ('land of the Blacks', in this case probably northern
Mali). He stayed for many years, married a local woman and had
a daughter. He then returned to his home qsar, inherited part of
his father's land and passed away. Years later, another trans-Saharan trader shows up in the qsar, brandishing a document by
which he asserts that he has bought parts of the land from 'Abd
al-'Azīz's Sudanese daughter, his rightful heir, and that some
of the family's prosperous garden is thus his by law. The qadi
vigorously refutes this claim, using all possible and impossible

legal arguments at his disposal.[6] But one wonders: surely this was not just a onetime occurrence but a constant threat. How many 'Sudanese daughters' (and sons) did Tuwātī traders sire over time? How many came to the Tuwāt to claim their inheritance? And what could be done about this?

Given these difficulties, it is perhaps not surprising that qadis' judgements and other legal provisions were often honoured primarily in the breach. But then, why have them in the first place? The answer lies perhaps in the overall paradox sketched in this chapter: how did the Sahara, considered by urban scholars as at best a missionary frontier, at worst an unruly wilderness, produce so many religious institutions, tarīqas, manuscript libraries and scholars who could vie with the best of their peers throughout the Islamic world? Why did it produce such a surplus of Islamic scholarship in the middle of the desert, where *any* kind of surplus is downright miraculous? The faithful would probably point to God's baraka and not be completely wrong. The frontier produced missionary zeal and the consciousness of being judged deficient. This encouraged sincere local investment in sharī'a – in endless attempts by locals to lift themselves out of the cursed state of ignorance to which the environment (and northern prejudice) seemed to relegate them.

Contemporary Quarrels

On 22 August 2016, Ahmad al-Faqi al-Mahdi, a member of the northern Malian Islamist organisation Ansār al-Dīn, was brought to trial before the International Criminal Court (ICC) in Brussels, accused of war crimes by the Malian government. He was indicted for leading the destruction of nine shrines and parts of the Sidi Yahya mosque in Timbuktu, one of which was a UNESCO-certified World Heritage site. He was sentenced to nine years in prison and fined €2.7 million in compensation for his victims, although the identity of these victims was not specified in the judgement. By 2015, in any case, the shrines had been re-built with UNESCO funding, and a ceremony was held to hand the keys back to their 'traditional owners'.[7]

The physical destruction of zāwiyas has become something of a trademark of radical Islamists throughout the region (and beyond: as noted above, Afghanistan, also a frontier region, shares both a similar zāwiya tradition and attraction to would-be mujahidin). In Western media, these incidents tend to be described as radical, dynamite-toting foreigners attacking local heritage, which is seen as standing for 'moderate Islam'. The destruction of manuscripts in Timbuktu tends to be read in the same vein and for many clearly put 'Islamist terrorists' beyond the pale of any civilised intercourse, even more so than their other unpleasant habits – the terrorising and killing of civilians. These attacks were cited as irrefutable proof of Islamists' ignorance and hostility towards learning, knowledge or even 'Islam' itself.

This interpretation might be partially true, but as always, things were rather more complicated. Ahmad al-Faqi al-Mahdi was in no way a 'foreigner' ignorant of local tradition but was very much home-grown. He hailed from the suburbs of Timbuktu, where many nomadic pastoralists had been forced to settle during the droughts of the 1970s and 1980s. These suburbs were often little more than makeshift slums, and their inhabitants still remain excluded, socially and economically, from the heart of the city. He blew up the shrines of saints whose prestige, like that of all other Saharan saints, derived from their foreign origin and their inscription in a religious topography that was anything *but* local. Rather, it reads like a list of the most prestigious centres of learning in the Islam world – many of them places which by now have become virtually inaccessible to ordinary Malians. Sidi Yahya himself was reputedly from Andalusia.

We can surmise that the real targets of Ahmad al-Faqi's wrath were not the shrines themselves but the saints' contemporary descendants. Centuries after the saints' demise, these people are still at the heart of the current Timbuktu elite. After all, shrines, like zāwiyas, are, as we have seen throughout this chapter, not just monuments to the dead but also active nodes in vast networks of power and wealth. They stand not only for a particular form of religiosity – which, as we have seen, can vary from one zāwiya to the next and over time – but also for a particular socio-economic and political order in which people like Ahmad al-Faqi can only occupy an inferior position. Islamic reformism of the kind that usually inspires attacks on shrines states that everybody, regardless of origin, race, class or status, can achieve direct access to Islamic knowledge without the intercession of local elites. This, then, was a conflict not between nasty universal ideas and cosy local realities but between different kinds of universalisms and the harsh local socio-economic realities they have long legitimised.

Although Ahmad al-Faqi's means of action were radical, he was in no way alone in his hostility. For many contemporary Saharans and North Africans, zāwiyas stand not just for 'superstition' but for a 'feudal' past and its hierarchical prejudice that it is high time to abolish. This perception is made worse by current attempts by all North African and many West African governments to instrumentalise the zāwiya tradition for their own (usually conservative and deeply authoritarian) ends, for instance, by using them to gather votes and for electoral campaigns. In exchange, they often promise funds and the restitution of land that was nationalised earlier. If we consider that zāwiyas have, over time, accrued considerable power as landowners and in many cases as slave-owners, there is in fact much for ordinary people to worry about in the current alignment of interests between authoritarian governments and revived Sufi orders and their zāwiyas.

We seem to have come a long way from the sleepy qsar of Talmin and the eerie beauty of the ahellil as it ebbs and flows through the Saharan night. Yet as much as the ahellil was both intensely local and invoking the universal and absolutely crucial to the making and survival of Talmin as a place, the question of Islam in the Sahara will always overflow any neat conceptual cage that we might wish to impose on it. Criticisms levelled today against the zāwiya tradition are not just about 'theology', the opposition between spiritual and juridical approaches to a godly life, or even just divergent interpretations of orthodoxy. They are primarily, perhaps, about political and social power, the kind of social order people wish to live in and the relation between spiritual and worldly truth and influence – questions that were already hotly debated among the Almoravids and the Almohads in the eleventh and twelfth centuries and that will probably never find definitive answers.

PART THREE

MARGINS OF EMPIRE

7

LAND OF DISSIDENCE

Government is an institution which prevents injustice
other than such which it commits itself.
Ibn Khaldūn, *Muqaddima*, 1377

In the last week of January 2012, the small settlement of Zouar,
wedged between the Chadian borders with Niger and Libya,
was teeming with cars. This was unusual: Zouar is located in
the foothills of the Tibesti Mountains, the Sahara's highest
mountain range. This makes it a stunningly beautiful place but
also one that is difficult to access. The busy trans-Saharan route
that connects Chad to Fezzan in southern Libya runs instead
through the improvised marketplace of Zouarké on a dusty
plain 30 kilometres further east. Few people have any reason to
visit Zouar's few administrative buildings (unfinished, largely
abandoned or both), the handful of mud-brick dwellings or the
former French – or was it Ottoman? – military fort that has
proved surprisingly resilient to the passage of time, all of these
far too scattered throughout the valley to form what one would
describe as a village.

On this particular day, however, people, most dressed up
rather elaborately in white robes and impressive turbans, were
coming and going in the vast spaces between the few houses.

Soldiers were parading in four-wheel-drives with sawn-off roofs and bundles of rockets stuck to their sides. The few market stalls were for once thriving, with traders hardly knowing how to keep up with business. The new *derdé*, or 'customary chief' of the Teda (a sub-group of the Tubu), who straddle the border area between Chad, Libya and Niger, was about to be officially 'enthroned', and Zouar was where the ceremony would take place. Everybody who was anybody among the Teda had to be present. With profound political changes in neighbouring Libya – Qadhafi had just been ousted and killed, with Western military support – everybody knew that a new political order was about to be negotiated throughout the region, but nobody really knew what it would look like.

People flocked to Zouar to pay their respects to the new derdé. He, however, hardly looked the part of a future regional power broker: he was a fragile-looking elderly man, crouching on a mat on the floor in the house put at his disposal for the occasion, still looking rather surprised by the honour that had suddenly been thrust upon him. Many people who had ostensibly come to witness his enthronement did not even bother to pay their respects to him. They stayed in the vast camp set up for the occasion twenty minutes' walk away, where guests were housed in large shared tents made out of mats, segregated by sex and marked out according to their socio-economic status: the more important the temporary resident, the bigger the tent, the fewer people had to share it, the more food was brought in and the more impressive the arsenal of guns displayed outside. Here, negotiations went on day and night.

The camp was, by local standards, lavishly equipped, bearing witness to the wealth recently accumulated in the area by trans-border traders. The tents contained carpets, hangings, heavy Libyan blankets (one of the central prestige objects

in every Teda bride's trousseau and a great comfort in cold
Saharan nights) and twice as much perfume, skin cream, oil,
incense and henna as all the women present could possibly use.
Nobody really bothered washing up dishes, as there were always
new ones to hand; vast quantities of fizzy drinks replaced the
usual murky well water, with empty cans piling up. Food almost
uniquely consisted of sweets, imported chocolates and meat,
in striking contrast to the usual boiled flour or Libyan pasta.
Thirty-five camels had been killed to honour the derdé, more
than ever before, or so it was claimed. The place where they had
been slaughtered near the campsite was running with blood,
and everybody's belly was pleasantly filled with fresh boiled
intestines and meat, washed down with unlimited helpings of
tooth-tingling sweet tea.

On the day of the ceremony, 29 January 2012 – by which time
the party had already been going on for several days – everybody
dressed up at their most beautiful. Those who could flocked to the
local 'landing strip', a flat piece of ground surrounded by acacias
4 kilometres from the village, to welcome the official delegation
flown in for the occasion from N'Djamena on two French and
one Chadian military transport planes. About a hundred official
guests arrived in this way, most of them Chadian, including the
ministers of the interior and of culture and other high-ranking
civil servants. Among the foreigners invited for the occasion
were several members of the French embassy and military
detachment, the US ambassador and his wife, and the EU representative in Chad. International attention to this celebration
of the 'Teda community' and of the central figure supposed to
hold it together, at least symbolically, was clearly of some importance to the organisers. The international guests clearly thought
that they were witnessing a key moment in the redistribution of

power in the border region, one in which 'traditional authorities' rather than state officials were calling the shots.

The members of the delegation from N'Djamena were ushered to chairs in the shade of a small purpose-built shelter facing an empty pad of soil guarded by armed soldiers, 2 or 3 kilometres west of Zouar. The derdé was carried in on a chair and set down next to his newly-wed (third) wife on a small mound of sand covered with a carpet at the foot of a big acacia tree. Palm leaves were brought in and then a short whip made of wood and leather with which the derdé nonchalantly beat the air around him. The crowd of spectators, overpowering the many police officers and soldiers, had drawn in. People were jostling to get a good view, the youngest among them trying to get as close as possible without being hit or pushed back. The aim of the game was to touch the derdé, never mind where, or to be photographed next to him. It was impossible to see anything from the official seats, and people were gesticulating wildly as they attempted to catch a glimpse or even film these moments, said to be the heart of the ceremony.

Meanwhile, the minister of civil service had launched into a speech, in French, reminding those (few) who cared to listen that the derdé was an employee of the Chadian state. His voice was drowned out by the crowd, who clearly had little time or patience for any display of state power; indeed, who loudly wondered why the minister had bothered to show up at all at what they considered to be a celebration of long-standing Teda autonomy and self-governance. Elaborately dressed camels were ridden straight through the crowd. Praise-singers started playing their drums, well aware that their singing was inaudible in the general turmoil. Women pushed forward to pay their respects to the derdé's second wife in her tent (she had been 'Miss Chad' many years before); others started to pack up and leave, as there was no sign of the orderly singing and dancing announced in the official programme, although especially younger women and girls had eagerly looked forward to this occasion to display their finery.

Dancing finally took place in the evening. The young women and praise-singers took turns singing, illuminated by small electric torches and the blinding headlights of the many jeeps parked nearby. For many, this was what the ceremony was really about: an occasion to party, to show off, to flirt. The praise-singers made up for lost time and sang until late at night, to the greater glory of everybody generous enough to remunerate their efforts. Giving money to singers is a public act and inherently competitive. This time, amounts quickly went up, reaching up to 1 million CFA francs (1,700 USD) handed out by local smugglers 'in blocks of money', or so people whispered in awe. Those, men and women who had carefully prepared their bundles of fresh-from-the press 1,000- or even 5,000-franc notes hence had no occasion to use them and put them back into their pockets or handbags (bought for the occasion) with a resigned shrug. Far from there, the derdé was squatting on the ground, talking to an old lady. People who walked past greeted him simply, clearly much more interested in the party than in the old man.

African states seem to be failing. Consult any edition of the Fragile State Index, produced annually by the World Peace Foundation, and you will not only see pictures of northern Mali on their title page but also much of the African continent, tinted an alarming hue of bright red ('very bad'), on their maps. Conflict seems to be everywhere, and to even speak of 'African states' conjures images of corruption, stagnation, fragility or the kind of wild jostling for power by various local and regional strongmen that the derdé ceremony seems to exemplify. International bodies such as the EU therefore not only send delegates to out-of-the-way places to attend 'traditional' ceremonies such as this one, hoping (and usually failing) to find more reliable and effective intermediaries in the 'traditional authorities' who stage them, but also invest millions of dollars in programmes to 'strengthen' regional states, especially by shoring up their military and coercive apparatuses. To little avail, it seems, as with every dollar spent on African 'security', insecurity seems to actually increase – as we will see, in more detail, in chapter 9.

In the early 2000s, the Ugandan political scientist Mahmood Mamdani noted that 'the African state' is, with a few modifications, the state left behind by European empires.[1] Perhaps, then, we should pause to think before we shed tears for the demise of state machineries established by colonial powers mostly for extractive and coercive purposes and instead adopt a strictly empirical and agnostic approach. Might not the one-size-fits-all notion of 'state failure' hide a much more complex political history and obscure actually existing political arrangements? Rather than state failure, might the derdé ceremony not be part of a different but nonetheless coherent political order in the region, one which global narratives struggle to contain?

In order to find elements of an answer to these questions in the Sahara, we need to look both at the genesis of states in the region and at alternative political traditions. Saharans have for centuries, if not millennia, lived in the vicinity of states without necessarily submitting to their rule, at least not all the time and everywhere, developing complex forms of exercising political power and ordering their collective lives. Local states have had to come to terms with these alternative traditions, shaping both states and their margins in specific ways. Mamdani might be right that much of the African state is colonial, but colonial states themselves were locally specific and born out of endlessly negotiated compromises between local power holders and European invaders. In many cases, they also drew on and co-opted pre-existing political traditions, some of which – like the derdé – now seem to 'reappear' in moments of crisis. In this chapter, we will therefore pick up the historical narrative in the late sixteenth century, a time when the deep foundations of many contemporary Saharan states – and the non-state political structures with which they had to contend – were first laid.

The Age of Empire

On 30 May 1591, Timbuktu was forced to open its gates to Jawdar Pasha (né Diego de Guevara), leader of a motley crowd of Moroccan and Andalusian soldiers, English sharp-shooters and other European renegades, slave soldiers or re-enslaved Moroccan harātīn, all fighting in the name of the Moroccan sultan Ahmad al-Mansūr. Jawdar Pasha had left southern Morocco more than six months earlier with an army of 4,000, many of whom had perished on the way or reached the Niger River in anything but fighting shape. Despite their losses, they had beaten the army of the Songhay empire, to which Timbuktu then belonged, in the famous battle of Tondibi, mostly because they had firearms and the Songhay did not. After a few months under Moroccan rule, the city of Timbuktu rose in revolt. Having crushed the rebellion, the Moroccans forced the entire population, including the Islamic scholars who had until then been the de facto political leaders of the city, to swear an oath of allegiance (*bayʿa*) to their new sultan.

After they had all assembled in the city's great Sankoré mosque to pronounce their oath, the Moroccan commander stealthily closed the gates of the mosque, in one stroke depriving the city of its elite. Most were permitted to return home after a few days, but seventy were sent into exile to Marrakesh, where they arrived in chains in spring 1594, many never to return. One of these prisoners was Ahmad Bābā al-Timbuktī, whose opinions on race and enslavement we considered in chapter 4. Ahmad Bābā's fame was such that even in his place of confinement in Morocco, he attracted a large number of students and fellow scholars who avidly listened to his weekly lessons, despite his pronounced stutter. Al-Mansūr kept Ahmad Bābā under house arrest until his own death in 1603. By the time the scholar returned home, the Moroccan presence in Timbuktu was all but forgotten: a new group of rulers, the Arma, had taken over, claiming to be descendants of Moroccan soldiers (another example of the 'spliceability' of genealogies noted in chapter 4). Timbuktu's scholarly circle, however, never quite recovered.

What did Ahmad al-Mansūr want in Timbuktu? For contemporaries, the answer was obvious: he wanted gold. Indeed, after his conquest of Timbuktu, he added al-Dhahabī, 'the golden', to his earlier surname, al-Mansūr, 'the victorious'. He probably also wanted slaves, partly but not exclusively to staff his army. Rather, he wanted to control trans-Saharan trade routes, which brought him both. Officially, the quarrel between him and the Songhay emperor had started over the right to levy taxes on salt extracted at the mines of Teghaza, halfway between Timbuktu and Morocco, so he probably wanted some taxes, too. Lastly, and this was what he told Ahmad Bābā when he finally granted him an audience, he wanted to unify the Islamic world, as befitted his status as righteous caliph, leader of all the faithful, right on time for the new Islamic millennium.

In all this, al-Mansūr was a man of his time. The Christian 'reconquest' of the Spanish peninsula had been completed, barely a century earlier, with the fall of Granada in 1496. The

Spanish (or rather the Habsburgs) were now putting pressure on the North African coast, establishing one fortified outpost (*presidio*, but we could also call them ribāt) after another, all the while looking west towards their new possessions in the Americas. Imperial conquest was in the air. Barred by the Spanish and the Ottomans from going north or east, al-Mansūr turned the only way he could: south to Timbuktu. Although al-Mansūr's actual domination of the former Songhay empire was brief, lasting barely twenty years, the imperial effort it implied, and the restructuring of his state and army that preceded it, laid the foundations for the modern state of Morocco.

Thirteen years earlier, in 1578, the sultan of the Ottoman empire, Murad III, who, like al-Mansūr claimed the title of caliph, sent a letter to Birni Ngazaramu, capital of the Kanem-Bornu empire, in response to an earlier Bornuan embassy. Ibn Furtū, the leading imam of the city, who witnessed the receipt of the letter in person, was delighted, as he believed that this proved his own emperor's greatness and recognition as an equal by what had by then become the major Mediterranean power. Diplomatic relations between Bornu and the various powers that had claimed to rule the Maghrib were long-standing: an earlier Bornu emperor had sent a giraffe to the Hafsid king in Tunis in the early thirteenth century at a time when Kanem-Bornu stretched all the way to Fazzān in what is now southern Libya and nobody had even heard of the Ottomans. Mai Idris had also long imported muskets from North Africa and probably also European slaves who knew how to work them.

The Ottoman chancellery has a copy of Murad III's letter, penned in Arabic. It indeed contained 'the bestowal of a greeting, perfuming the regions by the wafting of its odours'. Beyond this, however, we can see that, then as now, successful diplomatic relations over time require a working misunderstanding: Murad addressed Mai Idris as a 'king' (*mālik*) and an 'honourable person of princely rank' but also as the governor of one of his provinces (a clear demotion) and exhorted him to work 'in the most faultless harmony' with his colleagues, the Ottoman governors of Libya's southern provinces. He also rejoiced in his, Idris's, recognition of Murad's 'brilliant' and 'shining Caliphate' and dispensed advice on how best to govern his – both of their – subjects. For Ibn Furtū, on the other hand, the Bornu empire was clearly the centre of the world, Mai Idris not a king but the caliph himself and the Ottomans a peripheral power.

Ibn Furtū can be forgiven for his parochialism. After all, when Mai Idris sent his embassy to Istanbul, the Ottomans were but newcomers to the region. Asked by local dignitaries for help against the Spanish threat, they had taken Algiers in 1519, Tripoli (from the Knights of St John) in 1551, Tunis in 1572 and Fazzān in 1577. It was probably the last of these events which triggered the original Bornu embassy. Mai Idris clearly wanted to see where exactly he could position his own realm within the new world order. And he judged rightly. The Ottomans were there to stay; their arrival was part of a broader imperial reshuffling in northwest Africa which shaped the political landscapes that we still know today, laying the foundations of the three contemporary nation-states of Algeria, Tunisia and Libya, all former Ottoman regencies.

So far so good for the 'big history' of the Sahara and its margins at the cusp of the long seventeenth century. By then, the whole region clearly was surrounded, north and south, by large empires with global reach or at least ambitions. But what do we mean when we speak of 'empires'? To what extent, beyond mutual diplomatic recognition, were the Ottoman and the Bornu empires instances of the same thing, and is it useful to think of them as states, direct precursors of their contemporary avatars in the region?

Conventionally, an empire is defined as a 'state of states', and an emperor is a 'king of kings'. By this measure, it is not clear whether any of the early modern North and West African empires – including the Moroccan and Ottoman but also the Songhay and Bornu – really qualifies, as they were often superimposed on pre-existing political structures but not necessarily on states. Nor are they themselves best described as 'states' if we consider the latter to correspond to the Weberian ideal type: an organisation that holds a monopoly on legitimate force over a given territory or indeed a centralised administrative apparatus relying on regular taxes. Many of the northwest African empires were rather more fluid and mobile entities with no borders or limited territory, based on control over people rather than land. They rarely held a monopoly on legitimate violence but tacitly delegated local peacekeeping to others. They did not rely much on the taxation of peasants. Instead, they produced and reproduced themselves through slavery: by raiding slaves and selling them on or by settling them on uncultivated land in agricultural colonies that owed tribute directly to the emperor.

We should not see this as an 'African failure' to produce 'proper empires' but rather as an invitation to rethink our own political models, heavily influenced by the legacy of Roman and then European imperial history. Many empires in world history were probably rather more similar to northwest African polities, and they did not necessarily evolve into states as we know them today. Nor was their lack of territorial fixity a shortcoming: rather, given their universal aspirations, to reduce empires to their geographical expression was to demean them. For Murad III, to be addressed as 'the lord of Istanbul' or 'the king of Turks' would have been an insult. Similarly, the sultan of Morocco was, like his Almohad predecessors, *amīr al-muʿminīn*, the leader of *all* the faithful, and his spiritual realm did not necessarily overlap with the (rather limited) area that was under his direct political control. Which is why, at Moroccan independence, the borders of Morocco were so heavily disputed, as members of the Moroccan independence movement wanted the new nation-state to cover much of their sultan's pre-colonial spiritual realm, including parts of northern Mali, Algeria, Mauritania and of course Western Sahara.

Premodern empires nonetheless had a lasting impact on the political, cultural, social and linguistic landscape of northwest Africa. They participated in global networks of exchange, funnelling funds to them and reaping profits from them. Based on conquest, they divided populations into more or less well-defined status groups, often personally linked to the ruler. Examples of occupational groups with roots in imperial history are praise-singers and metalworkers, who still exist as recognisable and often in-marrying groups throughout West Africa, and *makhzan*, or 'government', tribes in the Maghreb. Empires created slaves, and therefore also freedmen and -women, on a large scale. They produced many of the people and languages that still structure northwest African landscapes through more or less forcible incorporation. Most importantly, perhaps, they restructured conceptual spaces, dividing them between political heartlands and their peripheries – including the greatest periphery of all, the Sahara, whose economy and people were central to all of the northwest African empires but always just beyond their reach.

Barbarians at the Gates

In summer 1962, the secretary of the assembly of the Algerian qsar of Tit faced a conundrum. Algeria had just been granted independence after eight years of brutal warfare, most of which – praise be to God – had taken place hundreds of kilometres further north. The new national administration – which, seen from Tit, looked quite a lot like the old one (but praise be to God that the French infidels and their cruel folly had finally been thrown out of the country) – had taken up residence in the Aoulef. Although this meant that they were quite a distance from Tit, there was no guarantee that they would stay there. On the contrary, there were already rumours afoot about secular education for all, the expropriation of religious institutions, even land reform – all words that the French had used but (praise be to God once again) had never even tried to implement. Some of these rumours were good: there would be justice and perhaps even financial help for outlying communities struggling with the upkeep of their basic infrastructure. And, God be our witness, there could be little doubt that Tit was struggling.

The secretary was himself a considerable landowner, with many children and other assets to lose and much to gain from state help with infrastructural updates, but the question he was pondering at the moment was much more practical. He was about to open a new page in the qsar's register, which contained all important collective decisions, expenses and regulations. The register itself was a standard-issue French exercise book filled with painstaking details of communal earnings and expenses and occasional internal trouble and conflict averted. It could stand up to any internal scrutiny, but what about prying state officials? The secretary knew very well that assemblies, such as the one he served, had no formal existence in the newly prom- ulgated Algerian constitution and might well be abolished, with their treasuries disappearing to God knows where. He shrugged and, in his neat scholarly handwriting, wrote, 'Praise be to God, and blessing and peace be upon Him who has no prophet after him. Patriotic greetings and revolutionary peace. These are the deliberations of the assembly of Tit, the parliament of the people who meet for the general interest of the people, and their names are below'.

Four hundred fifty years earlier, almost 1,000 kilometres further west in what is now southern Morocco, a local scribe faced a similar conundrum. After decades of courtly in-fighting, resulting in military and political impotence, the Moroccan makhzan had once more been consolidated under a new dynasty, the Saʿdīs (who two generations later would produce Ahmad al-Mansūr, conqueror of Timbuktu). They had moved closer and had recently even appointed a *qāʾid* (governor) in the nearest valley. How best to keep this new governor at bay without offending him and thereby attracting the makhzan's wrath, which might, as the scribe well knew, have dire consequences? He called in the local notables, who called a general assembly and sat down together to draft a list of customs and privileges to be presented to the qāʾid, thereby at once recognising his sovereignty, promising to pay taxes, discouraging him from meddling in internal affairs – why would he if all were taken care of anyway, cheaply and efficiently? – and incidentally also achieving de facto recognition for themselves. This was in 1512. They did not know then that this document, and the laws it contains, would survive the Saʿdīs' glory and demise, the rise of another dynasty, the Alawites, and long periods in between when the makhzan was far too distant for anyone to worry about. The document, with many amendments and add-ons, was still in use when it was collected and published by a French colonial official in 1934.

In the Sahara, assemblies could be found on all levels. Some made laws; others did not. Some were heavily institutionalised, as in the Algerian Mzab; others held rather ad hoc meetings, as in much of southern Morocco. Some were based in villages or qsūr, others in town quarters or around irrigation systems or collective storehouses, markets, seasonal fairs, zāwiyas or even roads. What makes them comparable is that they all referred to themselves with a similar vocabulary, usually drawn from the Arabic root *jamaʿa*, 'to come together', and that they all shared a collectively endorsed responsibility for a particular place or infrastructure. Indeed, the oldest customary law codes that we know of were produced not by village assemblies but by management committees of collective storehouses.

It is important not to idealise these assemblies as instances of 'primitive democracy' (there is no need to stress, I hope, that there was nothing 'primitive' about them).Assemblies of this kind were clearly exclusively male affairs. They were everywhere restricted to property owners and in some cases to the 'notables' of a given community (however this term might be defined locally). Nor were they 'democratic' by contemporary standards: although in some contexts, all adult men were required to attend, not everybody could speak in the same way or received the same kind of attention. Decisions were usually taken not by vote but by consensus. Nonetheless, these assemblies still translated into practice one fundamental principle of politics that is persuasive in its simplicity: what concerns all must be decided by all – both because this is right and because, in the absence of centralised coercion, this is the only way in which some level of compliance might be hoped for.

In many rural areas of northwestern Africa, these assemblies continue to function even now, accommodating themselves rather well to decades and in some areas centuries of state rule.

During the COVID-19 pandemic, for instance, village assemblies in northern Algeria were so efficient at gathering funds and medical supplies and at imposing a curfew that the central government, furious at being put to shame, forced them to share. Even more remarkable than their adaptability, longevity and shape-shifting quality is that, on the one hand, nobody ever seems to have anything good to say about their own particular assembly on the grounds of alleged corruption, nepotism, or worse, and on the other hand, most people I have met are immensely proud of the institution itself, citing it as a sign of their continuing – although by now in most cases severely limited – political autonomy. We can surmise that people have had similarly mixed feelings ever since assemblies first gathered.

June 2020. The photograph shows about twenty young men, wearing tight-fitting T-shirts, a scattering of broad-brimmed Australian sun hats, and military-issue bulletproof vests, in two overcrowded cars, one a jeep with its roof sawn off, driving through the streets of what looks like Tripoli. They are smiling at the camera, making victory signs. The headline reads, 'Head of Libyan Tribal Council: We Are Ready to Repel the Turkish Attack'. This was a reaction to the Egyptian president 'Abd al-Fattāh al-Sīsī's earlier announcement that he was ready to arm and train 'the Libyan tribes' to fight 'Ottoman colonialism' (the ongoing Turkish military intervention) on their soil, posing for the occasion for a photo shoot with a group of venerable old men in long robes. Other 'tribal leaders' intervened immediately, publicly scoffing at al-Sīsī's offer and denying those old men in robes any representative mandate. Instead, they pointed out that first, they were already well armed; second, they were already well trained; and third, they were the ones who controlled the border between Libya and Egypt in the first place, and al-Sīsī had better watch it. Further south, the Tuareg Tribal Council chimed in, happily letting everybody know that they were ready to 'cut off the nation's resources' if their own urgent political demands were not met. Their threat rang true in a context where tribal federations, large and small, routinely shut down oilfields to make their voices heard on the national stage.

June 2014. A somewhat dusty but large courtyard on the outskirts of Beni Walid, a small town less than 200 kilometres south of Tripoli. The courtyard is surrounded by cars, mostly white desert-going jeeps, and throngs of people. A police escort arrives on motor bikes, followed by several jeeps, city cars and a large, brand-new white bus. Sirens screech; a camel bleats in distress. The tension is palpable: on an earlier occasion, the expected visitors had been violently turned back at a check-point near the town. Today, however, they arrive without incident and are hustled towards a low platform on which four men are holding down a struggling camel. A fifth approaches and slits the animal's throat. The camera zooms in on the blood that flows abundantly down to the ground. A man starts cheering, fist raised to the sky: 'Warfalla, Zawiya, the enmity is dead, dead, dead; Warfalla, Zawiya, brothers, brothers'.

The chant is briefly picked up by others while the visiting dignitaries are ushered towards the entrance of the courtyard, lined with men in white robes and skull-caps or turbans below a banner proclaiming 'Welcome to our honoured guests'. They shake hands, each and every one, at times embrace. Bodyguards in dark suits, wearing shades and with mobile phones pressed to their ears, pace nervously. What looks like a tribal festival is in fact the official reconciliation ceremony between the Warfalla and the city of Zawiya. The Warfalla, Libya's largest tribal federation, was over-represented in the late Colonel Qadhafi's army, and Warfalla and militias from the city of Zawiya, strongly associated with the opposition, had clashed violently during the 2011 revolution and its aftermath. Now it is time to stop counting the dead and to reconcile, among other reasons because neighbouring groups, such as the town of Misrata, were becoming too powerful for comfort.

With ongoing conflict in Libya, the 'truce' and 'brotherhood' between Zawiya and the Warfalla has since been broken many times, but what matters are three things: first, that 'tribes' and 'tribalism' provide an idiom both for bitter oppositions and for reconciliation with a kind of conscious archaism that lends them weight but rather curiously also makes them highly adaptable to contemporary circumstances. Second, that the logic of 'tribalism', much like that of nation-states, shapes the world in its own image: once you start reasoning in terms of tribes, tribes will appear everywhere, even in places – such as the coastal town of Zawiya or the very bourgeois and historically Ottoman city of Misrata – where they have no historical antecedent. Third, following from this, tribes are in no way a thing of the past, nor do they describe an unchanging or even atavistic reality that reappears when the 'thin veneer' of statehood is peeled away. On the contrary, tribes are closely bound up with contemporary political institutions, including the state. They are particularly prominent in contemporary Libya not because they resurfaced after state collapse but because Qadhafi's state had consciously fostered them (and other local non-state institutions) throughout his reign.

'Tribe' is a complicated term and should be used with much caution. Since colonial times, it has been employed to denigrate certain populations, to imply that they live in a 'lower' or 'less evolved' phase of social and political evolution. 'Tribe' used in this sense is a fiction. It corresponds not to actual fact, nor indeed to local self-descriptions, but rather to a putatively universal evolutionary grid ranging from 'simple' to 'state' societies. As such, there can be no use for the term. In a few contexts, however, the Sahara among them, the term does correspond to local categories, and it is therefore difficult to do without. In a very different setting, the British historian E. P. Thompson famously distinguished between 'class' as an external ascription (a group defined by its place in a broader system of property relations) and class as a conscious feature of self-definition: between a 'class in itself' and a 'class for itself'. 'Tribe' is too vague a category to correspond to any reality 'in itself', yet we can find tribes that exist *for* themselves, inasmuch as people proudly define themselves as belonging to them. This also means that we need to extract the term from evolutionary suppositions and carefully reconstruct its meaning from the bottom up, based on historical evidence.

If we do this for the Sahara, we can see the many different kinds of groups that have been referred to or refer to themselves as 'tribes', ranging from small independent village federations to large and only loosely bound groups of hundreds of thousands of people. The Warfalla are said to contain, today, over 1 million 'members' grouped in 52 'sub-tribes', of different origins and belonging to different 'ethnic groups' – although, depending on self-identification and commitment, questions of membership are always uncertain and contextual. As an urban Libyan civil servant, you might never have cared much about which tribe you might claim as your own until promotions were distributed based on a tribal quota or your neighbours started threatening you with expulsion from your house and you needed help. The terms used to refer to 'tribes' can also vary from one case to another, from the classical Arabic *qabīla* or *'arsh* to words that refer to smaller units, often derived from body parts: thigh, pelvis or womb (for matrilineal Tuareg) or symbols of close ties: a round trap or a woven mat.

Despite these differences, a few basic principles emerge. Tribes are based on bonds of mutual protection, on the idea that the people closest to you are the ones who ought to help you if things go wrong, because you would do the same for them and because, collectively, you are responsible for a name, a set of people and often also for a more or less well-defined territory and other resources attached to the name. (This makes them rather similar to the assemblies described above.) In contemporary Libya, these can include oilfields or international banks. Tribes exist not because of a central authority that holds them together but because people mutually recognise each other as capable of protecting their own in a rather neat inversion of Weber's 'monopoly of legitimate violence': here we find a 'polypoly of legitimate violence' that promises some kind of recognisable order through mutual acknowledgement and agreement on a set of rules of engagement. This is also why the people of Zawiya had to hire a bus to attend the reconciliation ceremony; a simple handshake by their 'leaders' would not have been enough.

The contemporary 'tribal map' of northwest Africa, that is, the association of certain tribal names with certain areas, mostly goes back to the early modern period. This means that it was forged at roughly the same time as the North and West African empires described earlier. Tribes are thus in no sense 'prior' to states and empires; rather, tribe and state have evolved in a dialectical relationship right from the start, alongside and in mutual relation with other political institutions, such as the assemblies, discussed earlier, or the zāwiyas, discussed at length in chapter 6. Indeed, 'jamā'a', 'qabīla' and even the term 'bilād al-sība', Ibn Khaldūn's 'land of dissidence', are not words derived from some presumptively primordial popular culture but are part of a learned vocabulary: their 'barbarity' is thus intellectually high-brow and the result of centuries of close interaction and mutual awareness, if not interdependence. This is perhaps best exemplified by a ritual that was long at the heart of Islamic statehood: the bayʻa, or oath of allegiance, that all Muslim subjects had to swear, individually, to the righteous caliph, if one was available – the same ceremony that, in the late sixteenth century, led to the mass imprisonment of the Timbuktu elite by the Moroccan sultan mentioned earlier.

Mechouar Square, Tetouan, northern Morocco, 31 July 2023, outside the royal palace. The square is filled as far as the eye can see with men wearing bright white burnouses, the traditional pointed hood on their heads. The few women, veiled in white from head to toe, hardly stand out in the crowd. Everybody is aligned: the royal guards, dressed in smart green uniforms and mounted on horseback, have clearly done their job well. On the other side of the square, a red-and-green marquee shelters privileged guests from the merciless July sun. After hours of waiting, the sultan finally appears. Muhammad VI is standing in an open white limousine advancing at walking pace, immobile and unsmiling behind his signature sunglasses, clad in a golden-beige robe, hand on his heart, the ceremonial royal parasol unopened behind him. By the car walk his security guards and high-ranking army officers, in suits, and his three sons, also in golden-beige robes, Ottoman-style red tarbushes on their heads. They are followed by a horse-drawn and richly decorated carriage, the king's crown emblazed upon it – a present from Queen Victoria to her fellow monarch Hassan I, the current sultan's great-great-grandfather, on his accession to the throne in 1873.

This is the yearly commemoration of Muhammad VI's accession to the throne, occasion of the annual renewal of the bayʻa to the amīr al-muʼminīn, leader of the faithful. In its current form, the ceremony is an invention of the 1930s, an attempt by the

French colonial government to channel and control growing nationalist sentiment in the country. (As such, it was largely modelled on the 1920s Egyptian 'festival of the throne', which in turn followed British precedent.) The image it conveys is one of a homogeneous nation united in shared submission to the sultan, unquestioned sovereign and bearer of baraka for his people. (Many Moroccans do not identify with this image, of course, but that is a different story.) As the loudspeakers drone out the names and regions of origin of all those who have come to renew their allegiance, adding to this the long list of state functionaries working for the Ministry of the Interior, the police, the armed forces, the territorial administration, the ideal Moroccan nation-state comes into view, well organised, strong and imposing, with fixed and undisputed boundaries.

Before the current triumph of centralised state power, however, the bay'a – institutionalised in the sixteenth century by Ahmad al-Mansūr, conqueror of Timbuktu – stood for something rather different. While it is notionally an obligation of all Muslims, for obvious practical reasons, it was sworn not by everyone but only by those who mattered: representatives of the many diverse local political institutions that could guarantee loyalty and apportion responsibility on the ground. The term 'bay'a' itself is derived from the reciprocal form of the Arabic root *bā'a*, to sell, a transaction that always implies – at least formally – two independent parties who freely agree to an exchange whose exact terms are known to them in advance. While the bay'a is notionally for life and its breach blasphemy, its repetition – annually, as now, or simply if and when the sultan happened to pass by on one of his tax-raising excursions, as in the past – shows that allegiance was in fact context-dependent; that it could be withheld, transferred or negotiated or fade with time and distance.

This makes it rather different from the European tradition, where social contract theory implies an irreversible transfer of sovereignty (or, for Hobbes, an original act of submission), creating both the people and the sovereign forever more. It also means that the limit between the bilād al-sība and the bilād al-makhzan, the land of dissidence and the land of government, was never as stark as urban intellectuals like Ibn Khaldūn made it out to be: we can surmise that life rolled on regardless in the hands of local political institutions, whether or not these had sworn allegiance to a distant sultan. These political institutions, moreover, were clearly never all-inclusive. There were always, at the bottom of the pile or in the margins, people who were excluded. Despite their strong association with states, most slaves were one example, and harātīn and other landless peasants considered to be of 'lowly' extraction were another. With a few notable exceptions, women also played little part in public politics. They simply fell through cracks between the categories, which also mostly made them invisible in the written and oral histories that could be collected locally.

Others might have more consciously excluded themselves. Where state formations are primarily predatory, there is much benefit in having no recognisable political institutions at all, as this makes it impossible for regional states and empires (and other outsiders) to get a hold on local society. Something like this seems to have happened among the Tubu in northern Chad, whose contemporary attitudes towards their own 'sultan' (as the derdé is called in Chadian Arabic), and to the national state that now endorses him, were invoked at the beginning of this chapter. Here, people, although conversant with all the usual Saharan political principles, such as genealogies, assemblies, sultanates, empires and Islamic legal and political rhetoric, draw on them only tentatively, sporadically and without fully committing themselves. This has clearly long made local political life – nego-tiations over access to pasture, rights to date-palms and water, compensations for accidents and theft – impervious to greedy empires and states, including the contemporary Chadian variety. Who, in such a context, would be asked to swear the bay'a, and who would feel bound by it? We can surmise that in the margins of the institutions described so far, much political life in the Sahara was probably more like the 2012 derdé ceremony than like the orderly ranks of impeccably white-clad provincial repre-sentatives present in July 2023 on the Tetouan *mishwār*.

The Colonial Conquest

In the last years of the nineteenth century, the rivalry between the French and the British empires on the African continent was at its peak. In 1898, the French had been forced by the British to retreat from Fashoda, today in southern Sudan, to their great ire and embarrassment. The same year, the French secretary of state for the colonies decided to finalise the conquest of much of West, North and Central Africa, and to advertise it to the world, by a junction of three armed columns at Lake Chad. One was to start from Algiers, one from Senegal and one from the Congo basin. The column leaving Senegal was under the orders of the Capitaines Voulet and Chanoine, aged thirty-three and twenty-nine, respectively. They had already proven their ruthless brutality in earlier campaigns among the Mossi in what is now Burkina Faso. They left Senegal in January 1899 with a handful of French officers, 600 African colonial soldiers, and 2,000 porters, wives, and children,: the largest military column ever to travel across the northern Sahel. They carried provisions for only about a third of their journey. Things went wrong very quickly, as the column burned, looted, raped and massacred its way east.

By April, rumours of these activities reached Paris, where the reputation of the French army was already shaken by the Dreyfuss affair, a matter that was weighing heavily on Chanoine's father, then minister of war. He sent two officers after the column to clear up matters. They found that it was quite easy to follow the column's trail, marked as it was by the dead bodies of malnourished and ill-treated porters and the occasional remains of young girls strung up in trees. Three months later, as they finally approached the marching column, Voulet and Chanoine opened fire immediately, killing one officer and leaving the other for dead. Two days later, Voulet and Chanoine and most of the other French officers were themselves killed by their own soldiers. Voulet and Chanoine, it was said, had turned crazy, touched by a severe case of '*soudanite*', this mysterious malady that transformed otherwise decent and reasonable Frenchmen into delirious madmen if they spend too much time on African soil – as described in Joseph Conrad's *Heart of Darkness*, published in the same year.

Until the late nineteenth century, the European empires, which had started to establish colonial footholds on the northwest African coast from the fifteenth century onwards, had shown little interest in conquering the Sahara proper. The French conquest of Algiers in 1830 mostly concerned the coastal lands, and even the Ottomans only sporadically visited the Fazzān, notionally their southernmost belongings. This changed with the infamous 1884–85 Berlin conference, when the whole continent (with the exception of Ethiopia) was divided among European pretendants. From an empty and unprofitable 'wasteland', control over which was more trouble than it was worth, the Sahara was suddenly transformed into a strategically important territory as every major and minor European power scrambled to colour in as much of the map as possible. This coincided with technical advances in Europe that gave European armies – for the first time in history – a decisive technological advantage over their African counterparts. The Maxim gun – the world's first automatic machine gun – was invented in 1884, making it possible to kill people at a never-before-experienced rate and speed with little prior training and skill. Voulet and Chanoine's porters had lugged a similar cannon across the Sahel.

The French started to push south across the Atlas Mountains beginning in the 1880s. They reached Tamanrasset in what is now southern Algeria by 1902 and Djanet in the southeast by 1911. Timbuktu in northern Mali was occupied in 1893, northern Niger in 1905–1906, the Mauritanian Adrar in 1908–1909. The Tibesti in northern Chad was finally conquered in 1929 (after an earlier stint of colonial rule in the 1910s). Kitchener vanquished the Sudanese mahdī for the British in 1898. Southern Libya was formally annexed by Italy in 1911 and occupied under Mussolini in the 1920s and early 1930s. Western Sahara, claimed by the Spanish from 1884 onwards, was effectively annexed by 1934. These dates imply that different parts of the Sahara had substantially different colonial experiences, some starting in the late nineteenth century, others in the 1930s. In some cases, colonial rule – which came to an end mostly in the 1960s – therefore lasted less than a lifetime; in others, it more deeply restructured local political realities over time.

In comparison to the rest of the African continent, the Sahara was conquered late, often against the better judgement of government officials and for purely strategic reasons: the aim was to put boots on the ground so that others couldn't get there first. By the 1900s, official metropolitan enthusiasm for new colonies had largely run out of steam, and the consensus was that imperial conquest ought to pay for itself. Troops had to feed off the land and relied heavily on unpaid local auxiliaries animated by their own grudges. The Sahara was generally treated as a punishment post or as a posting suitable for hot-headed young soldiers who wanted to become heroes. Neither was conducive to administrative efficiency or even just to basic respect for human life and dignity. There was thus nothing exceptional about Voulet and Chanoine's methods. Until they shot their fellow French officer, all they could have been accused of from the point of view of a seasoned colonial soldier was excessive thrift and perhaps a lack of discretion.

The conquest did not take place in a political void. Due to colonial pressure, the repercussions of the transatlantic slave trade and internal political changes, the nineteenth century had been a century of revolution and warfare throughout West, Central and East Africa (mirroring in its own way the contemporaneous European 'age of revolutions'). From the late eighteenth century onwards, a wave of jihads had swept West Africa from west to east, culminating in the creation of the Sokoto empire in the early nineteenth century. In the 1870s, Sokoto stretched from contemporary Mali to northern Cameroon along the southern edge of the Sahara, with a population of perhaps as many as 20 million, a quarter to half of whom were enslaved. The creation of these empires, their resistance to French colonial incursions and internal warfare produced large numbers of displaced fighters, many enslaved. These in turn filled the ranks both of the imperial armies, largely recruited locally, and of those who resisted them, to the point that the military strategies of both colonial and anti-colonial fighters were the result of deep mutual entanglements and reciprocal learning processes.

In addition to formal recruits, European officers, who were usually totally ignorant of local terrains, relied heavily on local auxiliaries, whom they remunerated in kind. Beyond the opportunity for plunder, these auxiliaries had their own reasons for joining, partaking in political strategies that European officers perceived only dimly. Subordinate groups might wish to acquire arms and to emancipate themselves; dominant groups might recognise a military alliance with the conquering European armies as the only way that they could hold on to their power. Others might have seen in the European forces nothing but a passing menace, able to wreak great havoc and destruction but, like others before, unable to stay on afterwards. Yet others might have hedged their bets, placing their children on different sides, just in case; others were quite simply press-ganged. Whatever their motives, the choices made at the moment of conquest threw long shadows over later political and economic relations throughout the region.

This continued as European colonial rule became more permanent. Given their small number, insufficient means and incomplete grasp of basic local topography and sociology, imperial armies could only rule by relying on local intermediaries. They therefore eagerly appointed chiefs wherever they could. From the bottom up, for many Saharans, colonial rule was therefore experienced mostly not as direct rule by European officers – although some of them were usually about, often (judging by their monthly reports) doing very little – but by local intermediaries backed by the superior military force offered by the imperial regime. This was much easier in areas where, as in the former jihadi empires and emirates of northern Nigeria, the remnants of the Kanem-Bornu empire or indeed Morocco, the Europeans could identify a prince, king or emperor whom they could co-opt. It was much harder in areas where political arrangements were less recognisable. In northern Chad, notorious, as noted earlier, for its absence of institutionalised leadership, French colonial officers constantly complained about the lack of authority of the local 'chiefs', the derdé among them – 'chiefs' whom they had largely created themselves and who were now 'met with cutlasses drawn' every time they attempted to collect taxes.[2]

However ineffective, imperial endorsement or appointment profoundly changed political relations. Tribal notables became tribal leaders, backed no longer by popular consensus but rather by a foreign army with superior fire power; the Teda derdé, for instance, who until then had been mostly a symbolic figure, was turned into the state-appointed supreme chief that he still is, and heads of assemblies became colonial civil servants. Former 'warrior' elites had often been quite literally wiped out during conquest or had had to redefine themselves. A few local groups and families, often clerical or commercial groups who found it easier to correspond to colonial expectations, were quick to seize the opportunities offered by the resulting void and presence of a new, and militarily powerful, political player in the region to durably improve their own standing. Hence the Ifoghas, a scholarly Tamacheq-speaking group based in the Adagh Mountains in what is now northern Mali, managed to shake off the rule of their former overlords, the Ahaggar Tuareg from what was now southern Algeria, by persuading the French that *they* were in fact the 'traditional' leaders of the Adagh – with much success, as, one national independence and series of armed rebellions later, the Ifoghas are still calling the shots in the region today.

Over time, then, French imperial rule created a new class of intermediaries. Together, they subsequently worked to maintain the Saharan territories in a limbo of 'tradition', however much this 'tradition' was in fact of their own making. This continued as political formations elsewhere on the continent started to take on more readily recognisable 'modern' political forms: parties, trade unions, armed independence movements in the Maghrib.

Saharans were more often than not excluded from them, which meant that once independence was granted to their countries, French local functionaries were usually replaced by people from beyond the Sahara proper. As we will see in the next chapter, Saharans' resulting marginalisation still shapes political relations in the region today.

The French came with their own ideas about 'the desert' and what they considered to be its 'true' inhabitants: 'the nomads'. They were deeply fascinated by the latter, especially the Tuareg, whose 'aristocratic' demeanour and lifestyle gave many a French officer occasion to indulge in fantasies of chivalry and nobility that the French Revolution had long made unfashionable back home. This romantic infatuation was nostalgic and coexisted with the conviction that nomads were relics of the past that would be swept away by the ineluctable march of progress triggered by the French military conquest. All the French could do was ease that transition and exclude trouble-makers. At the heart of the French colonial regime was thus the attempt to divide populations into neat categories and to confine them to their 'proper' place, nomads in the desert and sedentary farmers on the desert's edge, with the centres of power solidly anchored among the latter.

As a consequence, Saharan space was actively and often violently divided into the different 'zones' that are still familiar to us: sedentary agricultural regions, including oases, were cut off from the pastoral economies on which they relied for their survival; the Sahel was severed from its north, and nomadic pastoralists were, as seen in chapter 3, barred from entry to the agricultural regions of the North African tell. Algerian space more generally was, in the Franco-Algerian geographer Marc Côte's terms, 'turned inside out': until the French conquest,

Algeria had turned on an east-west axis running inland along the northern limits of the Sahara, but French investment, infrastructure and settlement brutally shifted the country's economic, political and social centres of gravity towards the cities of the coast – to the Mediterranean and, beyond it, the French 'motherland'.[3] Populations who had, for a majority among them, lived in the mountains and drawn their livelihoods from their access to a variety of ecological zones were resettled in the valleys, now redefined as productive (agricultural) rather than commercial zones (and drained of much of their water through hastily installed eucalyptus plantations). Cut off from its northern connections, the Algerian Sahara was redefined as non-productive, hostile and futile.

Similar logics were at play in the southern Sahara, where colonial policy actively excluded nomads from pastures in the Niger Bend. 'During the fighting between our troops from Timbuktu and the Tuareg of the Niger bend', noted the colonial officers Mangeot and Marty in 1918, 'the latter were gradually pushed into the interior and every one of our victories diminished their prestige, while depriving them of a stretch of land. These lands were given to villagers to put them under cultivation'.[4] This was partly a way of winning the war – the French well knew that left to the Sahara's scarce resources alone, Arab and Tuareg pastoralists would starve. But it was also a way of durably restructuring territory and severing alliances between different population groups. Colonial policies thus put into practice a deep-rooted Mediterranean prejudice about the 'age-old' and 'intrinsic' opposition between sedentary and nomadic lifeways – images that still colour contemporary perceptions of the Sahara and, as noted throughout, render sedentary Saharans (often classified as 'Black') strangely invisible in popular perceptions.

In 1952, Libya was the first Saharan country (bar Egypt,

nominally independent since 1922) to achieve independence, under British patronage and a Sanūsī king (yet another 'invented tradition', but one that in this case proved to be short-lived despite active interference on the king's behalf by Hassanein Bey, the Egyptian traveller we met earlier). Sudan, Morocco and Tunisia followed suit in 1956, the latter two after a period of armed struggle; Mauritania, Mali, Niger and Chad, following a referendum, in 1960. Algeria won its independence in 1962 after a long and bloody war. Spain relinquished Western Sahara in 1976, followed by immediate reoccupation by Morocco, which is still ongoing.

Despite these rapid changes, the shadow of imperial state-building, conceived for export rather than national integration, still looms large. This is strikingly visible in the contemporary map of the region: with the exception of Mauritania, all post-colonial northwest African countries literally turn their backs to their Saharan territories, with capitals, major cities, road networks and other infrastructure situated either on the Mediterranean coast or, for Sahelian countries, on their southern borders. This is why, although the 1950s discovery of oil and gas in the northern Sahara turned the region into a vital economic asset, political decisions about it are still made elsewhere, often by people who might never have set foot in the Sahara. Contemporary Saharans, meanwhile, have to find ways to get by in the interstices of national and international state systems that tend to ignore them.

8

WHEN CRISIS BECOMES PERMANENT

> Youth of the Sahara, we inform you
> Do not believe that the contemporary
> world is superior to us
> although they oppress us, because
> they rose before we did.
> ...
> We have a history that begins with the sword.
>
> Mosa ag Akhmudan 'Bozwish', 1979[1]

I first visited Bani w-Iskut, an informal settlement on the out-skirts of the southern Algerian town Adrar, with my friend Jamal. Jamal is from a well-respected religious family from a qsar 70 kilometres south of Adrar; a devout Muslim and teacher at a local high school, he had put me in touch with several shaykhs and Islamic scholars in the area who were knowledgeable in local history and happy to talk to me. One, Sīdi Muhammad, had been the shaykh of the Algerian Kunta, a meeting I recounted in chapter 4. The Kunta are one of the most prominent trans-Sa-haran religious families in Algeria, Mali and Mauritania. They used to be influential Saharan traders, and many still are. They have also been associated with their own, Saharan branch of the Qādiriyya Sufi order since the sixteenth century and run many prestigious zāwiyas throughout northwest Africa. The Kunta have, in other words, substantially shaped the history, economy and religious traditions of the wider region.

Sīdi Muhammad thus seemed like the perfect teacher. Great was my surprise, therefore, when, after he had finished reciting the genealogy reproduced above and I asked for information about Mali, he professed ignorance. Instead, he asked Jamal to take me to Bani w-Iskut to look up Sīdi N'Goma, a 'very knowledgeable cousin' of his. Bani w-Iskut, 'Build and keep quiet about it', is the largest informal settlement in Adrar. With its anarchic layout and architecture; with its dirty mud roads, rubbish heaps and spontaneously constructed houses made out of all kinds of possible and impossible materials; and with its goats, chickens and intense street life, Bani w-Iskut stands in stark opposition to the clear and well-built town centre of Adrar, whose massive empty public squares, broad paved roads, right angles and large administrative buildings, all uniformly painted terracotta, breathe in the rhythm of the Algerian nation-state.

Jamal was at first reluctant to take me, as he feared for his car, he said, but one day during Ramadan, we finally went. We started asking for directions as soon as we turned off the broad paved road behind Adrar's main market and were sent down various wrong turns by veiled men squatting in the shade of trans-Saharan trucks, looking at us with suspicious curiosity. Goats feeding on large rubbish heaps in the streets were periodically chased away by children dressed in rags. 'Look at them', Jamal said sadly before he was mesmerised by large plates of steaming lentils carried past – in the middle of Ramadan!

When we finally found the house, we were ushered into a large mud-brick building, past three well-nourished ladies dressed in colourful *malāhif* (full-body veil, singular form *milhafa*) – 'See! And I can barely afford *one*', Jamal whispered – and then across a courtyard full of chickens and goats to a small square room with few furnishings, lit by a tiny window just below the low ceiling. Sīdi N'Goma was squatting on a cheap carpet, clutching his prayer beads; he mumbled in hardly audible Hassaniya that he knew nothing of Mali, had indeed hardly ever been there, but that he might be able to afford me 'protection' (in the form of an amulet) if I really wanted to go there – but then of course I would have to pay. Jamal quickly pulled me away, past the giggling women, into his car and back to 'civilisation'. 'These people sleep on pots of gold', he mumbled all the way back, and days later still, 'and they live in holes like animals'.

The second time I went to Bani w-Iskut was almost a year later, after having been to Mali and back. I had come on my own this time to visit Mahjouba, the elder sister of my northern Malian host Zahra. The veiled men still seemed to be squatting where I had left them, but this time, I recognised them straight away: I had met most of them either in Gao or al-Khalīl, both trading towns in northern Mali, and they were little surprised that I had made good my promise to visit. Sīdi N'Goma was Mahjouba's next-door neighbour, and his three daughters (not wives) insisted that I stay for dinner, gave me one of their malāhif as a present, and re-introduced me to their father, who spoke Algerian Arabic fluently and was now rather chatty. In Timbuktu, I had spent much time with one of their cousins and fiancé, and the girls were eager to hear family gossip. They did not recognise me, of course: last year's foreign visitor introduced by an elite Adrari visitor had long slipped their minds.

On acquaintance, what had seemed like the heartland of debauchery turned out to be an ordinary Timbuktu household, were it not for the slight markers of distinction that the girls had borrowed from Algerian mainstream culture: fizzy drinks, for instance, and elaborate sweets and dry biscuits rather than meat to greet the visitors. Bani w-Iskut as perceived by Jamal – and as I had seen it the first time, viewing it as I was through his eyes – thus disappeared at first touch, revealing itself as nothing but an illusion based on southern Algerian prejudice and latent xenophobia. Without a prior visit to Timbuktu, this 'normality' was simply not visible. Yet, as my visit with Jamal made clear, Bani w-Iskut as imagined by southern Algerians plays an important part in local self-perceptions as a way of defining and publicly underlining what one is not.

In reality, distinctions are much less clear-cut. Inhabitants of Bani w-Iskut run stalls and shops in the market, where they sell goods of more or less dubious provenance that, with their low prices, bring relief to strained middle-class household budgets. Sahelian labour is crucial to all aspects of local economic life, and many women work as cleaners or nannies for wealthy Adrari families and so know their lives intimately. Bani w-Iskut's female population specialises in certain services that have become indispensable to Adrari cultural life: they braid hair, for instance – a recent fashion among the Adrar wealthy – or supply amulets and love magic, foretell the future and cure depression or sterility.

As we have already seen, trans-border trade is never just in the hands of Sahelians but relies on the collaboration or at least the tacit endorsement of a whole cross-section of the Algerian population, and many Adraris are more familiar with Bani w-Iskut's tangled streets than they might like to admit. Most importantly, perhaps, most Adraris are but one generation removed from their own trans-Saharan past, and family connections can as easily be found across the boundaries between slum and town as across the border with Mali and Niger. Of course, such intimacy makes relations more strained rather than less.

This was perhaps the real lesson that Sīdi Muhammad wanted me – and Jamal – to learn when he sent us to look up his cousin in Bani w-Iskut. Pride in historical transregional connections and far-reaching genealogies comes with contemporary cousins attached, whether you like it or not.

The contemporary Sahara is cosmopolitan, urban and multi-lingual, buzzing with economic innovation and activity, fashion statements and artistic creativity. Places such as Bani w-Iskut are not accidental appendages to it but, much like the smuggling outpost of al-Khalīl described in chapter 5, at its heart. Yet they have their roots in a moment of existential crisis: the Sahel droughts of the 1970s and 1980s, when refugees from the southern edge of the Sahara arrived in great numbers in the Maghreb, irreversibly transforming its Saharan cities. The aim of this chapter is to sound out this apparent paradox: the decades when the Sahara as it still is today started to emerge were also the moment when 'traditional' Saharan lifeways were put under existential pressure; when harsh economic differences between the northern and the southern Sahara became entrenched, strengthening the perception of an unsurmountable 'Saharan divide'; and when the southern Sahara and adjacent regions came to be known to the outside world as an endemic crisis zone, marked by extreme poverty and environmental disaster. Contemporary Saharans have no choice but to build a life somewhere in the interstices of these narratives of catastrophe and the harsh realities that they reflect. The arrangements they have found still underpin much life in the region today.

From Development to Crisis

It is difficult to remember today that until the Sahel drought, the southern edge of the Sahara, where most inhabitants of places such as Bani w-Iskut originate, had been imagined mostly in radically different ways: not as a zone marred by structural poverty, resource insufficiency and overpopulation but rather as a potentially rich agricultural zone whose development was stifled by a lack of people and infrastructure. Nothing that could not be solved – according to the French imperial and then the independent national governments – by 'development', brought about by a change in productive strategies from extensive husbandry to ranching or from pastoralism to agriculture or from mixed 'subsistence' agriculture to cash-crop farming.

In sub-Saharan Africa, the notion of 'development' harks back to late colonial times. Until the 1930s, colonies were supposed to enrich the metropolis and otherwise pay for themselves. Their economies were thus mostly extractive, and infrastructure was kept at a minimum (unless it served military purposes). With growing social unrest in the colonies and an increasingly vociferous international labour movement, and then even more so with the massive contribution of imperial soldiers and economies to the Second World War, this situation became untenable. The only way that the European powers had any hope of holding on to their overseas territories was by convincing their populations and international observers of what the then French president, Nicholas Sarkozy, could still call, in 2005, the 'positive effects of colonialism'. This meant building roads, factories, hospitals, railroads and schools and restructuring local relations of production to make them more compatible with global capitalism.

Most of this was too little, too late. By the 1960s, most of the former French and British colonies in sub-Saharan Africa had voted or fought for independence. Yet both the belief in 'development' and the financial and commercial structures through which it was to be brought about survived the official dismantling of empire. This facilitated a smooth transition towards independence – under leaders who in many but not all cases had been part of the colonial political elite and who were now working with 'technical advisors' who only months earlier had been colonial administrators. This continuity was possible because 'development' was seen as an inherently technical process and therefore exempt from political debates. Belief in the power of technical solutions to social and political problems was shared across political dividing lines by socialist as well as by capitalist countries.

From the point of view of the Sahara, this emphasis on technocratic management had two major drawbacks: first, most Saharan territories, both northern and southern, had been colonised late, and many among them had stayed under military rule until national independence. This meant that few Saharans had attended colonial schools or been integrated into the colonial administrative apparatus or army. Given the strong continuities with the colonial state in terms of infrastructure, economic priorities and personnel, they tended to be under-represented in the new independent states as well. It is thus perhaps not a surprise that the first 'Tuareg rebellion' broke out in 1963 in northern Mali, barely three years after the declaration of independence, as northerners felt that the new nation-state could never represent them and grant them the political respect that they felt was rightfully theirs. The rebellion was brutally suppressed by the Malian army, which killed civilians, poisoned wells and slaughtered livestock as their owners watched helplessly, setting the stage for decades of more or less muted hostility and conflict.

The second major drawback was that technocracy did not work, at least not in the long run. From a developmentalist perspective, even drought and the inherent vagaries of Sahelian and Saharan ecosystems were mostly failures of management. This point of view was sustainable in the 1950s and 1960s, as exceptionally abundant rainfall throughout the Sahel made it possible to extend fields into the Sahara, to increase herds, to encourage nomads to settle, to turn pastures into private agricultural land and to invest heavily in monocrop intensive agriculture. This was a time of great abundance and agricultural optimism. In 1960, thanks to the success of irrigated rice cultivation in the Niger valley, Mali was a net exporter of staple crops.

In 1968, however, the rains didn't come, and things started to go awry. No rain fell in 1969 either, or in 1970. People lost their fields and their herds and trooped to refugee camps that were set up near the few towns in the Sahel. Many others crossed the borders into Algeria. According to official statistics, 100,000 people died. With television, all of this happened right in the living rooms of newly affluent post-war Europeans. International aid flowed in, mostly in the form of direct food aid. The term 'Sahel', which until then had been a floating signifier that could mean both the northern and the southern 'shores' of the Sahara, started to be used in European languages exclusively to refer its southern edge: an area where people were so poor that they were literally starving.

Just think of the staggering success of Bob Geldof's 1984 'Do They Know It's Christmas' single to raise funds for the Ethiopian famine (linked to the same drought) and subsequent Band Aid and Live Aid concerts, some of which featured explicit footage of skeletal and dying African children. To the paradigm of development was now added the idea of urgent humanitarian response. The image of the chronically poor 'African' always on the brink of starvation was born, and the southern shore of the Sahara was its first stage and setting.

The Problem with Statistics

There can be no doubt that from 1968 to 1974 and then again from 1983 to 1985, rainfall was particularly poor. This had disastrous effects on local societies and economies, irreversibly transforming them and causing incredible suffering. It is difficult, however, to express all of this in precise figures, as reliable statistics on rainfall, wealth and demography are simply not available. The only – very few – figures established by colonial governments date from the 1950s, a time of relative abundance. Figures, moreover, were extremely variable from place to place; they were 'efficient' – productive of a certain image – rather than reliable. The term 'famine' became widely accepted only towards the end of the first period of drought, in 1973. And contrary to the expectations that word might inspire, we now know that the population of the Sahel in fact grew by approximately 3 per cent between 1970 and 1973.

It was equally difficult to count refugees, as there were no reliable population figures to start with and few people could be identified beyond doubt (for example, had identity papers and the like). Many were thus probably not counted, others counted many times over. Furthermore, many travelled to regional capitals – where the camps were situated – not in order to receive handouts but to demand what they considered to be their right to assistance from state officials. They were thus not 'refugees', nor indeed passive victims of any kind, but rather citizens seeking out those whom they held responsible for their difficult situation in order to hold them accountable.

And this is perhaps the crux of the matter. The drought was generally portrayed as a natural disaster requiring an emergency response. Such a framing called for expert intervention, and most of this expertise – and the money to fund it – was found outside the countries concerned. The definition of the problem was thus separated from local experiences and the implementation of solutions removed from local structures of accountability. State sovereignty and self-determination, which had been acclaimed as universal principles a mere decade earlier, were now set aside in the name of overwhelming humanitarian concerns. This in turn gave rise to an identifiable industry of experts competing for bilateral and international funding. Local populations and even national governments were excluded from these processes. This later created the need to artificially involve them through 'local consultancy' or projects intended to 'raise their awareness' of problems that they had to cope with on a daily basis.

Yet, as the French anthropologist Claude Meillassoux, who witnessed the Sahel droughts first hand, noted long ago, while droughts might be considered an 'act of nature', this is never true of famines.[2] Famines are problems not merely of production but also of distribution; they are thus eminently political. This is why historically, droughts and famines do not necessarily coincide. Droughts are a common occurrence in the Sahel, and local and regional productive and political systems have always had to find ways to deal with them – hence their great flexibility. As seen throughout this book, one response to uncertainty was mobility, another the establishment of far-flung networks that might lie dormant in times of abundance but be called upon in times of need. Yet another was the hierarchical nature of Saharan and Sahelian societies, which made it possible to sporadically call in 'tribute', perhaps in the form of long-term hospitality, from former clients who might long before have settled in ecologically more resilient agricultural zones to the south.

All of these response mechanisms were severely curtailed with the establishment of national boundaries and the enforced separation of settled and nomadic economies, artificial barriers that were the legacy of colonial times. As the economic historian Stephen Baier put it, colonial interference meant that 'pastoral nomadism was frozen in time', stuck in the limbo of (often French-created) 'tradition', which had made the practice inflexible and unable to adapt to new circumstances, including drought.[3] Add to this the fact that the people who were now in power knew little of the local situation and felt no obligations to local families – indeed, might even have felt resentment towards those long portrayed as 'imperial stooges' (due to the French infatuation with the Tuareg) and 'former slave-holders'.

There can be no doubt that an important percentage of international aid was embezzled by local officials or by others who quickly learned how to work the system. Simultaneously, the sudden inflow of aid was such that the humanitarian business became a resource in and of itself, and one that was quickly absorbed into local livelihood strategies. Over time, the positionality of 'the Sahel' on the international stage – as a hotbed of poverty – became a source for a particular type of 'rent' for elites on both sides, similar to the term 'desertification'. As early as 1975, the Sahel Information Committee asked, 'Who feeds on the Sahel famine?'[4] This question has lost none of its relevance today.

Build and Keep Quiet About It

Mahjouba, my host in Bani w-Iskut on my second visit, arrived in Adrar in the 1970s with her husband after having spent several years in Mecca. Her house is situated in the oldest part of Bani w-Iskut, near the mosque. A shaggy door made out of corrugated iron opens into a large courtyard, where a satellite dish is suspended from crumbling walls, occasionally head-butted by goats feeding on plastic bags, and where a young niece is busy preparing large dishes of rice on an open fire, seasoning them with rancid sheep's butter imported from Mali. The little available electricity is used mainly to power the television and to charge the ubiquitous mobile phones.

The courtyard leads into a reception room, sparsely furnished and with its cheap blue paint peeling off the walls. The roof is made from corrugated iron. The walls are lined with mattresses covered in polyester sheets with a floral pattern; the low table which serves as a dining table is stored neatly in a corner, leaning against the wall. Handmade cushions are reminiscent of an earlier nomadic life further south in the once abundant pastures of northern Mali. The earthen floor is covered with colourful mats, woven in bright plastic thread and frayed at the corners. At night, this is where the women of the family sleep.

On every one of my many visits, the reception room was replete with family members and visitors, squatting on the floor and drinking endless rounds of strong, sweet tea. Bani w-Iskut acts primarily as a way station and relay for traders travelling through the border region, and as such, Mahjouba's house is perhaps best thought of as the feminine equivalent of Khalīlī gawārij, places of male sociability and business in the main smuggling outpost near the border between Mali and Algeria. Conversations turn on family members spread out between Gao, Bordj Badji Mokhtar and Adrar, on the ups and downs of trade and security in northern Mali and on Arab soap operas followed on either side of the border on satellite TV.

While they managed to resist the 1970s drought largely due to a small government pension paid to their father, since the 1980s, Mahjouba's family has lived scattered across the region. One sister lives in the Mauritanian capital, Nouakchott, where she trades in veils. A third sister, Halima, has settled permanently in Bordj Badji Mokhtar, on the border between Mali and Algeria, in social housing constructed – allegedly according to a

Soviet model that makes little sense in the desert environment –
by the Algerian government to alleviate the refugee camps that
sprang up in the 1970s and where the whole family remembers
having spent a few painful months.

'They treated us like beggars', Halima and Mahjouba's still
younger sister Zahra recalls. 'They made us queue up and beg
for food. They put these plastic bracelets on our wrists, bracelets that we couldn't take off, to keep track of us and so that we
wouldn't come and get another ration, as if one was ever enough.
Our older brother, who was then the head of our family, simply
refused to do this, stand in the sun and queue, being marked like
an animal – so we had to feed him too with our rations'. And as
hungry as they were, they didn't like the food: 'Sardines! It was
all sardines in tins. We don't eat fish, never have done. And bad
rice, the kind you wouldn't even give your animals. We were sick
all the time. That's when people became traders – some selling
the stuff further south so they could buy decent food for their
families. That's when they started, and ever since, the trading has
not stopped'.

Another sister has settled in Bani-w-Iskut near Mahjouba's
house; three others – Zahra and two of her younger sisters –
now live in a large urban compound in Gao's 'Arab' quarter. The
sisters are close and often visit each other for long periods; they
clearly conceive of their houses as forming part of one larger
whole, central for the survival of their family. Economically,
their life depends on revenues generated by their brothers, most
of whom are trans-border traders, who in turn rely on the safe
havens provided and maintained by their sisters – both in terms
of the actual physical buildings, the food and shelter provided,
and in terms of the active maintenance of the transnational
social networks that underpin their trade and the emotional
comfort they provide. Yet others look after the family's herds

– largely bought with profits made in the trans-border trade – somewhere in the northern Malian bādiya.

On a permanent basis, Mahjouba's house in Bani w-Iskut is almost exclusively inhabited by women: Mahjouba herself, her daughter Oumou, a young niece sent to Adrar to go to school, Mahjouba's daughter-in-law, a young girl from their home area in northern Mali, and Mahjouba's little granddaughter. This is without counting the many female visitors, who often stay for weeks or even months. Mahjouba's son Hamouda, a very active trans-border trader, rarely has time to stop over for long, while her husband, of a venerable age, generally keeps to his bed; Oumou's former husband lives in Bamako.

This predominance of women is typical of households in Bani w-Iskut: Mahjouba's neighbour Salima, a Tamasheq speaker from Kidal, lives with her two sisters and their three small daughters. Her only brother, a former trans-border trader, has set up house in Kidal, where I first met him; her husband, a smuggler, has 'disappeared' into the world of al-Khalīl and only rarely gives signs of life; and her brother-in-law, also a trader, works in a Khalīlī garāj and will be 'back shortly'. Next door, Sīdi N'Goma's three daughters look after their ageing father while their brothers and husbands-to-be work in northern Mali or on the road.

Like most of her neighbours, Mahjouba runs a business of her own, dealing in veils and other female paraphernalia. Some of these are sent to her from Mauritania by her eldest sister, who herself spends much time travelling between Nouakchott, Gao and Adrar; other goods are brought to her by exclusively female traders from northern Mali and Niger and in particular from Western Saharan refugee camps near Tindouf. Most are by now made in China and bought either in Dubaï or directly in China by enterprising Mauritanian ladies, whose names are known to all and who provide models of success even to the most modest of local tradeswomen. Mahjouba tends to sell her wares at the frequent women's gatherings or to neighbours and friends from her home.

Such gatherings – naming ceremonies, weddings, funerals – punctuate life in Bani w-Iskut. They take days of preparation; the house needs to be cleaned, mats and carpets borrowed from neighbours. Neighbours and relatives drop in beforehand to help with the cooking. For hours, the rhythmic pounding of millet can be heard through the street, mixed with cheap tape recorders – or, more recently, smartphones – blaring out *guitara*, contemporary Saharan music. Most residents of Bani w-Iskut have adopted their Algerian neighbours' culinary habits, eating industrially prepared couscous, rice or bakery-style baguettes most of the time. But for special occasions, only Sahelian food will do – mostly millet with a sauce made from dried okra – however much labour its preparation might take.

On the day itself, hosts and visitors are dressed in their finest, some with colourful and slightly transparent full-body veils – the malāhif that Jamal noted with some envy on our first foray into Bani w-Iskut. Others wear large boubous, long, flowing robes made of shiny *bazin* and richly embroidered with gold thread, a matching headscarf wrapped around tightly braided hair. After the first customary round of tea, large bags come out, filled with the latest fashions from Mauritania or Bamako, with gold-plated jewellery brought from Dubai and incense from Sudan. The beauty and elegance of these goods increasingly also attract women from the southern Algerian middle classes or even daughters of northern civil servants posted in Algeria's 'deep south'. This in turn encourages tradeswomen such as Mahjouba to adapt their wares: waistlines are pulled in, boubous shortened, embroidery diversified in colour. Whoever gets the mix between Saharan style and Algerian tastes just right stands to earn a fortune: a full outfit to be worn to a wedding reception by an Algerian client might come in at several million centimes (several hundred USD), or so women whisper in awe.

On paper, then, the 1970 and 1980 droughts accomplished what decades of colonial policies never could: the massive sedentarisation of nomadic pastoralists. Yet the term 'sedentarisation' can hide many different realities, especially in areas where, for ecological reasons, a purely sedentary existence is not in fact a viable option. As with Mahjouba and her sisters, what usually happened was something like this: parts of the family, often the women, settled, because somebody had to but also because they might not have wanted to return to the hard life of the desert, because they wanted to send at least some of their children to school, to benefit from health care, or just to be close to distribution centres should drought strike again. Other parts of the family, often the young men, remained mobile through migration, livestock husbandry or trade – or, most frequently, a combination of all three. This means that figures given for the sedentarisation of nomads – which, in Mauritania, for instance, are as high as 78 per cent – tend to hide more complex realities.

Most but by no means all of these now sedentary former nomads chose to settle in towns and cities, making the contemporary Sahara one of the most highly urbanised regions on the African continent. Take, for instance, Nouakchott, the capital of Mauritania, where Mahjouba's eldest sister, Rahmatou, has taken up residence. Nouakchott was created from scratch in 1957, and its inhabitants were initially counted in hundreds rather than thousands. In the 1970s, the town was expanded to house 8,000 people; then the Sahel drought struck and 70,000 former nomads settled in the capital within weeks. Many never left. By the late 1980s, Nouakchott counted 400,000 inhabitants. Today, it is home to more than a million people, more than a quarter of the country's overall population.

Saharan governments have rarely been able to keep up with this rapid growth, and a huge gap between urban infrastructures and population numbers remains even today. This means that places like Bani w-Iskut have become the norm rather than an exception. Attempts to remedy this are marred by financial difficulties as well as by political reluctance and bureaucratic uncertainty. As noted in chapter 4, North African countries are in the habit of considering themselves to be countries that send rather than receive migrants and, with the exception of Libya (where migration policy under Qadhafi was erratic and at times brutal, but at least there was official recognition that the country needed immigrant workers), resist the idea of legalising the large presence of Sahelian migrants – clearly there to stay – on their soil.

There was a time, as Zahra recalls with some nostalgia, when 'all you had to be was white' in northern Mali, 'and the [Algerian] consul [in Gao] would give you a passport ... and then you could go to the Libyan consul and he would do the same, just to spite the Algerians'. Or, as my friend Abdoulaye noted, 'If you have Algerian friends or in-laws, you ask them to come with you to the consul. And they will swear that you are their cousin so-and-so. Saharans always have lots of cousins somewhere, and most Algerian civil servants [who tend to be recruited in the north of the country] will never know the difference'. But since one Algerian consul in Gao was kidnapped by Malian rebels in 2012 and another killed six months later, obtaining 'Algerian papers' has become much more difficult. In any case, as all Malian and Nigerien nationals in Algeria know all too well, if you don't look the part, official papers are only of limited use. Algerian officials will rip up your Algerian passport right in front of you, laughing and calling you an 'Algérien Taiwan' – a fake. 'Which is what we are', Abdoulaye concluded.

In Algeria itself, some form of regularisation can be achieved through the integration of former slums into the municipal water or electricity network, thereby producing paperwork which for many residents is seen as a first step towards recognition of their rights both to property and to residence. On a later visit to Bani w-Iskut, I found Mahjouba happily smiling, waving a piece of paper at me: she had finally managed to obtain a legal claim to the shack where she had lived for the last thirty years. This in turn meant that she could claim subsidies to replace much of the corrugated iron roof and mud-brick walls with concrete and that she was to be connected to the municipal water and sewage network. Maybe soon she would even gain access to the public electricity network rather than buying what little electricity she had, at prime rates, from her neighbour who owned a generator.

Similar regularisation strategies are at work in Sahelian countries. Although here, the direct material benefits of title deeds to settlement sites – some of which have been established in places that quite simply do not permit a sedentary existence – might seem questionable from a purely economic perspective, residents often go to considerable length to obtain them. Many still remember that during the drought, they quite simply became non-existent, with no access to land; to the national administrative structures that were largely urban-based; or to humanitarian aid, which tended to be distributed in towns. The fact that they were, to the untrained eye, invisible in the local landscape made it all too easy for others to ignore their suffering or even their deaths. They are not going to make that mistake again, and they feel that the legally attested ownership of even the smallest piece of land will at least mean that they are recognised as belonging somewhere.

How to Get By in Tamanrasset

Nana was born in the golden days of the 1960s to an Arabic-speaking trading family in Timbuktu. During the first Sahel drought, when she was barely in her teens, her father married her off as a second wife to one of his regular business partners, a middle-aged trader from central Algeria, perhaps as a way of getting her out of famine's way. The newly-wed couple moved first to Niamey and then to Maradi in southern Niger to open a sweet and ice-cream factory. Nana grew up surrounded by Arabic-speaking Saharan traders, men and women for whom regular travel between Mauritania, Mali, Niger, Algeria and Morocco was routine and who – like her – had relatives everywhere. The term 'globalisation' had not yet been coined at that time, but for her, close connections across national borders were simply a fact of life.

As political conditions in Niger worsened with the second drought of the 1980s, Nana and her husband relocated to Tamanrasset, where Nana at first felt like a stranger. 'The Algerians were weird at first, and then the women were jealous: with my white skin, I was so much more beautiful than them!' she recalls now with a smile. Tamanrasset was then living through a period of great change. According to official figures, it counted 3,000 inhabitants in 1966, 42,000 in 1977, and 95,000 in 1987, with urban infrastructures and water supply struggling to keep up. By that time, more than half – some say two-thirds – of the population were Sahelian migrants despite occasional mass deportations – although here, as throughout the Sahara, it is often difficult to draw the line between migrants, family visitors and people with multiple claims of belonging. Nana and her husband soon found their feet in the rapidly growing city with the help of her husband's excellent social networks. The rather inconspicuous oasis town in central Algeria where he came from had in fact provided the trading elite of most of southern Algeria and beyond. Nana's husband died in the 1990s after a protracted illness.

Nana left the sickroom where she had nursed him to find the country once more changed: if the 1970s and 1980s had restructured social and economic relations in the Sahel, the 1990s were a time of great upheaval in Algeria, and refugees from the north of the country, uprooted by civil war, poured into Tamanrasset. Nana sold her late husband's business and invested all the proceeds in her own. Today, she is a conspicuous figure at all Malian Arab gatherings and family events; she knows everything and everybody, and her opinion is much valued. She owes this respected position not merely to her early arrival but also to her excellent connections to 'real Algerians': she is intimately acquainted with all parts of Tamanrasset society, partly because her cosmopolitan experience as a member of the wealthy business elite of Francophone Niger has taught her how to speak to everyone, including northern Algerians disgruntled by the 'backwardness' of the Algerian south.

Nana runs a sewing workshop, where she produces 'Sahelian' clothes of all possible styles for resident white Sahelians, but she also caters, as does Mahjouba, to the Algerian middle classes. Due to the large presence of sub-Saharan migrants, labour is cheap in Tamanrasset, and because of her experience in Timbuktu and Maradi, Nana is in an excellent position to appreciate the various skills that sub-Saharan workers might have. Her linguistic ability – she speaks Songhay and Arabic fluently, of course, as well as some Bambara, Hausa and French

– helps her here. Even though many of her workers are from Ghana ('That's where the really good tailors come from'), they are impressed by her 'local' knowledge of 'African ways' and trust her as one whose moral standards are intelligible to them. She may pay them a relatively low salary, but she provides lodgings and food, will cover medical expenses when needed and helps them in moments of distress.

Nana employs four to six tailors at any one time in a workshop inside her large compound. She is well aware that some of her employees are there to travel on, either to return home once they have earned sufficient money or to go to Europe once they are able to pay the fare – 'adventurers', she calls them with a resigned shrug. Most stay for six months to a year, but many come back after they have once again been picked up by the police and relieved of all their earthly possessions or once they have returned home for a while and run out of money. Her workers are of course aware that Nana's wealth is based on their labour and that she takes advantage of their difficult situation, but they know that she can protect them and that, in Tamanrasset, such protection comes at a price. 'If you work at the market', one of the tailors explained to me with a somewhat tired smile, 'the police will watch you and count every dinar you earn. Then, when they think that you have earned enough to leave, they will come and take it all. If you work for Nana, she takes her share, but if the police come for you, she will send them away; if they catch you outside, she will come for you and get you out of prison'.

Nana is not alone in taking advantage of the cheap labour offered by migrants, whether they are in Tamanrasset to stay or merely on their way up. The town's building sector is booming, fuelled by profits made in trans-border trade and the abundance of cheap and often highly skilled workers. Particularly conspicuous, or so everybody says, are the shiny new villas built by border police. 'It used to be that police officers and civil servants saw Tamanrasset as a punishment post', Sidi, an elderly trans-border trader and sometime diplomat, explained with a twinkle in his eyes. 'Now people are fighting to get these positions. If you want to get married, they say, go to Tamanrasset. If you want to set up a business, go to Timiaouine. If you want to earn your weight in gold, go to Bordj'. The chief of police in In Salah, for instance, runs the principal bus company providing services between Tamanrasset and In Salah. He picks up migrants in In Salah in his official capacity, sends them back to Tamanrasset at government expense and then, in his private capacity as a transport entrepreneur, sells them a ticket back north before they even get off the bus. Or so it is rumoured.

While the exploitation of West African migrants is thus rife, Sahelian migrants from neighbouring countries, less threatened, linguistically more versatile and with a longer experience of how things work locally, prefer to work independently. On the outskirts of town, the landscape is marked by traces of makeshift industries set up by Hausa- and Songhay-speaking migrants from central Niger with the purpose of taking advantage of Algeria's relatively wealthy consumer economy. Near the municipal slaughterhouse, workers collect animal skins that otherwise would be left to rot in ugly, odorous piles in the sweltering sun. They scrape and clean them by hand. Most are then loaded onto large trucks and sent to Kano in northern Nigeria, where they are used in the local leather industry. Others are tanned locally, using either cheap chemicals or local herbs known to Sahelian pastoralists, and then sold on to local Tuareg catering to the tourist industry or, since tourism collapsed in the 2010s, the international market in Tuareg paraphernalia.

Next door, several makeshift foundries have emerged. Workers scout the streets and municipal dump of Tamanrasset early in the morning and bring back empty aluminium cans by the bagful. These cans are melted down in hand-built ovens whose temperature is increased with the help of repurposed bicycle pumps. The liquid aluminium is poured into simple moulds made out of sand, modelled on traditional Saharan clay cooking pots; the aluminium cooking pots are then sold on the Tamanrasset market to immigrant Sahelians but also increasingly to Algerian customers who find these pots robust, cheap and easy to use. Further along, used oil barrels are cut open, cleaned and hammered into large suitcases and travel chests of the kind that can be found on all trans-Saharan trucks – containing provisions, tools and anything that needs to be kept away from the sand.

The town centre and adjacent quarters are similarly marked by the presence of Sahelian migrants. Many of those who have lived in Tamanrasset for long know how to take advantage of their intermediate position between 'real Algerians' and migrants from further afield. Sahelian-run restaurants offer West African food; 'ghettos' sell cheap accommodation and some degree of protection; Sahelian garages repair cars and trucks; and shops offer the equipment and expertise necessary for onward travel. Sahelian and West African women can be seen, in Tamanrasset's large 'African' market or simply walking through the streets, peddling lunch to the many migrant workers employed on local building sites as plumbers, painters and decorators or gardeners.

A few steps from Nana's house-cum-workshop, at the Catholic mission, Sister Margaret greets me with a sigh and a cup of coffee, served with an almost imperceptible tremble. The mission, founded by the legendary Père de Foucault, has long been part of Tamanrasset's urban landscape. Sister Margaret came here decades ago, during the first years of Algerian independence, as a very young and inexperienced nun, as she now recalls with a smile. She immediately fell in love with the place, glorying in its sheer physical beauty but also in its remoteness and solitude. Catholic missions, established in colonial times, are tolerated on Algerian soil as long as they do not try to make any converts. This suited her very well, but now things have changed beyond recognition: with the recent influx of migrants from ever further south, the numbers of faithful have suddenly exploded. 'If only they didn't have "immaculate conception" printed all over the colourful wraps they use to cover themselves', she sighed, pointing to a group of ladies from Benin, happily chatting as they prepared a large lunch over a small cooking fire in the courtyard of the formerly quiet Catholic mission.

Yet she probably knows, as do most residents of contemporary Tamanrasset and other Saharan cities, that this is just the way things will be from now on: after a short interruption of Saharan mobility in the middle of the twentieth century as Saharan borders hardened into imperial and then international borders, Saharan connectivity has once more come into its own. As Salma, my Tamacheq-speaking but impeccably Algerian lodger in Tamanrasset, told me with a big smile, Tamanrasset is 'Africa already': 'Women can go where they please; there is music, food and clothes of all kinds. Not like everywhere else in Algeria, where people are so dull'.

Solitudes Enlightened

In the late 1970s, when a group of young Tuareg migrants in southern Algeria started to meet regularly after work to pluck familiar tunes from their home region in northern Mali on the one acoustic guitar they shared among them, they had no idea that they were about to launch a new musical genre. Their main concern was with words, not music: they were reciting poetry intended for the uplift of others like them, young Tuareg thrown into exile as their parents lost their herds, the guitar riffs intended just to get their point across. They called themselves Taghreft Tinariwen, the 'enlightenment of the solitudes' (*tinariwen* is the plural of ténéré). Their first audio tapes, recorded at home, circulated widely in the slums of the fast-growing southern Algerian and Libyan cities but also in the pastures of northern Mali and northern Niger.

Many pastoralist families thrown into misery in the northern Sahel had opted to send their young men abroad in the hope that they would earn enough money to keep their families back home alive or, at the very least, be able to fend for themselves. Other migrants had come of their own accord, embittered by the shame they had lived through, preferring wage labour in the Maghreb to begging food from humanitarian organisations or the government or simply sitting by idly as their families slid into despair. They had flocked into the towns and cities of southern Algeria and Libya and quickly came to constitute the proletarian underclass, exploitable at will. Collectively, they came to be known as *ishumar*, a word derived from the French *chômeurs*, unemployed, indicating a deep shift, not only in status but also in self-perception, from pastoralists – who are never 'unemployed', or indeed 'employed', but quite simply live with their herds – to proletarians whose survival depended on the daily humiliation of wage labour in a hostile environment.

They were the people Taghreft Tinariwen wanted to touch. Many of the musicians had moved in the early 1980s to Libya, where at that time Qadhafi's military training camps were wide open to young men like them, offering jobs that seemed less shameful than cleaning, portering or fetching and carrying for others. There, they met like-minded musicians, a few of whom had been deployed to the battlefields of northern Chad and Lebanon as part of Qadhafi's Islamic Legion. They spent their military stipends on electric guitars. People imitated their songs, added others, and 'guitara' (as this musical genre came to be known locally), played on cheap instruments or even cheaper tape recorders, soon became one of the defining features of the culture of young northern Sahelians stranded in the Maghreb.

The ishumar sang of their loneliness in exile, of their longing for home, but also and especially about the wreckage of their home society that they had witnessed as teenagers: the shame brought about by the droughts and their global television coverage; their elders' inability to defend and protect themselves; the political corruption they had often witnessed first hand; and their own marginalisation both by Sahelian governments and by their elders. Much of this, they said, was due to their own weakness, which in turn was linked to internal divisions and prejudice according to place of origin, dialect spoken, race or status. Their songs were first and foremost calls for unity among Saharan people of different status, origins and nationalities, all now labelled 'friends'. They were born out of a new way of socialising in exile among Tuareg from different countries and distant regions, speaking different versions of the same language, who had all met in the Bani w-Iskuts of southern Algeria and Libya.

They were also, in their own way, part of the counterculture of the 1970s. They exhorted people to act in ways – including living in the desolation of the 'true desert', or ténéré – that traditionally would have been seen as a proof of madness:

I live in the deserts (tinawiren)
where there are no trees and no shade.
Veiled friends, abandon indigo and face veils

the deserts are expecting you
this is where our relatives' blood has been shed.
This is our land
in it lies our future.
Ibrahim ag Alkhabib, 1979[5]

While for their elders, the ténéré was a place of asuf, 'loneliness', these songs implied that true asuf was actually found in the factories, building sites and army camps of southern Libya, where it was all too easy to 'lose oneself' in alcohol, solitude and misery.

Most importantly, Tinariwen songs called for armed rebellion as the only possible way of restoring the honour that they had collectively lost:

We saw a small child
new born.
Men lifted it up
but it didn't cry.
It laughed his oath that
he would take revenge.
He picked up his weapons
the lance and the sword
Keddu ag Osadd, 1990[6]

The fire has been burning for far too long
In our lost slumbers
For the burnt animals and the aged dead
at the gates of Kidal we must assemble
And fight
Tinariwen, Chetma, 2004

Tinariwen returned to northern Mali when the second Tuareg

rebellion against the Malin central government broke out in 1990. This was when they crafted their legendary style: young men with wild hairstyles, what was left of their turbans wrapped loosely around their necks; an electric guitar over one shoulder, an AK-47 over the other; traces of mud – or is it blood? – on their faces.

Tinariwen's fighting career was short. Prominent band members were among the signatories of the controversial 1991 peace accords, and they were then 'discovered' by the French group Lo'Jo and started touring internationally. Their success contributed greatly to creating the category of 'Tuareg' music ('desert blues') on the world stage, with its own audience, concert circuits and festivals. Probably the most famous of these was the Festival in the Desert, first held in 2001 near Kidal and since 2003 near Timbuktu. Tinariwen recorded songs with Led Zeppelin and Cat Stevens. In 2010, they participated in the opening of the football World Cup in South Africa and won the Grammy Award for Best World Music in 2012.

However brilliant Tinariwen's career – and it certainly came with its share of humiliations, as it required to play up to the exotic niche that 'World Music' had reserved for them – it meant that their message of 'resistance' was fundamentally transformed from a very particular uprising against an authoritarian nation-state and its military organs to a more general resistance that is attributed by Western publics to 'indigenous' people of all kinds. Even their beatnik dress code has, somewhat ironically, come to stand for 'traditional Tuareg culture' on the world stage. Meanwhile, life in the places that gave rise to ishumar culture – Bani-w-Iskut and the Sahelian quarters of Tamanrasset, Sebha and Kufra – rolled on regardless, far from the glamour of the international stage.

*

Neither Tinawiren's songs nor their message have lost any of their urgency. Although large-scale Sahelian migrations, forced sedentarisation and concomitant urbanisation were initially seen as emergency responses to a temporary crisis, it became quickly obvious that they were here to stay. Partly, this was so because the underlying political problems that had turned the Sahel droughts into famine had not been solved as the rains returned in the 1990s. And partly because the 1970s and 1980s droughts, despite their iconic quality, were but expressions of larger changes which meant that historical survival strategies in the Sahara and the Sahel had become inadequate. Famine returned to parts of the Sahel in 2005 and in 2010 and 2012. The 2010 famine in Niger, some say, was in fact much worse than anything that had happened in the 1970s and 1980s.

The jury is still out, however, on what larger changes were behind these repeating droughts and famines. In the 1970s and 1980s, the droughts were read as primarily the result of the 'Sahel syndrome': population pressure coupled with poverty encourages people to put marginal lands under cultivation and thereby exhausts soils. Herds overgraze, destroying pasture. This in turn renders people even poorer than before, pushing them further into ever more marginal lands. Hence the many international projects to fight 'desertification', mostly by planting trees, that have emerged since the late 1970s. In January 2021, another 16 billion USD were earmarked for anti-desertification programmes; international programmes to slow demographic growth are similarly thriving.

Yet scientists today tend towards more nuanced responses. The Sahara oscillates, they say, between two possible 'stable states', one dry, one green; recent satellite images show that overall, the Sahel is currently 'greening', although this tells us little about biodiversity, which tends to be falling. Human occupation of land, including agriculture and mobile pastoralism, is not necessarily detrimental to the soil but might actually, when carried out carefully, improve it. Drought is linked primarily to ocean temperature and thus is caused by global rather than regional factors. Since the early 1970s, dry-season temperatures have indeed risen, in line with temperatures worldwide, reaching record heights in 2010. This has caused further aridity in some parts of the region and humidity in others, as the associated increase in carbon dioxide encourages plant growth. In certain areas, overall rainfall has increased, although the usually more torrential rains tend to have a negative effect on soil – as well as destroying historical mud-brick qsūr and threatening people's lives, as described in chapter 2.

Climate change, then, in the Sahara is not merely a future threat but has long been a reality that, despite long-standing attempts to lay the blame primarily on local populations held responsible for 'desertification', they can do nothing about, as they are generally among the lowest emitters of carbon dioxide on the planet. But locally, climate change is rarely perceived in terms of an 'advancing desert'; rather, it is seen as an increase in unpredictability and irregularity – not an overall lack of rain but too much of it in the wrong place and at the wrong time; not an absence of vegetation but too much of the wrong kind; not a regular increase in temperature but the kind of unpredictability that means that knowledge accumulated over generations now appears useless. What makes people's situation unbearable is their increasing lack of control over their own livelihoods and the gradual reduction of alternative strategies – usually related in some form to mobility.

Nor do local people necessarily agree that there are 'too many' of them, although demographic growth in the Sahel (but not the northern Sahara) is among the highest of the world. As the historian Barbara Cooper points out, there is something odd in the fact that countries such as France, with a rather aggressive pro-natalist policy back home, fund programmes aimed at the reduction of populations abroad, primarily in their former colonies in sub-Saharan Africa.[7] This oddity is rarely lost on the targets of such programmes. Women locally, she writes, are worried not about having too many children but, given the value placed locally on women's fertility and the total absence of any other form of social insurance (pensions, health insurance, unemployment benefits) about not having enough.

It is difficult in such a context to declare, as the World Health Organisation routinely does, that Nigerien women, for instance, are 'in need' of better contraception. What they are in need of is better health care that takes into account their own priorities, fears and desires, that makes it possible for them to be fully in control of their reproductive health, returning at least some of the control over their own lives that they feel they have lost. This is a profoundly ethical matter that raises issues of international power relations and the definition of other people's 'needs' according to global agendas and of the price poor countries currently have to pay for the transgressions of the rich.

Even if the Sahara and Sahel had returned or could ever return to their pre-drought state, we can be reasonably certain that people such as Mahjouba, Zahra and Nana would not really want to 'return' to a pristine past of mobile husbandry. As we have seen throughout this book, this past never existed: pastoralists and agriculturalists have always lived in complex economic systems that combine local productive strategies with more extroverted activities, such as trade and seasonal migration. As much as Mahjouba and others like her like to invest in livestock and spend a few weeks 'fatting up' with their animals during lactation, this does not mean that they see themselves primarily as pastoralists or that they would want to swap their urban cosmopolitan lives for the hardships of a year-round mobile pastoral life. This, they would all agree, is best left for the young men, like trans-border smuggling in illicit substances, to cut their teeth on before fully growing up.

The majority of contemporary Saharan populations today is urban, and this will continue to be the case in the decades to come. This does not mean that they are no longer 'true Saharans' or have betrayed their families' pasts. Rather, they have invented new ways of inhabiting this space, combining long-standing features of success – mobility, flexibility, the ability to build and maintain far-reaching connections over time – into novel forms. The tangled streets of Bani w-Iskut and the rich and complex life that people such as Mahjouba and her friends and family lead there and in similar places are thus not just an emergency response to a crisis but the epicentre of contemporary, dynamic and cosmopolitan Saharan culture. This culture is increasingly put under pressure by international interventions aiming to redefine trans-border mobility as a global threat, to which we will now turn.

9

IN SEARCH OF SECURITY

The Tenéré has become an upland of thorns
Where elephants fight each other
Crushing tender grass underfoot.

The gazelles have found refuge high in the mountains
The birds no longer return to their nests at night
The camps have all fled.

You can read the bitterness on the faces of the innocents
During these difficult and bruising times
In which all solidarity has gone.

Tenere taqqal, from the album *Elwan*, Tinariwen, 2017

Under the distracted eyes of a handful of soldiers, two teenage boys sweep the arrival lounge at Faya airport, which was then – in 2012 – the only airport in northern Chad with a paved runway. A security agent tapes two handwritten signs to nearby windows: 'Departure' and 'Arrival'. A few Chadian officials arrive, accompanied by two television crews, one Chadian, one French. A fire engine is parked nearby, dusty and shaken after the arduous 600-kilometre trek across the desert from Abéché in eastern Chad. A small contingent of French soldiers drive by, stop briefly, survey the situation and disappear in a cloud of dust. The hours pass slowly. Chadian soldiers attempt, unsuccessfully, to keep the runway free of marauding donkeys; security agents scrutinise the horizon and speculate about the likelihood of a dust storm. Finally, as the night is about to fall, there is a distant roar on the horizon. A plane appears, approaches, finally lands. Its passengers spill out: mostly European tourists interspersed with a few journalists. There is an audible sigh of relief.

This is the first time the Faya runway, paved in 1991, has been used for a civilian flight. It is also the first time that quite so many tourists, organised by the French travel company Point Afrique, arrive in Faya all at once. Although tourism has become a mainstay of a few local economies throughout the Sahara, it has long remained limited to certain countries considered to be safe and to particular places within them where both infrastructure and professional guides were available. Even though tourists come to the Sahara for an 'authentic' desert-trek experience, this requires preparation, supplies, infrastructure and trained personnel. For a long time, southern Algeria and northern Niger largely cornered the market, then Mali, and finally Mauritania. Never Chad, which, given its long civil war (1968–87) and subsequent series of military coups and rebellions, was generally considered to be beyond the pale for foreign travellers. Officially, only 800 tourists had visited northern Chad between 2000 and 2012, and most were expatriates who were resident in Chad anyway.

At a time when the rest of the Sahara was in crisis, with wars in northern Mali and Libya, kidnappings in southern Algeria and Mauritania and famine in northern Niger, one might wonder how and why northern Chad suddenly emerged as a 'safe' destination for tourists. Much of this impression of 'security' clearly was relative: the situation seemed even worse elsewhere, and Point Afrique, specialising in desert travel, was about to go bankrupt and needed a new outlet. The Chadian government, at the same time, was desirous to escape from its long-standing status as a war-torn pariah country and could afford to do so due to oil revenues that had started to come in since the mid–2000s. For the occasion, the Chadian government had organised a large festival 500 kilometres further east, in the then Chadian president's hometown of Fada, which was attended by quite as many (if not more) high-ranking government officials as tourists and was repeatedly broadcast on national television. The message was clear: Chad was on its way to becoming a 'normal' country; an important player, moreover, in regional diplomacy, where power relations were about to be redefined due to Qadhafi's demise.

The only people who were profoundly sceptical about this sudden redefinition of northern Chad as a 'safe' place were the French army, who in fact still – eighty years after official decolonisation – have a garrison in Faya and on whom Point Afrique had hoped to rely for logistical support. The French soldiers had turned out in numbers, and their commanding officer was cautiously scrutinising the horizon. 'They might have sol-air rockets', he mumbled, 'easy to obtain at the moment' (this was a reference to the ongoing civil war in Libya, a mere 500 kilometres further north). 'One bang and they are all shot down, and we have to clean up the mess'.

As it happened, there was no bang. The tourists landed safely and were quickly led away to the 'camps' that had been set up for this purpose. (The last hotel in Faya, dating from colonial times, had closed many decades earlier.) Yet despite the outstanding natural beauty of northern Chad, both tourists and locals were rather underwhelmed by their experience. Successful tourism requires much preliminary work in order to create 'sites' of particular interest and to train guides to show them to Europeans, in tune with their needs and desires. As, from the point of view of the Chadian government, tourism was primarily a political stunt aimed at an international audience, this work – necessarily delegated by Point Afrique to local institutions via the Chadian Ministry of Tourism – had not been carried out.

Locals, therefore, could not understand why all these people were coming merely to 'take pictures of rocks' and quite simply did not know how to relate to them – or could not even guess that these visitors wanted to be related to. Local conversation was much more preoccupied with the French military (whom they know well) and what they saw as the latter's attempt to 'denigrate' the security situation in international eyes by claiming that Faya was unsafe for tourists. It was around this time that the French words 'tourist' and 'terrorist' first became current in Faya, and it was easy to confuse one with the other ('terro-tourists'): two kinds of foreigners with uncertain motives whom the French army expected to show up that day at the airport. In any case, tourism in northern Chad never really took off, and national and international debates over Faya's 'safety' were of similarly short duration. Chad revised its diplomatic strategy, investing less in international tourism and more in international military interventions as, over the ensuing years, the Sahel and the Sahara gradually descended into chaos.

'Security' is a relative term. Places are 'safe' not just because of the absence of danger but also because they are perceived to be so. This perception, in turn, is the result of negotiation and competing interests. Nor are places ever 'safe' in the abstract; they are at best safer than others; once one starts worrying about security, threats appear everywhere, and nowhere is ever safe enough. Security, then, is always a matter of interpretation; it is largely socially and politically constructed and varies according to one's point of view. Even before the arrival of the tourist plane, local residents might have concurred that Faya was not a safe place, but they would probably have related this to local brawls or the instability of the political situation rather than to a 'global terrorist threat'.

Since the 2000s, 'security' has replaced 'development' and 'humanitarian aid' as the dominant paradigm through which Western powers interact with most African and hence also Sahelian and Saharan populations. Partly, this is so because 'security' has become the polite term to refer to military matters, and military forces are on the rise everywhere. In 2005, one-fifth of the US 'international aid' budget was managed by the Pentagon. In 2017, 29 per cent of it was directly earmarked for military aid, 11 per cent for 'political and strategic' sectors and 6 per cent for 'non-military security'. As a result, overall African military expenditure has increased by 65 per cent over the last decade.

Partly, the current popularity of 'security' is related to the way the term, and the military language that often accompanies it, has been extended to refer to almost everything. Martial language pervades public rhetoric on both sides of the Mediterranean (and the Atlantic), from the 'war against terror' to the 'war against irregular migration', against corruption, drugs, human smuggling, environmental degradation, Ebola, COVID – you name it, there will be a war against it. As a result, armed personnel and military techniques are increasingly prominent in all kinds of campaigns, from public health initiatives to anti-poaching efforts to migration control, gradually replacing civilian state actors or international NGOs. We can call these processes 'militarisation', a word that refers both to the growing importance of military personnel and expenditure and to the extension of military logic to all matters of social and political life.

To understand how the Sahara came to be militarised, this chapter traces the historical roots of the present situation, starting with events in northern Mali in 2012 and flashing back to earlier conflicts as necessary. As we embark on our exploration of these processes, it is important to remember that they participate in a global phenomenon, that they increasingly structure Saharan space and society and that, however little we might like guns, we need to approach them with a certain agnosticism: to see precisely what they produce on the ground, which might often have little to do with our initial expectations or their original remit.

Mali 2012

In January 2012, only a few weeks before Air Afrique's tourist plane landed in Faya, fighters from the Mouvement National de Libération de l'Azawad (Movement for the national liberation of Azawad, Mali's extreme north, MNLA) successfully attacked several army garrisons in northern Mali. They met with little resistance as they advanced, taking Gao on 31 March and Timbuktu on 1 April. On 6 April, they announced (from Paris) the creation of the independent state of Azawad in northern Mali. By then, rebel forces controlled two-thirds of Malian territory, although much of this area was desert and home to less than 10 per cent of Mali's overall population. In the meantime, the national government in southern Mali had collapsed following a military coup.

'Tuareg' rebellions have been an integral part of the country's history since independence from France in 1960, but they had never quite so successful. There were several reasons why things were different in 2012. Qadhafi's regime in Libya had collapsed, with international help, in 2011. As seen in chapter 8, many young Tuareg (and Arabic speakers) from northern Mali and northern Niger had lived in Libya, and some had been part of the armed forces. Identified as 'pro-Qadhafi', they now had to leave in a hurry, taking both their weapons and their military skills with them. Also, this time, the MNLA was not fighting alone in northern Mali but was first seconded and then rapidly displaced by groups fighting under an Islamic banner.

These included al-Qā'ida in the Islamic Maghreb (AQIM) but also a number of more local groups, such as Ansār al-Dīn (Companions of religion) and the Movement pour l'unicité et le jihad en Afrique de l'Ouest (Movement for unity and jihad in West Africa, MUJAO), which together seemed to be able to draw on a much more extensive pool of resources and recruits than the MNLA alone. Islamist involvement in the Central Sahara has a long history, starting with the Algerian civil war in the 1990s and notable feats such as the kidnapping of thirty-two mostly German tourists in southern Algeria in 2003 and the attack on the gas production plant in In Amenas in 2013. But until 2012, Islamist groups had used Mali as a safe haven, a place of refuge and respite, rather than as a battlefield.

After a short-lived alliance with the MNLA, Islamist groups expelled MNLA officials from Timbuktu in April and from Gao in June 2012 and started to administer both towns and their hinterlands according to sharī'a. In November 2012, the MUJAO also captured Menaka, thereby putting all major towns in the north under Islamist control. On 10 January 2013, Ansār al-Dīn launched an attack on Konna, a town in central Mali, beyond the desert proper. Following a demand for help by the then Malian president Dioncounda Traoré, the French army intervened on 11 January. By the end of the month, the French army, with the help of Chadian troops, controlled all major settlements in northern Mali. It was gradually, but never totally, replaced by the Multidimensional Integrated Stabilization Mission in Mali (MINUSMA), a UN 'peacekeeping' operation, from 25 April 2013 until, after yet another military coup in 2021, the Malian government asked most international forces to leave.

Although external military intervention was swift in removing Islamist control from towns and in killing perhaps one-third of the estimated 2,000 fighters in the area, its victory never extended to the countryside. Islamist groups under various labels and affiliations have since proliferated, including further south. Today, they control most of the rural areas in central and northern Mali, where they have implemented their own forms of territorial and legal administration centred on wells, Quranic schools and Islamic courts. From the outside, the whole area now appears to be a hotbed of radical Islamism, violence, drug and arms trafficking and human smuggling, crying out, it seems, for even more military intervention. Accordingly, international army bases have been constructed throughout the region, from Mauritania via southern Algeria to (until very recently) northern Niger and Chad. Algeria, home to a US army base near Tamanrasset, recently finalised the construction of 6,700 kilometres of wall, fence and ditch to protect its Saharan borders against unwanted incursions from the south.

How can we disentangle these various events? Let us first consider what it might mean for people locally to 'rebel'. After independence, many Saharan populations were left disgruntled, feeling underrepresented in the new states that were now supposed to govern them. As we saw in the previous chapter, the first armed rebellion in northern Mali broke out in 1963 to protest neglect and mistreatment at the hands of the central government a mere three years after independence was declared. This protest was brutally suppressed by the army. Subsequently, the Bamako government kept much of northern Mali under military rule until the 1990s. This meant that for most residents, with the exception of local elite groups now co-opted as unofficial 'customary chiefs', all avenues for political action – from government employment to enrolment in the armed forces – were blocked.

Rebellion broke out once more in the 1990s with the involvement of young ishumar (whom we met in the previous chapter), some of whom had been trained in Libya. The movement soon faltered as it split along dividing lines of status and race that, despite the nominal egalitarianism of the Malian state and ishumar appeals for unity, remained deeply entrenched. As early as 1991, parts of the rebel movement signed a peace agreement with the Malian state, which promised the partial integration of rebel groups into the Malian army and political decentralisation, usually to the benefit of local elite groups. Others followed suit later, while yet others denounced the whole process as a sell-out: a relinquishing of the ideals and region-wide solidarity of the rebellion in exchange for government or army positions or money.

After a wave of brutal repression, the Malian state responded to the rebellion of the 1990s with a double strategy: on the one hand, the integration of rebels into the army and of their leaders into important government positions; on the other, a careful nurturing, fostering and funding of local cleavages and hostilities in order to undermine any fragile solidarity between groups that could coalesce into another rebellion. Nevertheless, rebellion broke out again in the early 2000s, in 2006, 2007–2009, 2010 and, with more success, 2012. It therefore became quite ordinary for young men locally to join a rebel group, to 'make peace' in exchange for a position in the army, to subsequently join another rebellion and so on, in the absence, for most, of any other viable option of political or even just social advancement.

Over time, this created particular systems in which the threat, albeit not necessarily the reality, of armed violence fundamentally structured the political field and in which dividing lines between the official army and local rebels became increasingly blurred. Armed men, whether in uniform or not, emerged as central political actors throughout the region.

Take, for instance, Rhissa ag Boula from neighbouring Niger, which, like Mali, was shaken by a series of rebellions in the 1990s. Rhissa ag Boula was born in 1957 near the mining town of Arlit, described in chapter 1. He started his professional career as a tour guide. In 1983, at the height of the second Sahel drought, he co-founded, with the legendary Mano Dayak, the first tourist agency with headquarters in the Agadez region, Temet Voyage. Together, they joined the Nigerien Tuareg rebellion as soon as it started in 1990 and both distinguished themselves in leading positions. As in Mali, the 1995 and 1997 peace accords stipulated the 'integration' of former rebels into the armed forces or government. In a somewhat radical career change, Rhissa ag Boula was therefore nominated minister of tourism in 1997.

Seven years later, accused of complicity in murder, he was arrested and, while on temporary release, fled into exile in France. In 2008, a Nigerien tribunal condemned him to death. From his base in France, Rhissa founded a new rebel movement, the Front des Forces de Redressement (FFR). He returned to Niamey in 2010, after the then Nigerien president had been toppled in a coup, and found himself once more in prison. Rapidly cleared of all charges, he was elected regional councillor in Agadez in 2011 and then became the new president's special advisor in security matters.

Notwithstanding this long history of rebellion, international experts tended to describe the 2012 'jihadist' takeover in northern

Mali as sparked by external factors, by a heady cocktail of Algerian jihadis, Colombian drug smugglers and Libyan guns. The reasons were international rather than national: since 2001, the public enemy number one of the 'free West' had been 'Islamic terrorists', and the US and its allies had launched a 'global war on terror' (GWOT) to fight them wherever they might be said to raise their heads. Islamic terrorists were seen as particularly attracted to regions with poor government: events in northern Mali thus seemed to confirm what everybody already knew.

In fact, as already noted at the end of chapter 6, the majority of Islamist fighters in northern Mali were recruited locally, and local jihadi organisations occupied centre stage in the conflict. Even the handful of Algerians involved were often familiar with the region, either from a long shared history of trans-Saharan connections or through marriage (or both). The more spectacular jihadi activities dwelled on by foreign media, such as the destruction of saints' tombs, public floggings, amputations and the prohibition of football games, were usually carried out by local organisations and fighters, while the AQIM leadership attempted to calm their overzealousness in favour of a 'progressive application' of sharī'a. AQIM in fact repeatedly cautioned its fighters against the 'fanaticism' (*ta'assub*, which is perhaps better translated as 'factionalism') of their local allies, 'which is only useful when it is well directed and ruled by law', admonishing them to be as inclusive as possible in their recruitment and counsel.[1]

As we've seen, people locally had no need for others to encourage them to fight. Deep-seated cleavages and tensions continued to animate local political life, with added force due to ecological degradation and rising demographic pressure. Here as elsewhere, the universal rhetoric of Islam and its claims to justice and equality provided both a hope for unity and a powerful language to voice long-standing oppression and exclusion. In a context where notions of nobility are bound up with both martial and religious excellence, jihad offers the opportunity to claim both in a single gesture. In central Mali, Islamist groups fight for access to pasture and against former nobles who claim exclusive control over them, in the name of God but also for the benefit of former subordinates' languishing herds. Others might simply be looking for somebody to protect them, as life without such protection has become impossible. From their point of view, the difference between international soldiers and international jihadis might be primarily one of efficacy and reliability.

If political Islam conveys a powerful message to the downtrodden, local elites have been quite as quick to take advantage of the opportunities it offers for their own betterment and for strengthening the cause of region-wide unity under their own leadership. Take, for instance, the political career of Iyad ag Ghali. Iyad is a member of the Ifoghas, who have provided the rulers of Kidal in northern Mali since colonial times. He was born in 1958 in Boghassa near Kidal. Like many others, he migrated to Libya in 1973 and joined Qadhafi's army, fighting in Lebanon and Chad – where he also hung out with future Tinariwen musicians, some of whose first recordings he sponsored. Pictures from the time show him long-haired and moustachioed, his turban loosely draped around his neck, a cigarette perched precariously in the corner of his mouth, idly plucking a guitar. He was among the main instigators of the 1990 rebellion in northern Mali, but he was also one of the first signatories of the 1991 peace agreement with the Malian government, which was much criticised by the rank and file for primarily furthering elite interests.

After the rebellion, Iyad became increasingly interested in Islamic reform, forging ties with Saudi Arabia. When thirty-two mostly German and Austrian tourists were taken hostage in 2003 in southern Algeria by Abderrazak el-Para in the name of the freshly founded AQIM, Iyad offered his services as a negotiator and obtained their release for a substantial ransom. (There is still much speculation in the area about how exactly this ransom was spent.) He then acted as secretary for the 2006 rebellion in northern Mali. A year later, he was granted a position at the Malian embassy in Saudi Arabia, whence he was expelled to France in 2010 for alleged 'terrorist activities'. In 2011, his bid for the leadership of the newly created Ifoghas-led rebel movement MNLA, soon to be victorious against the defunct Malian national army, was unsuccessful. The same year, his application for the position of *amenokal*, or traditional leader, was also rejected by the late incumbent's close family (Iyad's own cousins). Disgruntled and frustrated, Iyad decided to create his own rebel movement, Ansār al-Dīn, of Islamist leaning and in close contact with AQIM.

By April 2012, Iyad was probably the most influential man in northern Mali, yet he had somewhat overplayed his cards. After the French military intervention in 2013, his Ifoghas cousins succeeded in negotiating a fragile equilibrium among the French military, the Malian state, remnants of the MNLA and a new 'non-jihadi' Islamist alliance run by the new amenokal, the Haut Conseil pour l'unite de l'Azawad (HCUA) – which today by all accounts governs Kidal according to the principles of sharī'a. Iyad, however, was declared a 'terrorist' and forced into hiding. He is currently the leader of Jama'at Nasr al-Islam wal Muslimin (JNIM), a federation of various local Islamist movements, and last made international news when he sent a congratulatory note to the Taliban in Afghanistan after their victory in August 2021.

'African Solutions to African Problems'?

The Chadian national television station rarely broadcasts anything beyond national politics, or rather the redistribution of goods that in Chad stands in its stead. It was thus remarkable when, in spring 2012, an international news bulletin was not only included but treated at length: a long report on the armed conflict in northern Mali backed up with footage that had been provided, presumably free of charge, by French news agencies. Although television audiences in northern Chad are mostly rather uninterested in foreign news, people this time followed the story with great interest: rebellion and war were things they knew about, and the décor looked familiar: rocks, dust, camels, desert-going four-by-fours and veiled armed men in tattered uniforms, some with chin-strap beards.

Their interest was not kindled for nothing. In January 2013, as the French president François Hollande unilaterally decided to send a contingent of French soldiers to northern Mali, his announcement was rapidly followed by a similar promise by the Chadian president Idriss Déby Itno. Barely a week later, 2,000 to 2,400 Chadian soldiers arrived in northern Mali from the east, having travelled overland across Niger. This intervention was unusual, to say the least: Chad, which is not even a member of the Economic Community of West African States (ECOWAS, linked to each other through mutual defence treaties), was intervening in a country more than 2,000 kilometres from its borders, with no international mandate and no justification other than a vague 'Islamist threat' that then had little substance in Chad itself. By mid-May 2013, as the first contingent of 700 Chadian soldiers returned to N'Djamena with great pomp and celebration – the Chadian president had declared a national holiday to mark the occasion – official figures showed that 38 Chadian soldiers had been killed in combat and 84 wounded (unofficial figures speak of roughly 100 killed). In 2023, Chadian soldiers continued to be part of the official MINUSMA mission, furnishing 1,419 soldiers, the largest contingent of men, and suffering the highest number of casualties.

The northern Chadian television audience thus had good reason to be interested in conflict in northern Mali, especially because the Chadian army recruits disproportionately among its Saharan populations. In Faya, there is a soldier in every family; the armed forces are probably the main local employer. After decades of internationally sponsored civil conflict and armed rebellion and the dismantling of most other public institutions, the Chadian army has pretty much come to stand for the state itself. Idriss Déby Itno, who ordered his country's military intervention in Mali in 2013 and who was himself from the north of the country, had come to power in a coup, toppling his predecessor and former comrade-in-arms Hissène Habré, a fellow northerner who had also come to power in a coup, toppling his former comrade-in-arms Goukouni Weddeye – a fellow northerner who had also come to power in a coup. Idriss Déby was later killed in a skirmish fighting rebels wishing to do unto him as he had done unto his predecessor and was – unconstitutionally but with French backing – replaced by his son, the general Mahamat Idriss Déby Itno. This is how Chadian politics works, as people in Faya are well aware.

For decades, this thorough militarisation of Chadian politics and society was something that was rather unavowable in international circles. The EU especially has spent vast amounts of money on disarmament and reintegration programmes in Chad, which invariably were followed by new recruitment drives by the army; the number of Chadian soldiers remained relatively stable, hovering between 45,000 and 60,000, many of them integrated ex-rebels. Mass enrolment was here, as in Mali and Niger, a way both of controlling local society and buying a fragile peace, but the numbers were incomparably larger.

Throughout the 1990s and 2000s, Idriss Déby had to cover the centrality of the army in politics in all sorts of ways, such as establishing a semblance of parliamentary democracy and appointing ministers and civilian officials. With the current militarisation of the Sahara and Sahel, however, Chad's plethoric and rather unruly army has suddenly been turned from the scourge of its nation into its primary asset. Accordingly, and in contrast to his father, Déby *fils* barely ever feels compelled to quit his uniform, whatever the occasion.

Since the early 2000s, Western powers have had to confront a paradox: on the one hand, they increasingly read most of the world through the lens of the GWOT and other security threats that can, or so many think, be contained only through the deployment of military force. On the other, they are reluctant to 'put boots on the ground' abroad, as soldiers returning in coffins from places that most citizens hardly know how to place on a map makes for bad publicity and attracts increasingly vociferous accusations of neo-imperialism. From the early 2000s onwards, the answer to both problems was summed up in the pithy slogan 'African solutions to African problems'. This meant that Western powers continued to fund military interventions on the continent but pushed the burden of actual fighting to the African Union or other regional organisations. This created a budding market for 'African peacekeepers' – a new kind of 'international mercenary', as the French political scientist Richard Banégas called them in 1998.[2]

In the Sahel, perhaps the most prominent expression of this was the creation of the Multinational Joint Task Force (MNJTF) with headquarters in N'Djamena as early as 1994 and of the G5 Sahel Joint Task Force in 2014: two mixed forces composed of soldiers from Cameroon, Chad, Nigeria and Niger and from Mauritania, Mali, Niger, Burkina Faso and Chad, respectively. (The G5 Sahel has since been dissolved after the unilateral retreat of Mali, Niger and Burkina Faso in 2022 and 2023.) They were funded primarily by the US and the EU, with budgets in hundreds of millions of dollars, poured into national contexts where often even the most basic school or medical supplies are chronically lacking. UN missions, although they remain international, follow a similar pattern. In Mali in 2023, 85 per cent of the 15,000 MINUSMA soldiers were recruited in Africa, with Chad and Senegal furnishing the largest African contingents; second in the list of top contributors was Bangladesh. Soldiers from richer or poorer countries do not have the same kinds of equipment, nor can they afford to avoid risk and danger in the same way. Of the 101 international soldiers killed in Mali during the first months of intervention, 7 were European and 91 African, with the Chadian contingent counting the highest number of casualties.

For African soldiers, volunteering for peacekeeping missions is risky but offers usually better pay than they can earn back home alongside other means of enrichment and promises of social mobility and promotion. From the point of view of national governments, external operations bring in considerable funds while keeping potentially troublesome units and officers busy elsewhere. They thereby solve the basic problem faced by poor countries wishing to keep large armies: how to maintain a large concentration of non-productive and potentially dangerous personnel over time without depleting national budgets or risking instability at home. In this way, the growing market for African peacekeepers has fostered the consolidation of highly militarised regimes throughout the region. Chadian military expenditure, for instance, soared by 663 per cent between 2000 and 2009 in a country where basic health care and education remain an elusive dream for many. International 'peacekeeping' and 'anti-terrorist' missions, moreover, are only two among the many opportunities open to skilled men with guns in the contemporary Sahara and Sahel.

This was brought home to me in Faya in the summer of 2012. While the war in Mali raged on, I visited Colonel Tinemi of the Chadian army at his home. He was happy to see me and immediately ushered me into his impeccably kept sitting room for tea. Beyond it, the house was mostly a building site, but it was quite clear that it would be large, with perhaps a dozen rooms and a large courtyard. Colonel Tinemi was not only hospitable and generous, with a deep belly laugh, but also liked to think big. Behind pink cushions and doilies, the walls proudly displayed a number of framed certificates, all for training missions that he had undergone with US military officers. As he talked us through them one by one, he chuckled at memories of US soldiers lost in the heat, teaching Tinemi and his fellow officers – all well seasoned after years of combat – how to look after equipment that they would probably never see again according to security standards that seemed to belong to a different galaxy. Nonetheless, he conceded, the Americans were tough, and the stuff they brought with them ... He chuckled again: if only they knew that half of their trainees would probably abscond north, joining the ranks of Islamist groups that they were supposedly fighting against, or offer their services to the highest bidder on the busy Libyan job market for well-trained and fearless men with guns.

To read what are essentially local conflicts exclusively through the lens of a global war against terror has several effects on the ground. It creates a market for fighters and tilts the field of political action in favour of armed men, who might or might not act according to their trainers' and funders' norms and desires. It shores up authoritarian and highly militarised governments. Given the high degree of plasticity of political and military careers, it also indirectly helps fuel armed rebel movements of all colours by providing more and better-trained and -equipped fighters; by endorsing local perceptions that most opportunities for social mobility are tied to one's military capacity; and by creating frustration, rage and a need for armed protection among those who do not fight. 'This is why we learn how to handle a Kalashnikov', northern Chadian high school students once told me in Abéché, in the east of the country, in between two games of Scrabble by candlelight, as the city's electricity network had once again broken down.

Authoritarian governments throughout the region benefit from this murkiness. All grievances against central government or the army can now be restyled, on the international scene, as 'Islamism' and thereby rendered illegitimate, warranting foreign intervention. In September 2018, the French army, on the demand of the Chadian president, bombed local rebels in the name of the GWOT, although these rebels clearly had nothing to do with political Islam – one of them was a card-carrying member of the French Socialist Party. The Moroccan government similarly has attempted to legitimise much of its political and military action in the Western Sahara and beyond in the name of its fight for 'moderate' Islam, to great acclaim by Western donors.

This makes any attempt at rebellion extremely dangerous. Take, for instance, the trajectory of the southern Algerian political activist Abdessalem Tarmoune. A native of Djanet in Algeria's southeast, he was a maths teacher at the local high school. In 2004, he founded, with others, the local branch of the Mouvement des enfants du sud pour la justice (Movement of the children of the south for justice), which had emerged from region-wide protests against what people perceived as the neglect of the south by the central government and their exclusion from lucrative jobs in the petroleum sector. Two years later, when Abdessalem Tarmoune presented himself as a candidate in local elections, his candidacy was rejected on the grounds of 'former involvement with a terrorist organisation' – namely, the Movement for Justice. Frustrated and angered, Tarmoune and a few of his comrades briefly took a plane at Djanet military airport hostage. Nobody came to any harm, but the local authorities were deeply and publicly humiliated. They retaliated by imprisoning Tarmoune and his brother and repeatedly intimidating his family.

On his release, knowing that he had no other option, Tarmoune fled to the mountains and took up arms against the central government. Public authorities declared him a 'terrorist' and divulged family ties with radical Islamists who were members of AQMI (this was a meaningless accusation: Tarmoune was from a large and influential Sha'anbī family and thus related to most people in this sparsely populated area). Locally, however, he continued to enjoy much popular legitimacy: according to one of his fellow militants, he 'represented, for all young activists in southern Algeria, an ideal. They all at some point dreamt to be him; they all at some pointed wanted to do what he did'.[3] Tarmoune was finally driven to seek refuge in Chad, where he was killed in 2018 by 'Tubu rebels', according to official accounts. His violent end was in a sense pre-programmed by the salience of international categories of enmity that justify all kinds of state violence in the name of counter-terrorism, thereby nipping democratic aspirations – which are very real throughout the area – in the bud.

Under Watchful Eyes

Ousmane was born in Guinea in 1996, to a family of relatively wealthy livestock owners. His grandfather had been a professor of mathematics at a local university, and his father had divided his time between his work as a primary school teacher and his commitment as an active member of the one opposition party in the country.[4] Both of his sons inherited his passion for politics and were active members of their father's party from an early age. Ousmane was a good student from a good family, just about to pass his high school diploma and enter university; all seemed to be going well for him. Until, in 2015, the Guinean president Alpha Condé, during a rather heated election campaign, started to crack down on his political opponents. Ousmane, despite his youth, was arrested, humiliated, beaten. He was released from prison only because his older brother pulled as many strings as he could, spending a considerable amount of the family fortune on his release.

On the day of Ousmane's release, his brother picked him up at the prison gate, a small bag with a change of clothes and a toothbrush in his hands. He put Ousmane straight on the next bus to the Malian capital, Bamako, to get him out of harm's way. Ousmane's plan was simple: he would travel overland to Oran in Algeria, find a job there, if possible finish high school and perhaps even enrol in university – he had always wanted to study sociology – and wait until things settled back down in Guinea so that he could return home. He duly took a bus from Bamako to Gao in northern Mali, but there he was forced to change plans: the ongoing armed conflict had made the direct road to Algeria impassable, or at least extremely dangerous. He had to go via Agadez in neighbouring Niger. So far, his travels had been relatively easy apart from the usual potholes, dust and long hours on overcrowded buses. As a Guinean national, he was entitled to travel freely in all ECOWAS member states, although at times border officials needed to be reminded of this right with a small sum.

In Agadez, however, things started to get more complicated: he was met right off the bus by professionals vociferously offering passages to the north. Ousmane was suspicious and preferred to spend some time in town to get his bearings, talk to those more knowledgeable than he and buy supplies: tins of sardines, dry biscuits and jerrycans to carry his own water. He finally settled on a transporter, paid and set out on his journey with another thirty migrants, all crammed together on the back of a pickup truck. 'You really have to hold on tight', he recalled. 'Those drivers are crazy; they go at 240 kilometres per hour, off-road, a can of beer in one hand – if you fall off, they will not stop for you'. On arrival, he was in for an unpleasant surprise: although he had asked for a passage to Algeria, the driver had in fact dropped him off just on the other side of the border with Libya.

Here, Ousmane had to pay another driver to take him to the nearest town: 'They all have their own territory; you have to pass from one to the next'. In addition to having to negotiate his fare anew every time, his route was littered with check-points manned by militia members, bandits, army personnel, you name it – 'They are all in cahoots, also with the drivers, and every time, you pay'. Ousmane was lucky inasmuch as his brother had given him a neat sum to make it through; those who could not pay at these check-points were arrested and made to 'work off their debt'. Ousmane had still not given up on his plan of going to Algeria. When he arrived on the Libyan coast, he looked for transport to Tunisia but was once more led astray: the driver simply dropped him off at the point of departure for boats crossing the Mediterranean. This was why, days later, he found himself on an inflatable boat with a leak, 300 people like him and no compass, drifting towards international waters – where he was finally rescued by a fishing boat, but that is a different story.

Until the mid-1990s, Agadez in northern Niger was a rather sleepy, dusty town where locals mostly watched as trans-Saharan trucks, loaded high with smuggled cigarettes, headed north into the desert. From the early 1990s onwards, a few sub-Saharan migrants were usually perched on top, heading north into Libya, where immigrant labour was in great demand. With economic crises and structural adjustment in the countries of West and Central Africa and increasingly restrictive immigration policies in Europe contrasting strongly with the open-door policy in Libya, more and more sub-Saharans arrived from ever further afield. Demand for onward transport quickly exceeded supply, and a few enterprising locals started to offer specialised passenger transport. By the 2000s, there were several dozen travel agencies in Agadez alone. These operated freely from offices in the centre of Agadez, advertised their services throughout town, paid taxes to the local town hall and offered more or less fixed fares and guarantees of relatively safe travel.

The town council and the management of the bus station introduced 'transit fees' specifically for passengers going to North Africa in addition to the many more or less institutionalised check-points they would encounter on the road. Brokers acted as intermediaries between migrants fresh off the bus and travel agents; others specialised in selling equipment for desert travel, such as food, protective clothing and jerrycans for water storage. 'Ghettos' offered cheap lodgings to migrants, restaurants catered to their tastes, and call centres and money transfer facilities followed suit. Construction boomed. Agadez had fewer than 50,000 inhabitants in 1988 and approximately 125,000 by the end of the 2000s as migrants injected several billion CFA francs (several million USD) into the local economy each year. An estimated 7,000 people in the region lived directly or indirectly from the migrant economy.

Most migrants were headed for North African destinations: Libya but also increasingly Algeria and Morocco. A few, however, decided to travel on to Europe, following the routes and connections forged by another well-developed migration system linking North Africa to the northern Mediterranean. Although this concerned only a small proportion of migrants – an estimated 10 to 15 per cent – they became the subject of intense international attention from the mid-2000s onwards. The populist European right and increasingly North African leaders as well started to brandish figures of hundreds of millions of sub-Saharan African nationals ready to come to Europe via the Maghreb. In fact, the numbers of sub-Saharan African nationals entering Europe via the Mediterranean have never exceeded a few tens of thousands per year, a drop in the ocean when compared to overall EU immigration figures.

Salif was born in 1998 in Ziguinchor, the capital of Casamance. Casamance is the part of Senegal that is cut off from much of the rest of the country by Gambia and which has fought, since 1982, a fruitless but no less bloody war of independence. Both of Salif's parents were killed during the war, and he was brought up by their neighbour, who also looked after his father's land while Salif was young. Salif quickly discovered a passion for football and wanted to become a professional, using revenue derived from his father's land to pay for his training. But his tutor refused and instead threatened him with the police should Salif attempt to get his land back. An only son of an only son,

Salif had nobody to help him. He fled to Dakar and from there to Bamako, Ouagadougou, Agadez and Libya. Less fortunate than Ousmane, he had to work at each stop to earn enough money to travel on. This was at first simple, he said, but became very difficult as soon as he reached Agadez, full of people just like him, ready to work for cut-throat wages.

Confused, like Ousmane, by the large number of people offering onwards travel, he decided to trust a Senegalese broker whom he met in the streets. At least they spoke the same language. But the driver his countryman had found for him, for a fee, abandoned him and the other passengers in the middle of the desert. They were saved by a Nigerien police patrol, which took them back to Agadez. As they went to complain to the driver, the latter offered to find them another car for half-price. Salif accepted this offer although he could pay only a fraction of the money demanded – he simply could not bear to spend any more time in Agadez. This time, the driver took him to Sebha in southern Libya, directly to a Libyan who forced him to 'work off his debt'. He severely and repeatedly beat Salif, injuring his knee in such a way that he had to abandon all dreams of a career as a professional footballer. One day, Salif managed to run away from a building site where he was working. He found refuge with another Senegalese in Sebha, who then exploited him quite as badly as his earlier Libyan captor. One day, Salif managed to creep into a group of migrants set to leave Libya for Europe, boarded a boat and arrived, a harrowing trip later, in Italy.

Since the 2000s, the EU has started to subject Saharan states to incentives and pressures to sign readmission and cooperation agreements to combat irregular migration. The signing of these agreements, at times within the framework of the European Development Fund (EDF), was generally accompanied by trade and development cooperation programmes, leaving the countries concerned little choice but to comply (at least on paper). From cities to desert check-points, Saharan spaces everywhere were thereby redefined as 'transit spaces' (once again erasing their historical and social specificity) in order to justify control over them. As this happened at roughly the same time that the GWOT was declared, these two processes combined to militarise Saharan spaces in a way that had been unheard of until then – even more so as the global wars against terror and migration often shared personnel and equipment and circulated information from one domain to the other.

Throughout the Sahara, visible economies of transit collapsed, to be replaced by more discreet underground economies. In Agadez, travel agencies and ghettos had to shut down to avoid being accused of taking part in the 'illicit traffic of migrants' and the concomitant arrest and confiscation of their jeeps and other assets. As demand for transport has continued unabated, many have kept operating, away from the public gaze, from the closed compounds of peripheral districts or villages. Routes have shifted to more arduous and often more dangerous locations, increasing the risk of fatal breakdowns, of getting lost or of being attacked by armed bandits. Much of the social controls that kept most drivers from simply dumping their fares in the desert have disappeared.

As a result, migrants' travel and working conditions have worsened throughout the region, especially in Libya. Here, migrants, especially those who, like Salif, find themselves in debt to transport providers, are routinely held captive to extort ransom from their families back home or, that failing, to work in inhumane conditions until their captors are satisfied. All of this is accompanied by routine violence against men but also and especially against women, who are tortured, raped and abused on their way north. Victory, whom we met in chapter 4, was one of the many who was caught, first by local merchants and then by 'state officials', who all use the same kind of brutality to squeeze ever more money and work out of hapless travellers and their families back home.

Throughout the region, those former transport agents who had the means to do so have reinvested in the new economic opportunities offered by the European 'war against migrants'. Former 'travel agencies' now sport posters declaring their commitment to the 'fight against irregular migration' to all who care to look and perhaps grant them a little funding on the side – all the while continuing in their old business. The Tubu militia leader Barka Chidimi made headlines in 2017 when he wrote directly to the EU to offer to protect the borders between Niger, Libya and Chad against migrants in exchange for a substantial payment, which would go towards funding his men. He was probably inspired by Libya, where militias have long discovered that the 'fight against migration' offers a lucrative sideline to their activities, attracting international funding, recognition and relative immunity – as was clearly the case with the Libyan prison warden quoted at the beginning of chapter 4. An added bonus is the ability to exploit the labour power of would-be migrants and to extort ransom payments from those held captive in (state-sponsored) camps.

William and Ndoumbé are both from Cameroon. Unlike Ousmane and Salif, when I met them in 2012 in the town of Faya in northern Chad, they were both in their late twenties. They were highly educated, well-spoken and hard-working, and they knew exactly what to expect on their trip north. They had both lived in Libya before and left it only temporarily when things threatened to go wrong in late 2011. They now wanted to return. William had left behind some money in a bank account and thought he ought to at least try to recover it; Ndoumbé had maintained friendly relations with his former boss and hoped that he would help him fall on his feet once they were back in Sebha. Both had picked up enough Arabic to get by. They knew that the current situation in Libya was dangerous, but they also knew that Libya always needed cheap and skilled labour – 'It is not because Qadhafi is dead that Libyans will suddenly acquire a taste for work!'

They were also keenly aware of why and how they had been put in the position of vulnerability that was their lot in life. Over tea in the long evenings spent waiting in Faya, they loved to analyse the injustices of the global economy that meant that their many talents would probably be wasted. A few weeks later, they rang me from Sebha: things were more difficult than they had expected, because of the civil war, but they had both found employment and a place to sleep. The conflict had not brought out the best in the Libyans they thought they knew, but they would hang in there just a little longer. Yet I could hear from their voices that they were scared; they knew well that if anything happened to them, they would have no one to turn to. Then their telephone numbers stopped working, and we lost touch.

Europe's border regime, as the anthropologist Ruben Andersson notes, succeeds mostly not in stopping migrants but in creating the category of 'illegal migrant' in a zone where many even today see migration not as a problem but simply as a fact of life.[5] This in turn fosters an 'illegality industry' that attracts exactly the same kind of people who also stand to benefit from the broader processes of militarisation described so far. The security expert Bruno Charbonneau suggests that we should see this not as a failure of EU policies in the area but as the construction of a new 'type of political order and regional governance that has been and is being built in the Sahel by international actors'[6] – and, we should add, by regional strongmen of all kinds and shapes, in government or outside it, who actively support, shape, transform and take advantage of the region's (and the world's) current fetishisation of 'security'.

The Problem with 'Security'

I started this chapter by observing that 'security' was largely in the eye of the beholder. As much as we can assume that the French tourists who landed in Faya in early 2012 had little idea of the political situation in Chad, their presence was part of larger international negotiations that ultimately decide whether a country is understood to be 'safe'. They were actors in a play whose script they had not read, much as local armed rebels might today be re-labelled 'Islamic terrorists' to cater to authoritarian governments in need of 'insecurity' in order to justify their own militaristic transgressions – and rising military budgets.

'Security' can mean different things to different people. From a local point of view, it means the ability to control and plan one's own life; it is a plea for individual and collective autonomy, for the ability to safely move about and make one's own decisions and for some assurance that the rules of the game will not radically change from one day to the next. For most Saharans, this kind of autonomy has become increasingly elusive over recent decades. Yet 'security' as understood by international funding bodies is more often than not conceived along purely military lines; it means funding and training more and better soldiers, police officers and other kinds of 'armed bureaucrats'.

Although many people on the ground probably would welcome a functioning and impartial police force, the actual effects of this militarisation are usually the exact opposite: the proliferation of weapons and of armed men who might (or might not) be loyal to the state and who might (or might not) see it as their duty to protect local populations, and rarely all of them equally. National militaries and other security personnel, once they have been trained, re-equipped and funded, do not necessarily do what their international backers would like them to do. The coupling of 'security' and 'insecurity' has itself become a narrative that functions in many ways like that of 'desertification' and 'development', with pernicious results that make short shrift of the largely democratic aspirations of the majority of the people in the region.

I started writing this book in the late 2010s. Things then looked rather different. The edges of the Sahara had been swept by vast popular movements against long-standing authoritarianism in the region: the *hirak* ('movement') in the Moroccan Rif in 2016–17; *Y en a marre* (We have had enough) in Senegal from 2011 to now; the *Balai citoyen* (Civic clean-up) that ousted the president of Burkina Faso after twenty-seven years of rule in 2014; the Sudanese *thawra* (revolution) that proved to be the unexpected downfall of Omar al-Bashir after almost thirty years in office; and the 2019 Algerian *hirak* that prevented the country's equally long-standing and moribund president Abdelaziz Bouteflika from taking on a fifth term in office.

Since then, national militaries everywhere have taken advantage of both the COVID pandemic and the global drive towards 'security' to strangle these movements and to brutally incarcerate those who were most prominent in them. The Sahel has been swept by a wave of military coups: Sudan in 2019 and 2021, Mali in 2020 and 2021, Chad and Guinea in 2021, Burkina Faso (twice) in 2022 and Niger in 2023. Although most of the new military regimes are decidedly anti-French, and indeed derive their (considerable) popular legitimacy from their anti-imperial claims, most have benefitted from international military aid and training prior to taking power. The coup in Niger happened not even two months after the EU had voted to allocate another €4.7 million to the Nigerien Armed Forces as part of its European Peace Facility, its current flagship anti-terror programme, bringing the total of funds directly granted to the Nigerien army since July 2022 to €65 million.[7]

As I finish this book, the vast majority of southern Saharans live under military rule. Most northern Saharans live in countries that, although nominally democratic, are de facto governed by the military and where any expression of dissent has become dangerous. Year after year, Algeria funds, on its freshly walled southern borders, a war effort without being at war. Morocco's military colonisation of Western Sahara seems to have achieved its end, while in Libya, the only North African state not tributary to an ever-growing national army, the very possibility of engaging in politics with any means other than violence seems to be but a distant memory. So far, the West's 'fight for freedom' has had the opposite result for most of those who line its (Saharan) battlefields. If this is 'security' (and in most cases, it is quite the opposite), the price is simply too high.

TRACING THE LION'S FOOTPRINTS

Dûgili dutti ši gôyindik.
(We can see the lion, but [as we are afraid of
him] we only trace his footprints.)
Tubu proverb

On one of my first trips on a fully loaded date truck from southern Algeria to northern Mali in 2009, we stopped for the night, exhausted from a day of rattling over bumpy tracks and endless repairs. As we stretched out on the ground, looking up at the night sky, the conversation veered to Europe. Did it look like this? No, the stars are arranged differently, and they are less bright. Were the roads quite as bad? Not really. Could you just stop somewhere for the night and be as comfortable as we were now? You can't, as almost every patch of land is owned by somebody – even if you camp, you have to pay a fee or risk being chased away. Silence ensued. My interlocutors were too polite to express their evident incredulity and horror at this thought. Finally, the youngest apprentice, a lad of perhaps fifteen from a nearby Tuareg camp, blurted out, 'But – if this is really true – where do you keep your camels?'

Everybody laughed, but his question was clearly to the point. Where do Europeans keep their camels, or rather, what has happened to their shared resources and their management that, in the young apprentice's mind, were an essential condition for collective prosperity and hence a good and fulfilling life? Where are the 'wastelands' where people go to stretch their legs at night? I did not have the heart that night to mention that most Europeans do not have any livestock – or large families, for that matter – as the obvious conclusion of dire poverty and abjection that he might draw from this seemed simply wrong, surrounded as I was by people who, in European terms, owned very little and whose material existence was often precarious.

The answer, then, would have to lie deeper. What would Europe, and indeed the world, look like, or rather what would the stories we like to tell ourselves about it be like, if we took the lessons that emerge from Saharan history and ethnography seriously? In a recent book, the anthropologist David Graeber and archaeologist David Wengrow ask how contemporary state-based societies came to be quite so 'stuck', set in one way of living and working and of organising their collective lives to the point that their members struggle to imagine any other form of life and tend to project their own rather impoverished idea of human possibilities onto other places and other times.[1] As I have shown throughout this book, Saharans have never had the luxury of getting stuck, and Saharan history and contemporary life are thus a tale of constant improvisation, movement and adaptation to new challenges. This means that their experience can open up new, precious visions if one only takes the time to listen.

Throughout this book, three key terms have drawn together Saharan livelihood strategies: mobility, connectivity and flexibility. There can be no doubt that the people on the truck that night knew all three first hand and largely took them for granted. Travelling was for them a way of life, and their connections stretched far and away on both sides of the border. They all had many skills, had been herders one day and traders and mechanics another, and excelled in a broad range of occupations. Even the most ordinary repairs of their ancient desert-going trucks called on almost magical creativity. They all spoke several languages and routinely lived in a variety of settings, from the bustling southern Algerian towns where they all had family to weeks spent in near solitude in the bādiya. They clearly relished both, and their ability to switch between them.

Yet they also had direct experience of Algerian border guards, forced family separations, exploitative labour relations, sometimes even imprisonment. They had watched television and had some idea of what life in Europe, or even just in northern Algeria, looked like. They had probably been part of it in some ways, when visiting friends and relatives, and might indeed be tempted to try more of it. They knew all that there was to know. What they could not imagine, however, was that this could be all of life: that one could not just get away, once one had had enough, to a space where mobility and the very basic freedom it grants is the norm and enclosure the exception.

This book has attempted to provide an account of Saharan history and social and political life, wherever possible, from the bottom up. Part One opened with a chapter on geology, dispelling the notion that the Sahara is everywhere the same and mostly full of sand. It then moved on to the paradox that the Sahara contains some of the world's largest reserves of sweet water, but they have for most of history been largely inaccessible or accessible only with great ingenuity and hard labour. We then turned to the animals that humans have relied on, both to make use of a broad range of resources that tend to be widely dispersed in space and time and to further their own mobility. In the face of a difficult landscape, we saw diversity, variability and interdependence and the highly skilled and flexible ways in which humans, collectively and in symbiosis with other living creatures, have arranged their lives.

Part Two focussed on the idea of movement, beginning with the stories people tell of their external origins in a place where nearly everybody claims to be from somewhere else. From these stories derive the categories of region-wide oppositions, more political than 'ethnic', as well as an array of far-flung networks of solidarity, mutual aid and, potentially, intimacy and exploitation. In a world where connectivity and mobility are valued as essential constituents of autonomous personhood, denying either or both literally strips people of humanity. It is thus not surprising that slavery remains the central trope, region-wide, of social hierarchies, domination and exploitation – one that resurfaces with great force when new conflicts erupt.

Similar tensions apply to the movement of things: exchange is necessary for life and is also a pleasure; movement is therefore always logically and temporally prior to place. But too much exchange creates debt and dependency. Thus, there is always a temptation to do without, if necessary, through raiding and theft. Much Saharan life is best understood as situated within the tension created by these two obligations: to connect and to protect. From a local point of view, Islam similarly resembles a story of connectivity, of reading local events through universal categories of value and spiritual worth and of maintaining this connection without relinquishing local control. Over and over again, movement has meant much more than just arrows on a map: it is ethically charged, morally judged, highly praised or understood to be threatening. Yet it is always a necessity rather than a luxury.

Part Three was concerned with external relations of a different kind. The first chapter described how Saharans have managed their collective lives and what imperial and then national states have made of this. It showed that stories of straightforward incompatibility and domination ignore much local complexity, leaving us unable to understand current developments. The next chapter examined post-independence developments in the region, marked by growing economic disparities between the northern and southern Sahara, successive droughts and migration north, leading to a particular urban cosmopolitanism that flavours much of Saharan life today. The final chapter was concerned with narratives of security and insecurity and the concomitant militarisation of the Sahara. It is difficult to develop analytic distance from events and processes that are still happening as I write, but we can say with some certainty that all of these developments are working towards greater closure of Saharan spaces, causing people to lose the one thing they perhaps cherish most: their ability to lead and foresee relatively autonomous, self-determined and coherent lives.

Overall, the aim of the book has been to do away with common misconceptions about the Sahara and deserts and drylands more generally: to question the standard bird's-eye view, to zoom in and look at the details, to propose an alternative to the all-too-common telescoping of Saharan history into a somewhat mystical ethnographic present. To achieve this, I have attempted to write a history not so much *in* the Sahara but *of* the Sahara, taking into account its ecological, social and cultural complexity all at once and as one. I have attempted to develop a fully historical and therefore also political ecology, which in turn challenges and undermines the many long-standing assumptions that still underpin most reporting on the region.

This, however, is not all. Deserts and other 'wastelands' have long been seen as the antithesis of civilisation; to ask questions about the former indirectly implies asking questions about the latter. Answers will vary according to time and context: each historical period, each setting has created its own 'desert' as a way of defining civilisation against it. Yet all of these ideas are related, as they tend to sediment in contemporary perceptions, making them layered, complex and not always coherent. Any conceptual history of the desert is thus also a history of the idea of civilisation.

In classical times, the distinction was primarily about politics. Mediterranean civilisation was well aware of the nomadic 'barbarians' who haunted its borders and indeed were indispensable trading partners, allies or even soldiers. But the 'civilised' people found it difficult to fathom the barbarians' political lives – indeed, as they were defined by their live outside the city, outside the *polis*, could they be said to have a *political* life at all? From a Greek point of view, clearly not, and nomadism early on became a trope to describe the limits of politics and hence fully human life.

Some of this prejudice is still with us and emerges both in usually firmly held beliefs that pastoral nomadism is just not sustainable in the modern world and in the great difficulties that we have in trying to imagine life beyond a centralised state in any but disparaging terms. The Saharan material presented here encourages us to rethink politics not as based on a polis, a bounded and exclusive territorial community, but as a more interactional and fluid process where political personhood derives from interpersonal relations and recognition and where sovereignty is not exclusive and permanent but negotiable, multiple, scattered and limited in time and space. It gives us a glimpse of life beyond the state, or rather on its margins, where state-based politics are only one among many other options.

From the seventeenth century onwards, in European

writings, the rhetorical opposition between the desert and the sown was mostly about land use. As noted in the introduction, in the English language, 'wastelands' are both lands open to all and lands gone to waste; they imply vastness and devastation. Their relation is not one of total opposition, however, but of potential transformation: deserts can be remedied, wastelands rendered productive through work, enclosure of some kind and technical ingenuity. This in turn confers exclusive rights of property: land becomes a resource. This was how Locke famously attempted to justify the European invasion of the Americas, but these assumptions have also informed the most common approaches by Europeans and northwest African political elites to the Sahara, with mixed results.

This book's story of the Sahara encourages us to uncouple the notion of land from that of productivity. After all, there is nothing natural about seeing land primarily as a resource and therefore of judging its value – or even its degree of 'desertification' – in terms of productivity. Saharan material further shows that scarcity should be an argument for common use rather than for individual appropriation. After all, currently dominant Roman law–derived notions of private property stand out from other, more flexible property regimes by their inclusion of the right not only to use a given piece of land but also to 'abuse' it, that is, to destroy it. In the Sahara and beyond, this 'abuse' is currently in full swing, but it is simply not something humanity will be able to afford for long.

Today, post-structuralist philosophers and political theorists, with usually cursory reference to scholarship on actually existing desert societies, coin terms such as 'nomadology' or advocate for a 'new barbarism' in order to create a conceptual space for critical thought, one that goes beyond the rigidity of state-imposed categories and concomitant restrictions. They identify not only a nomadic way of life but also a particular form of social organisation and even thought: one that is about flow, not fixture; universality, not national particularity; fluidity, not laws. Others turn to the 'barbarians' of the past to try to understand where we all went wrong, although they often and somewhat disingenuously stop short of advocating a return to the pre-sedentary distant past. This book should be sufficient proof that the realities of desert life are far too complex and too intertwined with the world to be summarised in simple thought experiments. But the productive potential of these thought experiments remains. We just need to take care not to confuse one with the other and to get our facts straight.

Drylands – areas with an aridity index of below 0.65 – today cover 41 per cent of the global land-mass. Over 2 billion people, or 38 per cent of the world's population, currently live in them, and their numbers are expected to rise. Due to ongoing climate change, experts predict that drylands will increase in size by 11 to 23 per cent by the end of this century, which means that they will soon cover more than half of the world. Not all drylands are deserts, of course, and there is no need to repeat here the problems of the term 'desertification'; nonetheless, deserts, as an extreme form of dryland, might point towards some of the structural features of dryland ecologies.

In a recent review paper, a group of US-based ecologists provide a list of common misperceptions about drylands that they hold responsible for the widespread mismanagement of these areas.[2] Most of these should be familiar by now: the idea that drylands have no intrinsic value, no impact on the global ecosystem; that they are inhabited mostly by poor people whose activities further degrade them; and that technical innovation combined with strong centralised governance is the best way

of improving the situation. Approaches to drylands, they con-
clude, have for too long been informed by equilibrium models,
notions of stable state and carrying capacity that are simply of no
use in areas that are intrinsically marked by heterogeneity and
spatial and temporal variability. What we need instead is more
flexibility, awareness of regional variation and interactions, a
celebration of mobility and more attention to local knowledge.

Correct as these ecologists certainly are, it is impossible to
simply isolate questions of ecology and to subsume them under
headings such as 'land management'. Ecologies are always also
human, and land is much more than a resource to be managed.
If we want to take Saharan examples seriously, we must consider
them in their totality as propositions about social and political life as a whole. These propositions are never fixed, nor are
they any more coherent than Western social theory: they are the
result of centuries-old experimentation, consultation and collective deliberation. As such, they provide plenty of inspiration
should we wish to revise our own implicit models of the world.

There can be little doubt that these models, based on the
idea of stable, bounded, territorial and exclusive political communities, on equilibrium models and calculations of yield and
productivity, are increasingly inadequate as we hurtle towards
new social and ecological realities. Saharans have long lived in
an environment where mobility and flexibility are essential,
where human-animal relations are at the roots of social life,
where dealing with outsiders is what makes you fully human and
where crises are always to be expected and isolation or occupational rigidity is simply not an option. Soon it will no longer
be possible for us to keep this world at bay through fictions of
civilisational oppositions and heavily policed national borders,
because it is ours also.

*

To question old models, we need new ideas. And to have new ideas, we need to be able to see beyond the old ones, to reflexively move outside ourselves. Often, this can be done only if we change positions, move away from the self-evidence of the centre and look at the world from a more marginal perspective. This is also where Ibn Khaldūn's description of the desert beyond civilisation as a 'land of dissidence' takes on a broader meaning: if much of our current predicament is in fact a failure of the imagination, a failure to pay attention to others, then the unruly margins of long-standing 'centres of civilisations' might be a good place to remedy both, as they are unfamiliar enough to spark new thought and familiar enough to make sense of it.

My argument is emphatically *not* that the Sahara presents some kind of 'exotic other' or that Saharans are akin to the 'noble savages' of Western lore and therefore provide fodder for a 'primitive critique' of the excesses of 'modernity' but rather that the Sahara (and through it sub-Saharan Africa) has always been intimately connected to the Mediterranean, that it is part of the same (modern) world and that this is precisely why it can teach us so much – and why it is time to pay attention. As I have shown throughout, 'dissidence' (literally, to 'sit apart') – or its Arabic counterpart, the *sība* – are dialectical categories that speak of a relation between consciously different political and social forms that mutually define each other. As Saharans have long known, admissions of relatedness might be difficult to stomach, but they are in the long run the only option.

Today, as mounting security concerns routinely broadcast Saharan television footage into European homes, the Sahara has, somewhat paradoxically, become ever more remote. Civil war and international intervention in Mali, a series of military coups through the Sahel, a failed revolution in Algeria and ongoing strife in Libya all have made empirical research in the area increasingly difficult, if not impossible, even for Saharans themselves. In the face of mounting levels of violence and a political landscape that even locals find impossible to fathom, they tend to have other priorities than talking to curious researchers. The days of leisurely peaceful truck trade across the border between Algeria and Mali are over, at least for now. Ghali and his men are themselves 'stuck', mostly in the slums of Tamanrasset and Adrar. In northern Mali, pastures are now won and defended with guns, and camels and cattle themselves have become not so much symbols of a particular form of life as a stake in war. But they are all still there.

NOTES

Introduction

1   Lt. Gen. Wallace C. Gregson Jr, commander of the US Marine Corps forces in the Pacific, cited in S. M. Powell, 'Swamp of Terror in the Sahara', *Air Force Magazine* (November 2004), p. 54.

2   Jeremy Keenan, 'The Banana Theory of Terrorism: Alternative Truths and the Collapse of the "Second" (Saharan) Front in the War on Terror', *Journal of Contemporary African Studies*, vol. 25, 1 (2007), pp. 31–58.

3   Muhammad Abū al-Qāsim b. Hawqal, *Kitāb sūrat al-'ard*; Abū Ishāq al-Istakhrī, *al-Masālik w'al-mamālik*; Abū 'Abd Allāh Muhammad b. Battūta, *Tuhfat an-nuzzār fī gharā 'ib al-amsār wa 'ajā 'ib al-asfār*; and Abū 'Ubayd 'Abd Allāh al-Bakrī, *Kitāb al-Masālik wa-al-Mamālik*, all cited in John Hopkins and Nehemia Levtzion (eds), *Corpus for Early Arabic Sources for West African History* (Cambridge: Cambridge University Press, 1981), pp. 45, 49, 304, 85.

4   Abū Zayd 'Abd al-Rahman b. Khaldūn, Franz Rosenthal (trans.) and N. J. Dawood (ed), *The Muqaddimah: An Introduction to History* (Princeton, NJ: Princeton University Press, 2015).

5   Georges-Louis Leclerc de Buffon, *Époques de la nature* (Paris : Imprimerie royale, 1778).

6   Charles Fourier, *Théorie des quatre mouvements et des destinées générales* (Leipzig, 1808), p. 246.

7   Augustin Bernard and Napoléon Lacroix, *Evolution du nomadisme en Algérie* (Algiers: Jourdan, 1906), p. 24.

8   Diana Davis, 'Desert "Wastes" of the Maghreb: Desertification Narratives in French Colonial Environmental History of North Africa', *Cultural Geographies*, vol. 11, 4 (2004), pp. 359–87.

1: Sand, Rocks and Yellowcake

1 James Giles, 'The Dustiest Place on Earth', *Nature*, vol. 434 (2005), pp. 816–19.

2 Georg Spittler, 'Wüste, Wildnis und Zivilisation – die Sicht der Kel Ewey', *Paideuma*, vol. 35 (1989), pp. 273–87.

3 Muhammad b. al-Qāsim b. Hawqal, *Sūrat al-ʾard*, cited in Joseph Cuoq (ed), *Recueil des sources arabes concernant l'Afrique occidentale du VIIIe au XVIe siècle* (Paris: Éditions du CNRS, 1975), p. 75.

4 Abū ʿUbayd ʿAbd Allāh al-Bakrī, *Kitāb al-masālik waʾl-mamālik*, cited in John Hopkins and Nehemia Levtzion (eds), *Corpus for Early Arabic Sources for West African History* (Cambridge: Cambridge University Press, 1981), p. 85

5 Mungo Parks, *Travels in the Interior Districts of Africa*, 5th ed. (London: Bulmer and Co., 1807), p. 214.

6 Paul Marty, *Études sur l'islam et les tribus du Soudan: Tome 1: Les Kounta de l'Est. Les Berabich. Les Iguellad* (Paris: E. Leroux, 1920), p. 244.

7 Mackenzie Knowles-Coursin and Joe Parkinson, 'Thousands Flock to Remote, Lawless Sahara in Search of Gold', *Wall Street Journal*, 17 October 2018.

2: Like the Deserts Miss the Rain

1 Abū ʿAbd Allāh Muhammad b. Battūta, *Tuhfat an-nuzzār fī gharāʾib al-amsār wa ʿajāʾib al-asfār*, cited in John Hopkins and Nehemia Levtzion (eds), *Corpus for Early Arabic Sources for West African History* (Cambridge: Cambridge University Press, 1981), p. 304.

2 Cited in Judith Scheele, *Smugglers and Saints of the Sahara: Regional Connectivity in the Twentieth Century* (Cambridge: Cambridge University Press, 2012), p. 35.

3 Alfred-Georges-Paul Martin, *À la frontière du Maroc: Les oasis sahariennes (Gourara, Touat, Tidikelt)* (Algiers: Imprimerie algérienne, 1908), p. 352.

4 Abū ʿAbd Allāh Muhammad al-Idrīsī, *Muzhat al-mushtāq fī ikhtirāq al-āfāq*, cited in John Hopkins and Nehemia Levtzion (eds), *Corpus for Early Arabic Sources for West African History* (Cambridge: Cambridge University Press, 1981), p. 125.

5 Paul Pascon, *La maison d'Iligh* (Rabat: P. Pascon, 1984), p. 9.

6   Geneviève Bédoucha, *L'eau, l'amie du puissant: Une communauté oasienne du sud tunisien* (Paris: Edition des archives contemporaines, 1987).

3: Cherchez le dromadaire

1   Cited in Nicolas Francis, 'Foklore twareg, poésies et chansons de l'Azawagh'. *Bulletin de l'IFAN*, vol. 6 (1944), p. 45.

2   Cited in Moussa Albaka and Dominique Casajus, 'Trois poèmes de la région d'Agadez', *Awal*, vol. 4 (1988), p. 147.

3   Auguste Geoffroy, 'Arabes Pasteurs Nomades de la tribu des Larbas', *Les Ouvriers des deux mondes*, vol. 1, 8 (1887), pp. 409–64.

4   Denis Retaillé, 'L'espace nomade', *Revue de géographie de Lyon*, vol. 73, 1 (1998), p. 73.

5   André Bourgeot, *Les sociétés touarègues. Nomadisme, identité, résistances* (Paris: Karthala, 1995).

4: To Be from Far Away

1   Mohammed Ennaji, *Soldats, domestiques et concubines: L'esclavage au Maroc au XIX siècle* (Casablanca: Eddif, 1994).

2   Nima Elbagir, Raja Razek, Alex Platt and Bryony Jones, 'People for Sale: Where Lives Are Auctioned for $400', CNN, 14 November 2017, www.cnn.com/2017/11/14/africa/libya-migrant-auctions/index.html.

3   United Nations Human Rights Office of the High Commissioner (OHCHR), 'Desperate and Dangerous: Report on the Human Rights Situation of Migrants and Refugees in Libya'(20 December 2018), p. 21.

4   Ramzi Rouighi, *Inventing the Berbers: History and Ideology in the Maghrib* (Philadelphia: University of Pennsylvania Press, 2019).

5   Orlando Patterson, *Slavery and Social Death* (Cambridge, MA: Harvard University Press, 1982).

6   Ennaji, *Soldats, domestiques et concubines*.

7   Chouki El Hamel, *Black Morocco: A History of Slavery, Race, and Islam* (Cambridge: Cambridge University Press, 2013).

8   M'hamed Oualdi, 'Commémorer l'abolition de l'esclavage en Tunisie. Les droits des citoyens noirs et l'histoire des esclaves d'origines européennes'. *Esclavages & post-esclavages*, vol. 4 (2021).

9   Martha Scaglioni, '"She Is Not an 'Abid"': Meanings of Race and

Blackness in a Community of Slave Descendants in Southern Tunisia'. *Anthropologia*, vol. 7, 1 (2020), pp. 117–39.

10 Benedetta Rossi, *From Slavery to Aid: Politics, Labour, and Ecology in the Nigerien Sahel, 1800–2000* (Cambridge: Cambridge University Press, 2015).

11 'Kais Saied veut fermer la Tunisie devant les "hordes des migrants clandestins"', 22 February 2023, https://anndz.dz/?p=24699&lang=fr.

5: Saints on Trucks

1 René Caillié, *Journal d'un voyage à Temboctou et à Jenné, dans l'Afrique centrale*, vol. 2 (Paris: Imprimerie Royale, 1830), pp. 446–47.

2 Muhammad Abū al-Qāsim b. Hawqal, *Kitāb sūrat al-'ard*, cited in John Hopkins and Nehemia Levtzion (eds), *Corpus for Early Arabic Sources for West African History* (Cambridge: Cambridge University Press, 1981), p. 45.

3 Cited in Judith Scheele, *Smugglers and Saints of the Sahara: Regional Connectivity in the Twentieth Century* (Cambridge: Cambridge University Press, 2012), p. 57.

4 Eugène Daumas, *Le grand désert* (Paris: N. Chaix, 1848).

5 Abū 'Abd Allāh Muhammad Ibn Battūta, *Rihlat Ibn Battūta al-musammāt Tuhfat al-nuzzār fī gharā'ib al-amsār wa-'ajā'ib al-asfār* (Rabat: Académie Royale du Maroc, 1997).

6 Abū Sālim 'Abd Allāh b. Muhammad al-'Ayyāshī, *al-Rihla al-'Ayyāshiyya* (Abu Dhabi: Dār al-Suwaydī li-l-Nashar wa-l-Tawzī', 2006).

7 G. Michael La Rue, 'Khabir 'Ali at Home in Kubayh: A Brief Biography of a Dar Fur Caravan Leader'. *African Economic History*, vol. 13 (1984), pp. 56–83.

8 Daumas, *Grand désert*, pp. 2–3.

9 Daumas, *Grand désert*, pp. 112–13.

10 Daumas, *Grand désert*, p. 4.

11 Mohamed b. Oumar El-Tounsy, *Voyage au Soudan oriental: Le Ouadây* (Paris: B. Duprat, 1851), p. 534.

12 Archives nationales d'outre-mer (ANOM), Aix-en Provence, box 22H68, 'Rapport de tournée du Capitaine Dinaux, chef de l'annexe d'In Salah. Ahnet, Adrar nigritien, Ahaggar, Aïr septentrional', 3 May to 29 October 1905.

13 Auguste Geoffroy, 'Arabes Pasteurs Nomades de la tribu des Larbas', *Les Ouvriers des deux mondes*, vol. 1, 8 (1887), pp. 409–64.

14 Jean Chapelle, *Nomades noirs du Sahara. Les Toubous* (Paris: Plon, 1957), pp. 211–12.

15 Ibn Battūta, *Rihla*, cited in John Hopkins and Nehemia Levtzion (eds), *Corpus for Early Arabic Sources for West African History* (Cambridge: Cambridge University Press, 1981), p. 301.

16 Didier Corbonnois, *L'odyssée de la colonne Leclerc* (Paris: Histoire et Collections, 2003), p. 69.

6: Qadis on Camelback

1 Mouloud Mammeri, *L'ahellil du Gourara* (Paris: Éditions de la MSH, 1984).

2 Rachid Bellil, *Textes zénètes du Gourara* (Algiers: CNRPAH, 2006).

3 A. M. Hassanein Bey, *The Lost Oases* (London: Thornton Butterworth, 1925).

4 Rosita Forbes, 'Across the Libyan Desert to Kufara', *Geographical Journal*, vol. 58, 3 (1921), p. 166.

5 Cited in Ismail Warscheid, *Droit musulman et société au Sahara précolonial: La justice islamique dans les oasis du Grand Touat (Algérie) aux XVIIe–XIXe siècles* (Leiden: Brill, 2017).

6 Abū 'Abd Allāh Sīdi al-Ḥājj Muḥammad b. 'Abd al-Raḥmān al-Balbālī, *Nawāzil al-ghuniya al-muqtasid*. Unpublished manuscript, consulted at the library of Mtarfa, courtesy of Shaykh Bilkabīr.

7 'Situation au Mali: Ahmad Al Faqi Al Mahdi remis à la CPI pour des accusations de crimes de guerre de destruction de monuments historiques et religieux à Tombouctou', International Criminal Court, 26 September 2015, www.icc-cpi.int/Pages/item.aspx?name=pr1154&ln=en.

7: Land of Dissidence

1 Mahmood Mamdani, 'Beyond Settler and Native as Political Identities: Overcoming the Political Legacy of Colonialism', *Comparative Studies in Society and History*, vol. 43, 4 (2001), pp. 651–64.

2 Cited in Julien Brachet and Judith Scheele, *The Value of Disorder: Autonomy, Prosperity and Plunder in the Chadian Sahara* (Cambridge: Cambridge University Press, 2019), p. 73.

3   Marc Côte, *L'Algérie ou l'espace retourné* (Paris: Flammarion, 1988).

4   Général Pol Victor Mangeot and Paul Marty, 'Les Touareg de la boucle du Niger', *Bulletin du Comité d'études historiques et scientifiques de l'AOF*, vol. 3 (1918), pp. 457–58.

8: When Crisis Becomes Permanent

1   Cited in Georg Klute, *Tuareg-Aufstand in the Wüste* (Köln: Rüdiger Köppe, 2013), p. 671.

2   Claude Meillassoux, 'Development or Exploitation. Is the Sahel Famine Good Business?' *Review of African Political Economy*, vol. 1 (1974), p. 27.

3   Stephen Baier, 'Economic History and Development: Drought and the Sahelian Economies of Niger'. *African Economic History*, vol. 1 (1976), p. 11.

4   Comité d'Information Sahel, *Qui se nourrit de la famine en Afrique?* (Paris: Maspéro, 1975).

5   Cited in Klute, *Tuareg-Aufstand in the Wüste*, p. 670.

6   Ibid., p. 682.

7   Barbara Cooper, 'De quoi la crise démographique au Sahel est-elle le nom?', *Politique africaine*, vol. 130 (2013), pp. 69–88.

9: In Search of Security

1   AQMI, l'Emirat de l'Organisation, 'Directives générales relatives au projet islamique djihadiste de l'Azawad', RFI, 6 October 2013, www.rfi.fr/fr/afrique/20131006-mali-vade-mecum-droukdel-mali-aqmi-terrorisme-al-qaida-sanguinaire.

2   Richard Banégas, 'De la guerre au maintien de la paix: Le nouveau business mercenaire', *Critique internationale*, vol. 1, 1 (1988), pp. 179–94.

3   El Madani Madani, Saharan political activist from Ouargla, 2018.

4   Ousmane's and Salif's trajectories are adapted from Matteo Fano, '"Quand tu n'as pas de papiers, tu ne peux pas choisir": Sociobiographie d'un groupe de jeunes migrants d'origine africaine à Marseille', PhD thesis, EHESS, Paris. All names have been changed.

5   Ruben Andersson, 'Hunter and Prey: Patrolling Clandestine Migration in the Euro-African Borderlands', *Anthropological Quarterly*, vol. 87, 1 (2014), pp. 119–49.

6 Bruno Charbonneau, 'Counter-insurgency in the Sahel', *International Affairs*, vol. 97, 6 (2021), p. 1806.

7 'European Peace Facility: Council Adopts Two Assistance Measures to Support the Nigerien Armed Forces', European Council, 8 June 2023, www.consilium.europa.eu/en/press/press-releases/2023/06/08/european-peace-facility-council-adopts-two-assistance-measures-to-support-the-nigerien-armed-forces/.

Conclusion

1 David Graeber and David Wengrow, *The Dawn of Everything: A New History of Humanity* (London: Penguin, 2021).

2 David Hoover, Brandon Bestelmeyer, Nancy Grimms, Travis Huxman, Sasha Reed, Osvaldo Sala, Timothy Seastedt, Hailey Wilmer, and Scott Ferenberg, 'Traversing the Wasteland: A Framework for Assessing Ecological Threats to Drylands', *BioScience*, vol. 70 (2020), pp. 35–47.

BIBLIOGRAPHY

Introduction

Andersson, Ruben. 'Here Be Dragons: Mapping an Ethnography of Global Danger'. *Current Anthropology*, vol. 57, 6 (2016), pp. 707–31.

Davis, Diana. *The Arid Lands: History, Power, Knowledge*. Cambridge, MA: MIT Press, 2016.

Di Palma, Vittoria. *Wasteland: A History*. New Haven, CT: Yale University Press, 2014.

Fromherz, Allen James. *Ibn Khaldun, Life and Times*. Edinburgh: Edinburgh University Press, 2011.

Grove, Richard. *Green Imperialism: Colonial Expansion, Tropical Island Edens and the Origins of Environmentalism*. Cambridge: Cambridge University Press, 1996.

Henry, Jean-Robert, Jean-Louis Marçot and Jean-Yves Moisseron. 'Développer le désert: anciennes et nouvelles utopies'. *Année du Maghreb*, vol. 7 (2011), pp. 115–47.

McDougall, E. Ann. 'Constructing Emptiness: Islam, Violence and Terror in the Historical Making of the Sahara'. *Journal of Contemporary African Studies*, vol. 25, 1 (2007), pp. 17–30.

McDougall, James, and Judith Scheele (eds). *Saharan Frontiers: Space and Mobility in Northwest Africa*. Bloomington: Indiana University Press, 2012.

1: Sand, Rocks and Yellowcake

Barich, Barbara. *People, Water and Grain: The Beginnings of Domestication in the Sahara and the Nile Valley*. Rome: L'Herma di Bretschneider, 1998.

Bisson, Jean. *Mythes et réalités d'un désert convoité: le Sahara*. Paris: L'Harmattan, 2003.

Bibliography

Boulay, Sébastien. *Pêcheurs imraguen du Sahara atlantique: mutations techniques et changements sociaux des années 1970 à nos jours*. Paris: Karthala, 2013.

Brooks, Nick, Isabelle Chiapello, Savino di Lernia, Nick Drake, Michel Legrand, Cyril Moulin and Joseph Prospero. 'The Climate-Environment-Society Nexus in the Sahara from Prehistoric Times to the Present Day'. *Journal of North African Studies*, vol. 10, 3–4 (2005), pp. 253–92.

Brunet, Michel, et al. '"Toumaï", Miocène supérieur du Tchad, nouveau doyen du rameau humain'. *Comptes rendus Palevol*, vol. 3 (2004), pp. 277–85.

Chevrillon-Guibert, Raphaëlle, Laurent Gagnol and Géraud Magrin. 'Les ruées vers l'or au Sahara et au nord du Sahel. Ferment de crise ou stabilisateur?' *Hérodote*, vol. 172 (2019), pp. 183–215.

Favet, Jocelyne, et al. 'Microbial Hitchhikers on Intercontinental Dust: Catching a Lift in Chad'. *ISME Journal*, vol. 7 (2012), pp. 850–67.

Grégoire, Emmanuel. 'Niger: un état à forte teneur en uranium'. *Hérodote* 142 (2011), pp. 206–25.

Kuper, Rudolph, and Stefan Kröpelin. 'Climate-Controlled Holocene Occupation in the Sahara: Motor of Africa's Evolution'. *Science*, vol. 313 (2006), pp. 803–807.

Mattingly, David J. (ed). *The Archaeology of Fazzân, vol. 1: Synthesis*. London: Society for Libyan Studies, 2003.

McDougall, E. A. 'Salts of the Western Sahara: Myths, Mysteries and Historical Significance'. *International Journal of African Historical Studies*, vol. 23, 2 (1990), pp. 231–57.

Meunier, Dominique. 'Le commerce de sel de Taodenni'. *Journal des Africanistes*, vol. 50, 2 (1980), pp. 133–44.

Musso, Marta. '"Oil Will Set Us Free": The Hydrocarbon Industry and the Algerian Decolonization Process'. In Andrew Smith and Chris Jeppesen (eds), *Britain, France and the Decolonization of Africa*. London: UCL, 2017, pp. 62–84.

Vikør, Knut. *The Oasis of Salt: The History of Kawar, a Saharan Centre of Salt Production*. Bergen: Centre for Middle Eastern and Islamic Studies, 1999.

Wengrow, David. *The Archaeology of Early Egypt: Social Transformations in North East Africa, 10,000 to 2650 BC*. Cambridge: Cambridge University Press, 2006.

2: Like the Deserts Miss the Rain

Allan, J. A. 'The Kufrah Agricultural Schemes'. *Geographical Journal*, vol. 142, 1 (1976), pp. 50–56.

Amrani, Khaled. 'Gestion de l'eau d'irrigation dans le bas-Sahara algérien: Le paradoxe hydrique de la palmeraie d'Ouargla'. *Annales de géographie*, vol. 738 (2021), pp. 77–104.

Battesti, Vincent. *Jardins au désert: Évolutions des pratiques et savoirs oasiens, Jérid tunisien*. Paris: IRD Editions, 2005.

Battesti, Vincent. 'Des ressources et des appropriations: Retour, après la révolution, dans les oasis du Jérid (Tunisie)'. *Études rurales*, vol. 192 (2013), pp. 153–75.

Bellal, Sid-Ahmed, Mohamed Hadeid, Tarik Ghodbani and Ouassini Dari. 'Accès à l'eau souterraine et transformations de l'espace oasien: Le cas d'Adrar (Sahara du sud-ouest algérien)'. *Cahiers de géographie du Québec*, vol. 60 (2016), pp. 29–56.

Bensaâd, Ali (ed). *L'eau et ses enjeux au Sahara*. Paris: Karthala, 2011.

Gonçalvès, Julio, J. Petersen, P. Deschamps, B. Hamelin and O. Baba-Sy. 'Quantifying the modern recharge of "fossil" Sahara aquifers'. *Geophysical Research Letters*, vol. 40 (2013), pp. 2673–78.

Grandguillaume, Gilbert. 'De la coutume à la loi: Droit de l'eau et statut des communautés locales dans le Touat précolonial'. *Peuples méditerranéens*, vol. 2 (1978), pp. 119–33.

Hamamouche, Meriem Farah, Marcel Kuper and Caroline Lejars. 'Émancipation des jeunes des oasis du Sahara algérien par le déverrouillage de l'accès à la terre et à l'eau'. *Cahiers Agricultures*, vol. 24 (2015), pp. 412–19.

Idda, Salem, Bruno Bonté, Hamidi Mansour, Sid-Ahmed Bellal and Marcel Kuper. 'Monuments historiques ou systèmes bien vivants? Les foggaras des oasis du Touat (Algérie) et leur réalimentation en eau par pompage'. *Cahiers Agricultures*, vol. 26 (2017).

Massuel, Sylvain, and Jeanne Riaux. 'Groundwater Overexploitation: Why Is the Red Flag Waved? Case Study on the Kairouan Plain Aquifer (Central Tunisia)'. *Hydrogeological Journal*, vol. 25 (2017), pp. 1607–20.

Palluault, Sébastien. 2012. 'L'achèvement de la grande rivière artificielle en Libye: Et maintenant, quelle gestion de l'eau?' *Méditerranée*, vol. 119, pp. 9–16.

Van der Meeren, Thijs, Pierre Deschamps, Florence Sylvestre, et al. 'Les lacs d'Ounianga: Mieux comprendre leur dynamique hydrologique et écologique par une approche interdisciplinaire'. In Christine Raimond, Florence Sylvestre and Dangbet Zakinet (eds), *Le Tchad des Lacs*. Paris: IRD Editions (2019), pp. 127–38.

Wilson, Andrew. 'Foggaras in Ancient North Africa'. In Virginie Bridoux (ed.), *Contrôle et distribution de l'eau dans le Maghreb antique et médiéval*. Rome: École française de Rome (2009), pp. 1000–21.

3: Cherchez le dromadaire

Almathen, Faisal, et al. 'Ancient and Modern DNA Reveal Dynamics of Domestication and Cross-Continental Dispersal of the Dromedary'. *Proceedings of the National Academy of Sciences*, vol. 113 (2016), pp. 6707–12.

Baier, Stephen, and Paul Lovejoy. 'The Desert-Side Economy of the Central Sudan'. *International Journal of African Historical Studies*, vol. 8, 4 (1975), pp. 551–81.

Barich, Barbara. *People, Water and Grain: The Beginnings of Domestication in the Sahara and the Nile Valley*. Rome: L'Erna di Bretschneider, 1998.

Bernus, Edmond. *Touaregs nigériens: Unité culturelle et diversité régionale d'un peuple pasteur*. Paris: ORSTOM, 1981.

Boukhobza, M'Hamed. *L'agro-pastoralisme traditionnel en Algérie: De l'ordre tribal au désordre colonial*. Algiers: OPU, 1982.

Bourgeot, André. 'Nomadic Pastoral Society and the Market: The Penetration of the Sahel by Commercial Relations'. *Journal of Asian and African Studies*, vol. 16, 1–2 (1981), pp. 116–27.

Clanet, Jean-Charles. 'Caravanes du Sahara'. *Outre-mers*, vol. 92 (2004), pp. 9–30.

Clanet, Jean-Charles. 'La dure école des petits chameliers du bassin tchadien'. *Journal des africanistes*, vol. 72, 1 (2002), pp. 149–64.

Corniaux, Christian. 'Le commerce du bétail sahélien: Une filière archaïque ou la garantie d'un avenir prometteur?' *Afrique contemporaine*, vol. 249 (2014), pp. 93–95.

Garcea, Elena. 'An Alternative Way Towards Food Production: The Perspective from the Libyan Sahara'. *Journal of World Prehistory*, vol. 18, 2 (2004), pp. 107–54.

Holl, Augustin. *Saharan Rock Art. Archeology of Tassilian Pastoralist Iconography*. Walnut Creek, CA: Rowman Altamira, 2004.

Keenan, Jeremy. *The Tuareg, People of Ahaggar*. London: Allen Lane, 1977.

Leach, Helen. 'Human domestication reconsidered'. *Current Anthropology*, vol. 44, 3 (2003), pp. 349–68.

Marshall, Fiona, and Elisabeth Hildebrand. 'Cattle Before Crops: The Beginnings of Food Production in Africa'. *Journal of World Prehistory*, vol. 16, 2 (2002), pp. 99–143.

Volpato, Gabriele, and Anna Waldstein. 'Eghindi Among Sahrawi Refugees of Western Sahara'. *Medical Anthropology*, vol. 33, 2 (2014), pp. 160–77.

4: To Be from Far Away

Cleaveland, Timothy. 'Ahmad Baba al-Timbukti and His Islamic Critique of Racial Slavery in the Maghrib'. *Journal of North African Studies*, vol. 20, 1 (2015), pp. 42–64.

Cleaveland, Timothy. 'Reproducing Culture and Society: Women and the Politics of Gender, Age, and Social Rank in Walâta'. *Canadian Journal of African Studies*, vol. 34, 2 (2000), pp. 189–217.

Duffy, Helen. 'Hadijatou Mani Koroua v. Niger: Slavery Unveiled by the ECOWAS Court'. *Human Rights Law Review*, vol. 9, 1 (2009), pp. 151–70.

Ensel, Remco. *Saints and Servants in Southern Morocco*. Leiden: Brill, 1999.

Fenwick, Corisande. 'The Umayyads and North Africa: Imperial Rule and Frontier Society'. In Andrew Marsham (ed.), *The Umayyad World*. London: Routledge, 2020, pp. 293–313.

Ghouirgate, Mehdi. 'Le berbère au Moyen Age: Une culture linguistique en cours de reconstitutions'. *Annales H.S.S.*, vol. 70, 3 (2015), pp. 577–603.

Hall, Bruce. *A History of Race in Muslim West Africa, 1600–1960*. Cambridge: Cambridge University Press, 2011.

Harrak, Fatima. "Abid al Bukhari and the Development of the Makhzen System in Seventeenth-Century Morocco'. *Comparative Studies of South Asia, Africa and the Middle East*, vol. 38, 2 (2018), pp. 280–95.

Lucas-Sánchez, Marcel, Jose M. Serradell, and David Comas. 'Population History of North Africa Based on Modern and Ancient Genomes'. *Human Molecular Genetics*, vol. 30, R1 (2021), pp. R17–23.

McDougall, E. Ann. 'A Sense of Self: The Life of Fatma Barka'. *Canadian Journal of African Studies*, vol. 32, 2 (1998), pp. 285–315.

McDougall, E. Ann. 'Visions of the Sahara: Negotiating the History and Historiography of Premodern Saharan Slavery'. *Comparative Studies of South Asia, Africa and the Middle East*, vol. 38, 2 (2018), pp. 211–29.

Mrad Dali, Inès. 'La mobilisation des "noirs tunisiens" au lendemain de la révolte de 2011: Entre affirmation d'une identité historique et défense d'une "cause noire"'. *Politique africaine*, vol. 140 (2015), pp. 61–81.

Rossi, Benedetta. 'Beyond the Atlantic Paradigm: Slavery and Abolitionism in the Nigerien Sahel'. *Journal of Global Slavery*, vol. 5, 2 (2020), pp. 238–69.

Scaglioni, Martha. '"She Is Not an 'Abid'": Meanings of Race and Blackness in a Community of Slave Descendants in Southern Tunisia'. *Anthropologia*, vol. 7, 1 (2020), pp. 117–39.

Stewart, Charles. *Islam and Social Order in Mauritania*. Oxford: Clarendon Press, 1973.

Taine-Cheikh, Catherine. 'La Mauritanie en noir et blanc: Petite promenade linguistique en hassâniyya'. *Revue des mondes musulmans et de la Méditerranée*, vol. 54, 1 (1989), pp. 90–105.

5: Saints on Trucks

Austen, Ralph. *Trans-Saharan Africa in World History*. Oxford: Oxford University Press, 2010.

Beck, Kurt. 'Roadside Comforts: Truck Stops on the Forty-Day Road in Western Sudan'. *Africa*, vol. 83, 3 (2013), pp. 426–55.

Bonte, Pierre. 'Faire fortune au Sahara: Permanences et ruptures'. *Autrepart*, vol. 16 (2000), pp. 49–65.

Drodz, Martine, and Olivier Pliez. 'Entre Libye et Soudan: La fermeture d'une piste transsaharienne'. *Autrepart*, vol. 36 (2005), pp. 63–80.

El Hakim, Sherif Mahmoud. 'Some Economic Consequences of the Libyan Oil Discovery on the Zeyadiya Nomads of Darfur, Sudan'. *Sudan Notes and Records*, vol. 56 (1975), pp. 120–29.

Haarmann, Ulrich. 'The Dead Ostrich: Life and Trade in Ghadamès (Libya) in the Nineteenth Century'. *Die Welt des Islams*, vol. 38 (1998), pp. 1, 9–94.

Heffernan, Michael. 'The Limits of Utopia: Henri Duveyrier and the

Exploration of the Sahara in the Nineteenth Century'. *Geographical Journal*, vol. 155, 3 (1989), pp. 342–52.

Kelley, Anna. 'Movement and Mobility: Cotton and the Visibility of Trade Networks Across the Saharan Desert'. In Leslie Brubaker, Rebecca Darley, and Daniel Reynolds (eds), *Global Byzantium*. London: Routledge, 2022, pp. 138–54.

Lesourd, Céline. *Femmes d'affaire de Mauritanie*. Paris: Karthala, 2014.

Lydon, Ghislaine. *On Trans-Saharan Trails: Islamic Law, Trade Networks, and Cross-Cultural Exchange in Nineteenth-Century Western Africa*. Cambridge: Cambridge University Press, 2009.

McCall, Daniel F. 'Herodotus on the Garamantes: A Problem in Protohistory'. *History in Africa*, vol. 26 (1999), pp. 197–217.

McDougall, E. Ann. 'Conceptualising the Sahara: The World of Nineteenth-Century Beyrouk Commerce'. *Journal of North African Studies*, vol. 10, 3–4 (2005), pp. 369–86.

Spittler, Georg. 'Caravaneers, Shopkeepers and Consumers – the Appropriation of Goods Among the Kel Ewey Tuareg in Niger'. In Hans Peter Hahn (ed.), *Consumption in Africa: Anthropological Approaches*. Münster: Lit Verlag, 2008, pp. 147–72.

Wilson, Andrew. 'Saharan Trade in the Roman Period: Short-, Medium- and Long-Distance Trade Networks'. *Azania*, vol. 47, 4 (2012), pp. 409–49.

6: Qadis on Camelback

Batran, Abd al-Aziz. *The Qadiriyya Brotherhood in West Africa and the Western Sahara: The Life and Times of Shaykh Mukhtar al-Kunti, 1729–1811*. Rabat: Institut des études africaines, 2001.

Bennison, Amira. 'Liminal States: Morocco and the Iberian Frontier Between the Twelfth and the Nineteenth Centuries'. *Journal of North African Studies*, vol. 6, 1 (2001), pp. 11–28.

Berriane, Johara. 'Intégration symbolique à Fès et ancrages sur l'ailleurs: les Africains subsahariens et leur rapport à la zaouïa d'Ahmed al-Tijânî'. *Année du Maghreb*, vol. 11 (2014), pp. 139–53.

Brett, Michael. 'The Islamisation of the Maghreb from the Arabs to the Almoravids'. *Journal of the Society for Moroccan Studies*, vol. 2 (1992), pp. 57–71.

Bibliography

Cleaveland, Timothy. *Becoming Walata: A History of Saharan Social Formation and Transformation*. Portsmouth, NH: Heinemann, 2002.

Fierro, Maribel. *The Almohad Revolution: Politics and Religion in the Islamic West During the Twelfth–Thirteenth Centuries*. London: Routledge, 2018.

Kane, Ousmane. *Beyond Timbuktu: An Intellectual History of Muslim West Africa*. Cambridge, MA: Harvard University Press, 2016.

Krätli, Graziano, and Ghislaine Lydon (eds). *The Trans-Saharan Book Trade: Manuscript Culture, Arabic Literacy and Intellectual Culture in Muslim Africa*. Leiden: Brill, 2011.

Moussaoui, Abderrahmane. *Espace et sacré au Sahara: Ksour et oasis du sud-ouest algérien*. Paris: Éditions du CNRS, 2002.

Oßwald, Rainer. *Die Handelsstädte der Westsahara. Die Entwicklung der arabisch-maurischen Kultur von Sinqīt, Wādān, Tišīt und Walāta*. Berlin: Reimer, 1986.

Ould Cheikh, Abdel Wedoud. 'Théologie du désordre: Islam, ordre et désordre au Sahara'. *L'Année du Maghreb*, vol. 7 (2011), pp. 61–77.

Picard, Christophe, and Antoine Borrut. 'Râbata, ribât, râbita: Une institution à reconsidérer'. *Civilisation Médiévale*, vol. 15, 1 (2003), pp. 33–65.

Saad, Elias. *Social History of Timbuktu: The Role of Muslim Scholars and Notables 1400–1900*. Cambridge: Cambridge University Press, 1983.

Triaud, Jean-Louis. *La légende noire de la Sanūsiyya: Une confrérie musulmane saharienne sous le regard français (1840–1930)*. Paris: MSH, 1995.

Ware, Rudolph. *The Walking Qur'an: Islamic Education, Embodied Knowledge, and History in West Africa*. Chapel Hill: University of North Carolina Press, 2014.

Werenfels, Isabelle. 'Beyond Authoritarian Upgrading: The Re-emergence of Sufi Orders in Maghrebi Politics'. *Journal of North African Studies*, vol. 19, 3 (2014), pp. 275–95.

7: Land of Dissidence

Ahmida, Ali Abdullatif. *The Making of Modern Libya: State Formation, Colonization and Resistance, 1830–1932*. Albany: State University of New York Press, 1994.

Bonte, Pierre. *L'émirat de l'Adrar mauritanien: Harîm, compétition et protection dans une société tribale saharienne*. Paris: Karthala, 2008.

Brower, Benjamin. *A Desert Named Peace: The Violence of France's Empire in the Sahara, 1844–1902*. New York: Columbia University Press, 2009.

Davis, John. *Libyan Politics: Tribe and Revolution. An Account of the Zuwaya and Their Government*. London: Tauris, 1987.

Dennerlein, Bettina. 'Legitimate Bounds and Bound Legitimacy: The Act of Allegiance to a Ruler (Bai'a) in 19th century Morocco'. *Die Welt des Islams*, vol. 41, 3 (2001), pp. 287–310.

El Moudden, Abderrahmane. 'The Idea of the Caliphate Between Moroccans and Ottomans: Political and Symbolic Stakes in the 16th and 17th century Maghrib'. *Studia islamica*, vol. 82 (1995), pp. 103–12.

Grémont, Charles. *Les Touaregs Iwellemmedan (1647–1896): Un ensemble politique de la boucle du Niger*. Paris: Karthala, 2010.

Hunwick, John. 'Ahmad Bâbâ and the Moroccan Invasion of the Sudan (1591)'. *Journal of the Historical Society of Nigeria*, vol. 2, 3 (1962), pp. 311–28.

Hüsken, Thomas. *Tribal Politics in the Borderland of Egypt and Libya*. New York: Springer, 2019.

Hüsken, Thomas, and Georg Klute. 'Political Orders in the Making: Emerging Forms of Political Organization from Libya to Northern Mali'. *African Security*, vol. 8, 4 (2015), pp. 320–37.

Kaba, Lansiné. 'Archers, Musketeers, and Mosquitoes: The Moroccan Invasion of the Sudan and Songhay Resistance (1591–1612)'. *Journal of African History*, vol. 22, 4 (1981), pp. 457–75.

Lacher, Wolfram. *Libya's Fragmentation: Structure and Process in Violent Conflict*. London: Bloomsbury, 2020.

Laroui, Abdullah, *The History of the Maghrib: An Interpretive Essay*, trans. by Ralph Mannheim. Princeton, NJ: Princeton University Press, 1977.

Martin, Bradford. 'Mai Idris of Bornu and the Ottoman Turks, 1576–78'. *International Journal of Middle East Studies*, vol. 3, 4 (1972), pp. 470–90.

Mouline, Nabil. 'La fête du trône: Petite histoire d'une tradition inventée'. In Baudouin Dupret, Zakaria Rhani, Assia Boutaleb and Jean-Noël Ferrié (eds), *Le Maroc au présent*. Casablanca: Centre Jacques Berque, 2015, pp. 691–701.

Taithe, Bertrand. 'L'affaire Voulet-Chanoine dans le sillage de l'affaire

Dreyfus: Massacre et tournant humanitaire'. *Temps modernes* (2017), pp. 693–4, 28–43.

Wilson, Alice. *Sovereignty in Exile: A Saharan Liberation Movement Governs*. Philadelphia: University of Pennsylvania Press, 2016.

8: When Crisis Becomes Permanent

Badi, Dida. 'Cultural Interaction and the Artisanal Economy in Tamanrasset'. In James McDougall and Judith Scheele (eds), *Saharan Frontiers: Space and Mobility in Northwest Africa*. Bloomington: Indiana University Press, 2011, 200–11.

Boesen, Elisabeth, and Laurence Marfaing (eds). *Les nouveaux urbains dans l'espace Sahara-Sahel: Un cosmopolitanism par le bas*. Paris: Karthala, 2007.

Bonnecase, Vincent. 'Retour sur la famine au Sahel du début des années 1970: La construction d'un savoir de crise'. *Politique africaine*, vol. 119 (2010), pp. 23–42.

Bonnecase, Vincent, and Julien Brachet. 'Les "crises sahéliennes" entre perceptions locales et gestions internationales'. *Politique africaine*, vol. 130 (2013), pp. 5–22.

Choplin, Armelle. *Nouakchott: Au carrefour de la Mauritanie et du monde*. Paris: Karthala, 2009.

Côte, Marc (ed). *La ville et le désert, le Bas-Sahara algérien*. Paris: Karthala, 2005.

Glenzer, Kent. '*La sécheresse*: The Social and Institutional Construction of a Development Problem in the Malian (Soudanese) Sahel, 1900–92'. *Canadian Journal of African Studies*, vol. 36, 1 (2002), pp. 1–34.

Kusserow, Hannelore. 'Desertification, Resilience, and Re-greening in the African Sahel – a Matter of the Observation Period?' *Earth System Dynamics*, vol. 8 (2017), pp. 1141–70.

Lecocq, Baz. *Disputed Desert: Decolonisation, Competing Nationalisms and Tuareg Rebellions in Northern Mali*. Leiden: Brill, 2010.

McDougall, James, and Judith Scheele (eds). *Saharan Frontiers: Space and Mobility in Northwest Africa*. Bloomington: Indiana University Press, 2012.

Nielson, Jonas, et al. 'Environmental Change in the Sahel: Reconciling Contrasting Evidence and Interpretations'. *Regional Environmental Change*, vol. 16 (2015), pp. 673–80.

Pliez, Olivier. *Les cités du désert: Des villes sahariennes aux Saharatowns*. Toulouse: IRD. 2011.

Rasmussen, Susan. 'Voices Above the Din: Tinariwen Musicians, the Media, and the Construction of Tuareg Cultural Identity in Northern Mali'. *American Journal of Semiotics*, vol. 29, 1–4 (2013), pp. 69–99.

Spittler, Georg. *Les Touareg face aux sécheresses et aux famines: Les Kel Ewey de l'Aïr*. Paris: Karthala, 1993.

9: In Search of Security

Andersson, Ruben. *Illegality, Inc.: Clandestine Migration and the Business of Bordering Europe*. Berkeley: University of California Press, 2014.

Bachman, Jan. '"Kick Down the Door, Clean Up the Mess, and Rebuild the House" – the Africa Command and Transformations of the US military'. *Geopolitics*, vol. 15 (2010), pp. 564–85.

Bencherif, Adib. 'Récits du conflit entre les Ifoghas et les Imghad: (Re-)positionnement, grammaire de la parenté et compétition entre élites politiques touarègues'. *Cahiers d'études africaines*, vol. 234 (2019), pp. 427–51.

Benderra, Omar, et al. *Hirak en Algérie: L'invention d'un soulèvement*. Paris: La Fabrique, 2020.

Benjaminsen, Tor, and Boubacar Ba. 'Why Do Pastoralists in Mali Join Jihadist Groups? A Political Ecological Explanation'. *Journal of Peasant Studies*, vol. 46, 1 (2019), pp. 1–20.

Brachet, Julien. 'Manufacturing Smugglers: From Irregular to Clandestine Mobility in the Sahara'. *Annals of the American Academy of Political and Social Science*, vol. 676, 1 (2018), pp. 16–35.

Charbonneau, Bruno. 'The Imperial Legacy of International Peacebuilding: The Case of Francophone Africa'. *Review of International Studies*, vol. 40, 3 (2014), pp. 607–30.

Debos, Marielle. *Living by the Gun in Chad: Combatants, Impunity and State Formation*. London: Bloomsbury, 2016.

Dieng, Moda. 'The Multi-National Joint Task Force and the G5 Sahel Joint Force: The Limits of Military Capacity Building'. *Contemporary Security Policy*, vol. 40, 4 (2019), pp. 481–501.

Frowd, Philip, and Adam Sandor. 'Militarism and Its Limits: Sociological

Insights on Security Assemblages in the Sahel'. *Security Dialogue*, vol. 49, 1–2 (2018), pp. 70–82.

Gagnol, Laurent. 'Géohistoire des frontières sahariennes: L'héritage nomade enseveli sous les murs'. *Bulletin de l'association des géographes français*, vol. 99 (2022), pp. 53–75.

Grémont, Charles. 'Dans le piège des offres de violence: Concurrences, protections et représailles dans la région de Ménaka (nord-Mali, 2000–2018)'. *Hérodote*, vol. 172 (2019), pp. 43–62.

Quidelleur, Tanguy. 'Les dividendes de la "guerre contre le terrorisme": Milicianisation, États et interventions internationales au Mali et au Burkina Faso'. *Cultures & Conflicts*, vol. 125 (2022), pp. 115–38.

Scheele, Judith. 'L'Afrique militarisée: Perspectives historiques'. *Politique africaine*, vol. 161–62 (2021), pp. 165–88.